D0340612

JUNK RAFT

JUNK RAFT

AN OCEAN VOYAGE AND
A RISING TIDE OF ACTIVISM
TO FIGHT PLASTIC POLLUTION

MARCUS ERIKSEN

NO LONGER PROPERTY OF
ANYTHINK LIBRARIES/
RANGEVIEW LIBRARY DISTRICT

BEACON PRESS
BOSTON

Beacon Press
Boston, Massachusetts
www.beacon.org

Beacon Press books
are published under the auspices of
the Unitarian Universalist Association of Congregations.

© 2017 by Marcus Eriksen
All rights reserved
Printed in the United States of America

20 19 18 17   8 7 6 5 4 3 2 1

This book is printed on acid-free paper that meets the uncoated paper
ANSI/NISO specifications for permanence as revised in 1992.

Text design and composition by Kim Arney

Library of Congress Cataloging-in-Publication Data
Names: Eriksen, Marcus, author.
Title: Junk raft : an ocean voyage and a rising tide of activism
to fight plastic pollution / Marcus Eriksen.
Description: Boston : Beacon Press, 2017. | Includes
bibliographical references and index.
Identifiers: LCCN 2017012072 (print) | LCCN 2016048806 (ebook) |
ISBN 9780807056400 (hardback) | ISBN 9780807056417 (e-book)
Subjects: LCSH: Plastic marine debris—Environmental aspects—Pacific Ocean.
| Microplastics—Environmental aspects—Pacific Ocean. | Marine
pollution—Pacific Ocean. | Eriksen, Marcus, 1967—Travel—Pacific Ocean.
| BISAC: NATURE / Ecosystems & Habitats / Oceans & Seas. |
NATURE / Environmental Conservation & Protection. |
BIOGRAPHY & AUTOBIOGRAPHY / Personal Memoirs.
Classification: LCC GC1471 .E75 2017 (ebook) | LCC GC1471 (print) |
DDC 363.738—dc23
LC record available at https://lccn.loc.gov/2017012072

For our Avani

CONTENTS

Prologue   ix

CHAPTER 1   Synthetic Seas   1

CHAPTER 2   Junk & Gyre   15

CHAPTER 3   IMUA   29

CHAPTER 4   Junk-o-philia: Our Obsession with Stuff   45

CHAPTER 5   Thrown Away   55

CHAPTER 6   Coming Unscrewed: The Little Fish in a Big Sea   67

CHAPTER 7   "Junk In, Junk Out"   73

CHAPTER 8   Guadalupe Loop: The Recycling Myth   81

CHAPTER 9   Too Wasteful to Value: ChicoBag vs. Plastic-Bag Lobby   93

CHAPTER 10   Waves and Windmills: A Case for the Eco-Pragmatist   107

CHAPTER 11   Wasting Away: The Fate, Fallacy, and Fantasy of Ocean Cleanup   119

CHAPTER 12   Synthetic Drift: Human Health and Our Trash   129

CHAPTER 13   Little Fish Bites Big Fish   143

CHAPTER 14   A Plastic Smog   157

CHAPTER 15   The Great Divide: The Linear vs. Circular Economy   169

CHAPTER 16   A Revolution by Design   185

EPILOGUE   Embrace   193

Acknowledgments   197

Notes   199

Index   213

PROLOGUE

2:00 a.m. Storm near San Nicolas Island
(Latitude 33°12', Longitude 119°26')

In darkness, another wave slams against the underside of the air-plane strapped to fifteen thousand plastic bottles. I pull the hatch closed to avoid more spray in my face. Water now sloshes under the plywood floorboard, between the bank of batteries and beneath our damp sleeping bags. The homemade rigging moans and whistles as fifty-knot gusts rip through. A wall of water engulfs the deck and blurs the windshield, and a cascade of echoing drips trickles through the holes I forgot to plug.

"Something's not right," I say.

"I think the airplane just slid across the deck," Joel replies.

In these dark and timeless hours, we're still huddled on a relatively horizontal plane, so at least we're not on the verge of flipping over. We were near San Nicolas Island, sixty miles west of Los Angeles. I don't know if we're still there. Like me, Joel is wide awake, trying to stay warm, nerves on edge. We jump with each new crack, moan, or sudden lurch of the raft. In the dim light of the coming day, I step outside into the sea.

One year earlier, Anna Cummins and I met in the kitchen doorway at Captain Charles Moore's sixtieth birthday party at his home in Long Beach, California. Waves of blond hair unfurled around her neck. Lit-tle did I know that in eight months we would sail across the North

Pacific Ocean to study plastic pollution aboard the Oceanographic Research Vessel (ORV) *Alguita*. Somewhere in the middle of that ocean I would climb up into the folded sails and ask Anna to marry me. "But there's one thing," I said. "I want to raft across the ocean."

We hatched a plan, asked the crew for volunteers. I sketched the final drawings of the raft. Joel Paschal, a fellow sailor on that same North Pacific research voyage, stepped forward and said, "I like it." Together, he and I would sail *Junk*, a raft made from plastic bottles, with thirty old sailboat masts for a deck and a Cessna 310 airplane as a cabin. Anna would be "mission control" on land. No motor or support vessel buoyed our journey—just us and the current, bound for Hawaii, imitating the path of trash into the swirling ocean gyre, those massive vortices of currents that suck trash into a stagnant center.

The *Junk* would turn out to be the first of many expeditions for Anna and me. In the years following the voyage of *Junk*, we'd establish the 5 Gyres Institute, a research and advocacy organization, sailing around the world to all five subtropical gyres. In over fifty thousand nautical miles of sailing on twenty expeditions, we'd invite some two hundred crew members, ranging from CEOs of plastic companies to educators, artists, activists, and policymakers, to help answer two questions: "How much plastic waste is in the world's oceans?" and "What can we do about it?"

Our fight is to end the throwaway culture. Science in this synthetic century, riding the coattails of the Industrial Revolution, avoided the question, "Where is *away*?" In 2013, plastic producers broke the three-hundred-million-ton benchmark in terms of the amount of new plastic produced in a single year, and production is expected to exceed a billion tons annually by 2050. The industry's global solution to plastic is incineration, perpetuating the linear economy, from extraction to consumption, then destruction. To secure demand for new plastic, the industry must make last year's plastic obsolete. Incineration is the essence of "planned obsolescence," a concept central to twentieth-century capitalism, but a practice that cannot continue if we are to have a healthy and just existence.

Natural history is rich with unhappy endings. As short-lived, short-sighted, bipedal, big-brained primates preoccupied with war and sex, we risk consuming and overpopulating until we collapse. We fossil fools, driven to global conquest, have—in the blink of a geological eye—made an enormous mess of things.

But I have tremendous hope. I am confident that we possess the collective intelligence and will to overcome the course that was set in the last century. I've witnessed a growing movement to end throwaway living. We're fighting for a "circular economy," in which little to nothing escapes unless it is benign to the environment. We need zero-waste and end-of-life design for everything we create; a world in which social and environmental justice becomes part of product and systems design. We want a world without waste—because there is no "away."

Are we capable of replacing the globalization of stuff with the globalization of new ideas to transform our culture of consumption? To rebut Kurt Vonnegut's epitaph for our species—"Nice try"—I argue: "Not done."

Another wave slams into the raft. I imagine it coming apart and sliding into the sea. I think mechanically through those seconds of impending catastrophe. The airplane, with only a few straps keeping it in place, will fall into the water and float for a moment as the tail rapidly turns downward like a bobbing cork. Four hundred pounds of batteries loosely arranged on the floor will come crashing onto Joel and me as the fuselage fills with seawater. It will be a quick drowning, and we'll likely never be found.

I remove the satellite phone from the dry bag and call Anna.

"Hey. . . . We're sinking."

CHAPTER 1

SYNTHETIC SEAS

Economists have a term for these costs. . . . They are "negative externalities": negative because they aren't beneficial and external because they fall outside the market system. Those who find this hard to accept attack the messenger, which is science.

—Naomi Oreskes and Erik M. Conway
Merchants of Doubt, 2010

Beginning in this century, news accounts painted a dire picture that captivated the world: images of drifting plastic masses, of marine mammals, sea turtles, and birds choking on plastic bags. Young entrepreneurs clamored to clean those mythical islands of trash, while industrialists rose to defend plastic. From this melee, a new field of science emerged to sort fact from fiction. A cast of characters—sailors turned scientists and scientists turned activists, and activists who turned to politics—set the stage for a dramatic comedy of fossil fools, as behemoth petrochemical corporations rose like phoenixes to counter a public relations nightmare.

I was one of those fools. I did not arrive at a career in science by the traditional rigorous academic path, but in haphazard leaps from one experience to another, wielding my ignorance like a quixotic sword. Just as there's no straightforward path to scientific knowledge, there's no one method of becoming a scientist. My path began with a naturalist's dream and took me through a war and a river home. Along the way I bore witness to an ecological atrocity and to the complexity of self-preservation through conservation and social justice.

In 2000, I visited Midway Atoll, the last island along the Hawaiian archipelago in what's now the Papahānaumokuākea Marine National

Monument, where I met biologist Heidi Auman and her collection of odd artifacts, items that had been swallowed by Laysan albatross, including light bulbs, armies of little green men, glow sticks, golf balls, and a syringe (found with its needle protruding from a living bird's chest). Auman's a young scientist, with long blond hair that contrasts with a tan from hours of fieldwork studying these birds. As we wandered the island we picked up toothbrushes, an asthma inhaler, half a spoon, an electrical-wire nut, an action-figure leg, and cigarette lighters from the bleached rib cages of dead albatross. One lighter bore the clearly legible phone number for some bar in Tokyo. I could have called them to say, "Hey, you dropped something."

"There are over four hundred thousand nesting pairs of Laysan albatross here on the three islands that make up Midway Atoll," Heidi explained. According to the US Fish and Wildlife Service, the Midway colony represents 71 percent of the species.[1] It's estimated that this species alone is responsible for transporting five tons of plastic to the island each year. There, it's purged from their stomachs into the bodies of fledgling chicks. Heidi and I stopped to watch a hungry albatross chick tickle a little spot under its parent's beak, prompting a slurry of sludge in the proventriculus—the first stomach—to be regurgitated. The adult albatross, both male and female, acts on an evolved sense of nurturing, giving away the majority of its nutrients. But the parents unwittingly feed our trash to their young, causing a false sense of satiation in the chicks, which leads to malnutrition, dehydration, and weakness, making them vulnerable to illness and death. When I left the island, my luggage held the contents of forty-five albatross stomachs—items that would be seen by tens of thousands of students in the years ahead.

Four years later, I arrived on the doorstep of Captain Charles Moore with my *Bottle Rocket* raft on a trailer behind my van and with a keen interest in the science of plastic pollution. It was my first plastic-bottle boat, set adrift on Lake Itasca, Minnesota, where the Mississippi River is ten feet wide and six inches deep, and arriving 2,300 miles later, past my home in southern Louisiana, at the Gulf of Mexico. During the 1991 Persian Gulf War I had promised myself to raft the Mississippi River if I made it home, and twelve years later I made good on that promise. In those five months living on the Mississippi, I witnessed a never-ending trail of plastic trash, which had its roots in the petroleum I had been sent to defend in Kuwait. Now I watched it drift to the ocean via America's greatest watershed.

"That thing floats?" Charlie asked with a chuckle, walking around the *Bottle Rocket*. He poked at the 232 two-liter plastic bottles that carried me down the Mississippi River the previous year. Charlie, the man credited with discovering the "Great Pacific Garbage Patch," stands about five feet nine. He has blue eyes and, usually, a haggard, thin beard, like any sailor should have. His hands are working hands, coarse and calloused, even though his family fortune would give him the option for them not to be.

I had driven the raft to the front door of Charlie's home in the Alamitos Bay area of Long Beach, California, weeks after I dropped a letter in the mail to the Algalita Marine Research and Education (AMRE), stating: "I've watched millions of plastic bags, bottles, and cups headed to the ocean. I need to see the garbage patch you discovered."

In 1997, Charlie had sailed his catamaran ORV *Alguita* to Hawaii in the Transpacific Yacht Race. On the return voyage—which typically follows a longer arc north from Hawaii to catch the currents rounding the central high-pressure system in the center of the North Pacific Subtropical Gyre—he was lured instead to power through the middle. As twin diesel engines motored into the balmy oceanic desert, the flat, glass-like seas revealed something unexpected: tiny light-colored flecks of plastic floated in sharp contrast to the dark canvas deep beneath the surface. They were endless, like a reflection of a starry moonless night, yet at midday.

Haunted, he returned in 1999 to conduct AMRE's first research expedition, this time with nets to skim the sea surface. He documented the count and weight of plastic particles in a study area he deemed "twice the size of Texas."

At the same time, Dr. Curtis Ebbesmeyer, an equally jolly and shaggy-bearded oceanographer famed for his study of thousands of rubber ducks lost at sea from a container ship, coined the term "garbage patch." Media accounts put "garbage patch" and "twice the size of Texas" together, giving the public something to visualize, something very different from sparse specks of plastic in a vast ocean: an image of a new subcontinent of drifting trash, something akin to the mass in Jules Verne's *Floating Island*.

This image of a thick island of floating refuse, looking as if you could plant a flag on it or buy real estate there, was reported on the five o'clock news with the drama of a plane crash or impending hurricane. A stream of photographs horrified the public—sea lions and whales entangled and drowned in nets, sea turtles choking on plastic bags, albatross rib cages filled with trash, and an adult snapping turtle from Louisiana with an hourglass-shaped shell (the result of having been stuck in a milk-jug ring as a hatchling). Equally gruesome were depictions of a human impact—children walking through plastic-covered beaches, living on landfills, and melting plastic to earn a few pennies.

Even if the "Texas-size island of plastic" was hyperbole, it spurred individuals and organizations to form a movement to address a problem caused by a man-made material that most of us routinely ignore.

Crack a barrel of fossil fuels, whether drilled here or stolen there, and you'll see the energy that powers everything from lawn mowers to jetliners, as well as the chemistry that becomes plastic—a long hydrocarbon in a solid form. While there's a growing industry of plant-based plastics, today most plastics are still derived primarily from fossil fuels. It's not crude oil itself that becomes plastic, it's the hydrocarbon gas liquids (HGL) extracted from the oil that do. HGL and natural gas are then "cracked," a term referring to the chemical processing that extracts monomers such as ethylene and propylene. These monomers are short-chain molecules that usually have a few atoms surrounding a carbon atom (an exception is silicone, which has silicon as the core atom). The monomers are then linked together as repeating units into longer chains, called polymers.

There are generally two types of plastics: thermoplastics and thermosets. Thermosets include epoxies and resins, such as polyurethane that is used to build fiberglass boat hulls and car body panels. They are "set" with a catalyst that changes the chemistry of the polymer, making it a permanent solid. They are not recyclable, but are sometimes shredded and used as fillers for new resins.

Thermoplastics, such as polyethylene and polypropylene, make up the vast majority of plastics on the market today, and they are the most versatile. Think of them like wax, in that they can be repeatedly melted and reshaped, unless the long-chain polymer is damaged or degraded. They have changed the way the world moves and preserves goods, and serve as the "lubricator of globalization," as Charlie calls them. And as the National Academy of Engineering puts it, "The products from petrochemicals have played as great a role in shaping the modern world as gasoline and fuel have in powering it."[2]

Plastic that trickles out to sea survives longer than natural materials set adrift, but it may degrade by ultraviolet sunlight, chemical oxidation, and slow biodegradation, though to a large extent, all plastic, unless incinerated, still exists. It floats, flows, and blows everywhere, downhill to the ocean, forming massive accumulation zones of microplastic trash in the subtropical gyres, fragmenting and cycling through entire marine ecosystems. Eventually it will settle on the seafloor or get washed ashore somewhere, returning to the layers of the earth. These are the externalities that are often more costly than the short-term benefits far upstream. This life cycle of plastic was largely unknown in its entirety until the turn of the twenty-first century brought the discovery of the global distribution of floating plastic.

It's June 2005—Charlie's fourth trip aboard the ORV *Alguita*, my first. It was as balmy, flat, and windless as I imagined in the middle of the accumulation zone, halfway between Hawaii and California. It took us one week to get here, traveling almost due west from Los Angeles and a little north to get to the center of the stable high-pressure system that defines the North Pacific Subtropical Gyre. Jody Lemmon, a filmmaker along to document the voyage, and I launched the manta trawl into the water for a three-hour tow.

A subtropical gyre is a wind-driven system of currents on the ocean surface centered on a stable high-pressure system. There are eleven gyres in the world's oceans: two subpolar gyres just below the Arctic Circle and three smaller gyre circulations above; the circumpolar gyre around Antarctica and five subtropical gyres in the Indian Ocean, and Atlantic and Pacific Oceans above and below the equator.[3] Much attention is directed toward the subtropical gyres, because that's where global currents accumulate floating trash.

Atmospheric currents, driven by the earth's rotation, are affected by the Coriolis effect: in the Northern Hemisphere, rotational currents push air to the left (to the right in the Southern Hemisphere, where air moves in an anticyclonic rotation). The Coriolis effect arises from a frictional force that drives surface currents toward the center of high-pressure systems—the subtropical gyres, where it's hot and dry, and where wind and ocean currents slowly fade. Five subtropical gyres cover vast expanses of the ocean surface—roughly 40 percent of the global ocean if you force boundaries on them, or a quarter of the earth's total surface.

On May 27, 1990, the *Hansa Carrier*, a cargo freighter leaving South Korea for Los Angeles, met a storm head-on and lost twenty-one containers into the subarctic current, like a dog shaking mud off its rump. Many containers split open as they crashed to the deck before going over. Five of the containers were filled with Nike shoes; four of them opened to release their cargo. Oceanographer Curtis Ebbesmeyer began tracking the shoes. He created a communications network to pair beachcombers who had found Nike shoes of a particular size and style with people who found the match. In several morbid instances, Ebbesmeyer received reports of shoes with decomposing feet still in them, evidence not only of the persistence of our human-made stuff, but of underreported casualties among maritime workers.

While there's no legal obligation to report lost containers for public record, the World Shipping Council surveyed the majority of shipping fleets between 2008 and 2013 and found on average a total of 1,679 containers had been lost at sea each year. A single catastrophic loss of 4,293 containers occurred when the *MOL Comfort* split in two in the Indian Ocean in 2013.[4] To Ebbesmeyer's amazement, on January 10, 1992, another cargo ship, the *Ever Laurel*, fighting hurricane-force winds just a couple of degrees east of the international dateline in the North Pacific, shook off a dozen shipping containers before recovering. One container spilled 28,800 bath toys, including plastic blue turtles, green frogs, red beavers, and yellow ducks. A year later, residents of Sitka, Alaska, began seeing the little plastic animals come ashore. "It was a game to find all four," Ebbesmeyer said. In following years, they were found in Hawaii, along the northwest coast of North America, and in South America. Some were frozen in Arctic ice, and three found their way to the North Atlantic as far as the United Kingdom.

Hours later, in the middle of the North Pacific Gyre, we winched in the manta trawl. In total we had skimmed roughly ten thousand square meters, an area the size of two football fields. The result was a half cup of multicolored plastic confetti. This is typically as thick as it gets, aside from the random fishing float or giant tangled ball of net and line that drifts by. There's no island, no garbage patch, but I was horrified to see these thousands of microplastic particles. This was much worse.

Charlie dumped the contents of the collection sock into a Pyrex cake dish, neatly spreading fish out in parallel form, like victims recovered from a battlefield, though these were covered in a kaleidoscope of microplastic, like sprinkles on cupcakes. This is the reality the media needs to see, but the inaccessibility of the middle of the gyres exacerbates the misconceptions we're trying to overcome.

The island myth is a consequence of science filtered through contemporary storytelling. As Jeremy Green describes in "Media Sensationalisation and Science," "In the process of transforming and re-packaging scientific knowledge so that it can be understood by non-specialists, the content of the knowledge becomes degraded, so that it is distorted and less true."[5] Would the world have cared about plastic marine pollution without the island myth? The discovery of plastic swirling in the ocean preceded Charlie's discovery by three decades; it took some science fiction to stoke the fires of public interest.

When Charlie published his results in 2001, ocean plastic was getting very little attention from the scientific community. The Scripps Institution of Oceanography and the Woods Hole Oceanographic Institution (WHOI), two prestigious marine research institutions, were not actively studying plastic marine pollution. Richard Thompson, a marine scientist in the United Kingdom, was looking at microplastics, and Hideshige Takada was working on pollutants that bond to plastic pellets and fragments. It was a continuation of the trickle of scientific publications since the 1970s, yet with few peers available to review anything.

Charlie's research awoke a sleeping giant. Media suddenly gave scientists airtime to talk about the mythical island of floating garbage, and by the mid-2000s, industry was fighting a growing public disdain for disposable plastic. National organizations, such as the Surfrider Foundation, the Natural Resources Defense Council, Sierra Club, the Environmental Working Group, and dozens of local organizations began talking about the efficacy of plastic-bag bans. This provoked counterefforts by plastic manufacturers, who formed lobbying groups and anti-environmental organizations, such as Save the Plastic Bag and the Progressive Bag Alliance. The plastics industry trade group, the American Chemistry Council (ACC), and scientists on their dole worked feverishly to undermine the validity of AMRE's research, accusing Charlie of not being a "real" scientist. Big Plastic takes cues from the tobacco industry by denying the problem, disrupting the work of critics, distracting the public, delaying action, and denigrating scientists perceived to be troublemakers. It's a war of public and policy persuasion that can be won only by persistent pressure from nongovernmental organizations (NGOs) and good science.

Hours after returning from sea to the ORV *Alguita* dock in Alamitos Bay, Charlie pulled me aside in his office. "If you're going to work in this field, you've got to start from the beginning," he said, handing me a dozen research papers, the slim sum of all research on plastic pollution that preceded his discovery. As my mentor, he invited me into the world of marine science.

Plastic marine pollution was first discovered in 1972 in the North Atlantic by Edward J. Carpenter and Kenneth L. Smith.[6] While aboard the WHOI ship *Atlantis II* in 1971, they discovered abundant tar balls and plastic particles in their neuston nets (a kind of fine-mesh surface trawl) when sampling the sea surface at eleven sites. These yielded an average of 3,500 particles weighing 290 grams per square kilometer, roughly a teaspoon of plastic for every football field of ocean surface.

Four decades later, I caught up with Edward at his office at San Francisco State University. I launched into a monologue about how he started a new field of marine science, and about his influence on my career. "Most people are surprised I'm still alive," he responded, with a faraway smile.

"At the time you published the first paper describing plastic in the ocean, what did other scientists think of the work?" I asked.

"I was called the 'plastic guy' and not really taken seriously," he replied. "That same year, in 1972, we also published a paper about the widespread distribution of polystyrene spherules in southern New England waters and ingestion of the spherules by eight different fish species. The director of my department at WHOI said that what I was doing wasn't real science."

"In the time between your first publication in 1972 and the discovery of the Great Pacific Garbage Patch by Captain Moore a quarter century later, there were only a handful of studies on ocean plastics, while the plastics industry more than quadrupled annual production," I said. "Why do you think the science of ocean plastics lagged behind the pace of industry for so long?"

Edward paused for a second, taking a long breath. "The Society of the Plastics Industry expressly flew out to meet me. They wanted to let me know that my findings were not relevant, useful, and were even un-American. They spoke to the higher-ups at WHOI and perhaps made the same criticisms. It was an intimidation tactic. I'm sure they did it to every scientist that took an interest in this. They did it again when I published the fish ingestion of polystyrene paper. They came to personally visit me again to let me know that I should stop what I'm doing because it's not real science. They also talked to my colleagues and the administration."

In 1937, the Society of the Plastics Industry (SPI) was born out of internal collaboration between the emerging giants—Dow, Monsanto, DuPont, Standard Oil, and others—that transformed their bitter disputes over who invented what into an industry-wide alliance to build market share against glass, metal, and paper. World War II drove powerful industries that transformed the domestic marketplace. What had been a culture of resource scarcity and conservation in the Depression years before the war shifted to embrace newfound wealth and prosperity, arising from the triumph of capitalist democracy over tyranny. The heirloom society that built things to last before the war was now the antithesis of modern consumerism.

Plastic defined "planned obsolescence," a necessary prerequisite of sustained consumer demand. Compromised quality and abbreviated product lives, in terms of fashion and function, make room for new sales. By comparison, a vintage O'Keefe & Merritt gas stove sitting in my kitchen was designed so well in the 1940s that few customers had reason to come back. The company depended on population growth for sales. Now it's gone. The post–World War II years were the golden age of advertising. Marketing mayhem convinced the public it needed a television and a washing machine, and that latest kitchen gadget, along with whatever products should stock a modern bomb shelter. Saran Wrap was marketed as a means of keeping polio at bay, in TV commercials that showed housewives wrapping sweaters. Plastic allowed companies to rapidly accommodate the demand they fabricated. Any threat to the rapidly growing plastic market was met head-on by the SPI, and Carpenter's work was a colossal threat to be denied and denigrated.

"You've started something that took four decades to understand," I said. "What do you think of the explosion in interest in the last fifteen years?"

Edward rocked back in his chair and said, "It's wonderful to see so much good work done by so many."

Edward Carpenter had been doing tremendous work, publishing feverishly, even helping to create the Sea Education Association (SEA) in 1971 to take university students out on the water through WHOI. Despite his career accomplishments—which included publication of a whopping thirteen papers in 1973 in other fields—his supervisor worked to have him ousted from WHOI. His contract was terminated, and he left Woods Hole, where the door had been flung wide open.

After Carpenter's work there was a long lapse in research on plastic, until 1980, when UK scientist Robert Morris described plastic pellets and fragments in the South Atlantic off the coast of South Africa. Then, in 1985, Robert Day and colleagues began a series of expeditions across the North Pacific.[7] They published a four-year data set in 1989 consisting of 203 sea-surface samples. One site yielded 316,800 individual pieces of plastic per square kilometer (imagine a cupful of microplastic strewn over a football field). The science of ocean plastic pollution inched along for another decade until 1997, when Moore unknowingly sailed through the one place in the North Pacific that

Robert Day had missed, the eastern accumulation zone of the North Pacific Subtropical Gyre.

It had taken a quarter century since World War II for annual plastic production to rise from zero to nearly 40 million tons in 1972, the year Carpenter made his discovery. Annual production had more than doubled, to 99 million tons, when Day described microplastics across the North Pacific in 1989, and doubled again to over 200 million tons each year by the time Moore arrived. With rising success, global plastic production gave no sign of slowing down, and reached 311 million tons annually by 2013. At 4 percent anticipated growth over the next few decades, the industry will surpass 1 billion tons of new plastic production by 2050 only through planned obsolescence. This linear economic thinking is the root of the problem we face today.

The ACC, which is much larger than the SPI, represents petrochemical industries and plastic product and packaging manufacturers—Dow, DuPont, Monsanto, Shell, Coca-Cola, PepsiCo, and a couple hundred other companies. Formerly called the American Plastics Council, it changed its name in the early 2000s when the public began associating the word *plastic* with pollution. In 2001, the ACC plastics division found itself fighting the Texas-size Garbage Patch mythology with multiple strategies seeking to moderate and manipulate public perception and counter regulation, through heavy lobbying of policymakers and public messaging. The organization launched communications campaigns and conferences, and offered funds to any scientist interested in plastic marine pollution.

In the early 2000s, the ACC even succeeded in inserting language into California textbooks asserting recycling and anti-littering efforts as primary solutions—with nothing about designing smarter or using fewer products. It is stereotypical of industry to argue that consumers are responsible for litter and taxpayers are responsible for waste management, but product and packaging design should go unregulated. While recycling is still widely supported by the public, it is a dismal failure in the United States—the recycling rate for plastics was only 9.2 percent in 2013 according to the US Environmental Protection Agency (EPA)—because there's no obligation to design for it.[8] Few people in the United States or Europe realize that we export unrecyclable plastic to developing countries where environmental standards and worker health are not regulated. If the public knew that their city's "waste diversion" rates are more about "waste relocation," they would demand greater transparency about true recycling rates.

The ACC held its own marine debris conference in La Jolla, California, in 2007. It heavily funded the 5th International Marine Debris Conference in 2008, and threw money at NGOs, including the Ocean Conservancy and SEA's research programs on plastic marine pollution. Municipal ordinances to ban plastic bags became the battlefield, and I found myself testifying often at city council hearings with other scientists to shed light on ocean impacts of plastic, while the ACC's foot soldiers stood next to us to counter our testimony. They protested producer responsibility and end-of-life design while spending millions on television, radio, and print ads with their absurd mantra "Bag bans raise taxes and kill jobs."

As the plastic pollution conversation hit the mainstream, the big oceanographic institutions had little science to offer on the subject and were wiping the tar off their ivory towers for not having answers before the public asked. Scripps began organizing its own expedition to study plastic, called the Scripps Environmental Accumulation of Plastic Expedition (SEAPLEX). In early 2009, the researchers boldly sailed where Charlie Moore had gone before. Science was playing catch-up.

Meanwhile, SEA Education out of Woods Hole analyzed a twenty-two-year data set from its archived plankton tows, and interestingly it found no increasing trend in plastic in the North Atlantic Subtropical Gyre over time, a finding that would later be retracted by the authors as new data came in. The US National Oceanic and Atmospheric Administration (NOAA), following the Marine Debris Act of 2006, began to dole out funds in competitive grants.[9] Recognizing the magnitude of the problem, NOAA laudably embraced citizen science, opening the doors for amateurs and small NGOs to apply for the same funding that larger academic institutions have access to.

The National Center for Ecological Analysis and Synthesis (NCEAS), a Santa Barbara, California-based working group on plastic pollution (funded largely by the Ocean Conservancy), invited thirty-seven scientists to answer key questions about plastic pollution, such as "How much is out there?" Years later I would be invited to coauthor an NCEAS publication after our organization, the 5 Gyres Institute, published the first global estimate of floating trash. One of the coauthors explained, "You had a data set we wanted, but it was already available when you published. Really, we figured you would likely be a reviewer of our revised global estimate and your politics might make you overly critical. It's a case of keeping your colleagues close and your critics closer," revealing one of the strategies of publishing in scientific journals.

I discovered that the culture and the methods of science permit plenty of subjectivity. In the Machiavellian world of scientific research there are bitter rivalries and strategic alliances, and there is stiff competition to publish ahead of your colleagues. If you take the golden carrot incessantly dangled in front of you by the industries that stand to lose, and you use it to fund your expeditions, employ staff, buy equipment, and pay to keep the lights on, then you become dependent. Years later, as a scientist on the inside, I'd follow suspicious studies to their common funding source—the ACC. I'd discover that another set of scientific methods existed, and that the plastics industry was all too familiar with the rules.

CHAPTER 2

JUNK & GYRE

The ultimate triumph of plastic has been the victory of package over product, of style over substance, of surface over essence.

—Stephen Fenichell
Plastic: The Making of a Synthetic Century, 1997

"This is where plastic comes home to roost and degrade," Charlie said as the first flecks of microplastic appeared beneath the hulls of the ORV *Alguita*. It was January 2008. This was my second voyage to the North Pacific Subtropical Gyre, Charlie's sixth, Joel and Anna's first. A few hundred miles northeast of Hawaii, we're close to Charlie's original sample sites.

Joel Paschal was at the helm while Anna and I deployed the manta trawl, tailored with a 0.33 mm mesh net to capture all of the zooplankton and some phytoplankton and plastic. Jeff Ernst and Herb Machleder, two other volunteer crew members, winched it in an hour later. Nine years ago a trawl sample from this site yielded 1.46 grams of plastic. The manta trawl came aboard and we dumped the contents into a Pyrex cake dish. This one easily yielded ten times the previous amount.

"If we were studying something more optimistic than the accumulation of plastic trash, I'd likely give everyone a high five after the dramatic results of this trawl," Charlie said. Every sample from here onward contained plastic.

"Net ball!" Joel yelled from the bow an hour before sunset. We're always on the lookout for the big stuff. Joel pointed toward it, while calling out distance and heading, guiding Charlie as he flipped the *Alguita* around.

"Bucket!" Anna yelled, followed by a barrage of trash sightings along a linear path. "Basket! Hanger! Crate! Another buoy! Light bulb!"

Everyone was yelling what they were seeing, while at the stern, above the stream of trash, I grabbed what I could with a net and hauled it on deck. This trail of floating trash is called a "windrow," formed by wind-driven surface currents, or regionally by larger current systems, called "Langmuir cells," which converge to form linear rows, aggregating everything buoyant.

This may be where plastic comes to degrade, but where is it all coming from? Who is responsible? While fishing buoys often have names and numbers embossed on them, everything else is fragmented and degraded to the point of obscurity, save for the rare brand recognition that occurs with the familiar shapes and colors of some objects, like red Coca-Cola bottle caps or yellow-and-red-striped McDonald's straws.

"You look at all of the big stuff collecting here in the middle of the gyre, and it's mostly fishing gear," Joel explained. Nets and buoys are designed to last. Plastic bags, Styrofoam, and other low-quality plastic products that leave shore fragment fast. They are rare out here. Only thick items, such as toothbrushes and lawn chairs, survive the long drift to the gyres.

Joel spent four months working for NOAA to remove more than forty tons of nets from the Northwest Hawaiian Islands just before coming here. He would hold on to a flat board tied to a rope, which was towed behind a small boat slowly patrolling the shallows near reefs to spy net balls. Often he would see a trail of broken coral long before the net, like a bowling alley leading to the pile of pins.

"There are restrictions in place to prevent these nets from being here," Joel said. The 1988 international agreement MARPOL (for "marine pollution") Annex V of the International Convention for the Prevention of Pollution from Ships restricts the dumping of all forms of plastic into the ocean from all sources—including sloppy fishing and fish-farming activities, offshore mining, illegal dumping, and shipping.[1] But monitoring and compliance, beyond oversight of some large military and commercial fleets and some cruise lines, are practically nonexistent.

We don't know how much is out there, but we do know that lost nets or "ghost nets" are indiscriminate killers, likely catching more fish when lost than when used for fishing. They become navigational hazards, tangling boat propellers, and wreak ecological havoc, bulldozing coral reefs and tearing coral apart, proving far costlier as waste than their initial price tag would suggest. The United Nations Environment Programme (UNEP) estimates that abandoned, lost, or otherwise discarded fishing gear (so common it even has an ungainly acronym, ALDFG) accounts for 10 percent of the plastic at sea, while another study estimates commercial fishing gear accounts for 5 percent,[2] with a more recent assessment at 18 percent.[3]

There's a frequently cited estimate that 80 percent of plastic pollution comes from land and 20 percent is from maritime activities.[4] Two fingers point to sea, to a fishing industry that needs to clean up its act, and eight fingers point to land. Jenna Jambeck, an environmental engineer from the University of Georgia, recently published a global estimate of plastic lost from land in 192 coastal countries, and arrived at a range of four to twelve million tons annually.

The American Chemistry Council interpreted this study as meaning that the world needs better waste management and should rapidly invest in incinerators, a view that feeds the group's collaboration with waste-to-energy companies and perpetuates linear economic thinking. It was a golden opportunity to dodge producers' responsibility to create end-of-life product and packaging chemistry and design. Again, they avoid negative externalities and put the blame and fiscal responsibility on cities and taxpayers.

When we look at all forms of plastic in the ocean—from trash leaving countries with poor waste management to fishing gear that's lost and illegal dumping at sea—what becomes evident is the way a global system of currents and gyres slingshots trash through international waters. It quickly becomes the ultimate "tragedy of the commons," whereby unrecognizable fragmented plastic claims no country or company—eternal vagabonds.

"Something big is swimming ahead," Anna yelled, and then it was gone. I netted a blob of red flesh, which turned out to be a three-inch-thick slab of the body wall of a giant squid. To Anna's dismay and the crew's amusement, I took a bite, then quickly spit it out as I almost gagged.

After an hour of chasing trash and piling it all on deck, we turned around and lassoed a giant net ball.

This tangled nest of mismatched nets and embedded debris was just the tip of the man-made iceberg. Underwater, the behemoth bolus sank heavily, providing shelter to abundant marine life. The variations in net and line tangled together were impressive. The ocean is a weaver, as decades-old fragments become entangled by chance encounters. The net ball easily weighed more than a ton. A black-footed albatross prodded curiously around the net, looking for wandering crabs that might emerge.

Joel winched the mass tight to stern, and we tied to it a satellite buoy, a gift from a NOAA program called the GhostNet project. Two years later, Greenpeace would find this buoy a few hundred miles away, still in the eastern North Pacific Subtropical Gyre, with less than half the netting still attached to it.

The sun set behind us, signaling the start of the greatest migration of life on the planet, when amazing things rise from the depths. Wildebeest moving across Africa or caribou across Canada are impressive, but the nightly vertical migration of the marine food web, rushing to the surface to feed and then descend back to the depths before sunrise, is breathtaking. We grabbed our dive lights to observe the vertical stampede. First a few pteropods, like Cavolina, akin to a giant lentil with wings, followed by Venus's girdle, an elongated jellyfish that looks more like the leather belt holding up my pants than the circular Medusa body-form of common jellies. Its translucent body bears short cilia around its periphery, and a bead of light zooms back and forth from end to end. Somehow, it sensed my presence and undulated rapidly, disappearing in seconds. Another life-form, the size and color of an apple with a starburst of radiating tentacles, noted my proximity—it withdrew its appendages, unfolded its wings, and gently swam away. At this moment, I turned off my dive light. I was deep, hovering quietly in complete darkness on one deep breath. I moved my arms and legs through hordes of zooplankton that raced upward, each contact with their bodies causing a flash of green bioluminescence. Thousands of collisions formed trails of light that poured off my fingertips. I spun around, euphoric. I extended my arms and swooshed to the surface, like a rocket with fiery green flames emanating from my feet. I was an astronaut among living stars.

I joined Anna and soon found Joel, who was busy filming fish as they darted around the net ball. I touched the UV-degraded fishing net and a slurry of microfibers immediately disintegrated in my fingers, an alien material amidst a kaleidoscope of life, and a contrast to the starry bioluminescent display around me. When we grabbed the net above water, our hands looked as if we'd dipped them into a bowl of plastic bread crumbs. This net was a propagator of microplastic particles, and over time it would degrade into millions of them. In the years ahead, we'd find them inside many of the animals that lived on this artificial reef, from the smallest zooplankton to barnacles and fish. Joel suddenly looked up from his camera and kicked his fins violently. Another long gray fin erupted below him, but it was not his. The second time it happened, I grabbed Anna and pointed: "Babe, there's a shark."

Her eyes widened as the shark approached us and, like a cartoon character, she raced back to the boat atop the waves. Anna has a fascination with sharks that is equal parts fear and wonder. I swam right behind her. Joel returned. "Yeah, it was a six-to-seven-foot mako shark," he said, with a degree of calm confidence I would grow to appreciate deeply in the months ahead. "They're known to attack. Never turn your back on them."

With the crew wide awake, we started the engines and began trawling. Fish were congregating on the surface, foraging, feasting, blinking their photophores—an orgy of gluttony, a nightly tradition millions of years in the making, and in a few hours we had them in our manta trawl. Among them were the Myctophidae, a family of fish known as lantern fish, occupying the title "greatest biomass of fish in the ocean." They feed the fish that feed the fish that are fished by the fishermen who feed the world.

"It's full of fish!" Joel yelled as he opened the cod end of the net. The six-to-one plastic-to-plankton ratio Charlie published in 2001, observed from daylight sampling, was now completely flipped around. Unlike any trawl from his previous expeditions, this time dozens of fish poured out, along with the same soup of microplastic and zooplankton.

We collected 671 fish from six species, to be dissected later to study their gut contents. Thirty-five percent were found to have swallowed microplastic.[5] The Scripps Institution would be critical of this study, on the grounds that fish in the throes of death gasp for breath and ingest whatever is around, and when their final moments occur in a net filled with plastic particles, such findings are not unexpected. Scripps would soon venture into the same area on the SEAPLEX voyage to replicate this study and find 9 percent had plastic in their guts.[6] In 2016, a similar study done in the North Atlantic would collect 761 fish, also primarily myctophids, and find 11 percent had plastic in their guts.[7]

Collectively, these studies confirm that wildlife are unwittingly engaging with plastic through entanglement and ingestion.[8] It's safe to say the majority of the world's biomass of fish are interacting with our trash. These interactions run up the food chain. It's not uncommon along the west coast of the United States to spot an unlucky sea lion with a rope or net scar around its neck, or to read a laundry list of swallowed plastic items in the necropsy report from a beached whale—it almost always includes a handful of plastic bags. It's unknown how many marine mammals and seabirds actually die from getting snagged and then drowning in lost fishing gear. Sea turtles are likely worse off. In a conversation with Wallace J. Nichols, sea turtle biologist and author of *Blue Mind*, a compelling argument for our psychological bond to the sea, he told me, "We used to say 'some sea turtles are interacting with plastic,' then it was 'all turtle species are impacted,' and now we find pieces of plastic in nearly every sea turtle necropsy, so it's safe to say that *all* individual turtles in the world's oceans are ingesting our trash in some point in their lives. That's a stunning statement: none should. It doesn't kill them all, but it hits them in many sub-lethal ways, including laying fewer eggs . . . which translates to fewer hatchlings." Seabirds have an equally horrific fate; an estimated 99 percent of species will have eaten plastic by 2050 if things don't change.[9] The impact of plastic on marine life, from entanglement in synthetic nets and line, to ingestion of particles, is not restricted to any organism by size or species.

In addition to the lantern fish we found in the middle of the North Pacific, other fish species are increasingly eating microplastics, including the ones that make their way to your dinner plate. A recent study of fish in markets found that 25 percent of those sampled in the United States and Indonesia had microplastics in their gut.[10] The steamed mussels you order as an appetizer might have nanoplastic particles swirling in their bloodstream.[11]

"Does this matter?" you might ask. Well, we know that plastics have the amazing property of absorbing (taking in) and adsorbing (sticking to) other persistent hydrocarbons drifting aimlessly about. Gas stations will sometimes use giant cloth socks full of polyethylene plastic pellets draped around storm drains to absorb those drops of fuel making their way along the curb. In the ocean, those tiny bits of plastic become little toxic pills, with up to one million times the concentration of pollution of the seawater around them.[12] The frontier of marine science today is uncovering sobering interactions between the toxicants carried by micro- and nanoplastic and the organisms that interact with them.[13] In one study, lugworms—a keystone genus with a critical role in maintaining the structure of an ecological community—ingested microplastic polyvinyl chloride (PVC), which reduced their overall energy levels as they suffered inflammation and reduced feeding.[14] Inside the gut of marine life there's a different environment than that of seawater. A difference in pH and temperature, and the presence of gut surfactants (things that emulsify fats), create a setting for desorption of those toxins and storage in tissues and organs.[15] In other words, the stomachs of marine life are chemically different from the ocean, so plastics are stripped of the chemicals they absorbed and adsorbed, and in some cases those chemicals are stored in the animal rather than being digested or passed. In another study, of a dozen short-tailed shearwaters (*Puffinus tenuirostris*) caught accidentally in fishing nets in the North Pacific, three had extremely high levels of flame retardants, or polybrominated diphenyl ethers (PBDEs), in their stomach fat.

In another 5 Gyres Institute expedition in 2011, we sailed from Rio de Janeiro to Cape Town, through the center of the South Atlantic Subtropical Gyre, with an eclectic crew of surfers, sailors, CEOs, and scientists, including Chelsea Rochman, an ecotoxicologist studying toxicants in the ocean and their impacts on wildlife. She pulled fish out of the net while we collected microplastics. Her results showed a correlation between concentrations of PBDEs in both fish tissues and plastic fragments as we entered the center of the gyre.[16] PBDEs are common in everyday life and are found in items from clothing and curtains to automotive interiors. Although they are being phased out in the products around us, their toxicological impacts are all around us, including evidence of reduced fertility in women[17] and of hormone disruption in developing children in and out of the womb.[18] PBDEs' resistance to biodegradation means they are here for a long while, and in 2009 they were added to the Stockholm Convention on Persistent Organic Pollutants (POPs). The convention is an international treaty that lists pollutants that don't leave the environment easily, including polychlorinated biphenyls (PCBs), DDT, and dioxins that the world should eliminate. It has been ratified by the European Union and 178 other states (the United States has yet to sign on, since much of the stuff is made here and lawmakers are heavily lobbied by industry).

Instances of entanglement and ingestion have risen, involving an estimated 267 species in 1997[19] and more than doubling, to 557 species, by 2015.[20] At the same time, marine life is hitchhiking on trash, riding plastic pollution from one continent or island to another. Invasive species are being transported to new continents at a magnitude unprecedented in the history of life on Earth.[21] Even the fallen giant redwoods of the Pacific Northwest, which are known to reach Hawaiian shores, never make it farther without degrading and sinking. Plastic has turned surface currents into biological highways. When the 2011 Japan tsunami sent unknown millions of tons of debris into the North Pacific, large items like fishing docks, boats, and buoys began washing ashore in the Pacific Northwest of Canada and the United States, with more than 150 documented nonindigenous species hitchhiking along, including crabs, starfish, oysters, and fish, and many plants and other invertebrates.[22] One sixty-six-foot section of a dock, composed of metal and foamed polystyrene, from the fishing port of Misawa came ashore in Oregon with 130 species attached, including the brown algae *Undaria pinnitifida*, a fierce competitor against local species.[23]

Floating plastic can give certain critters a population boost. The only insect genus to walk on the ocean surface, *Halobates sericeus* is a small long-legged black insect that preys on fish eggs. It has found new real estate on plastic trash to lay its own eggs in numbers far greater than ever before. Miriam Goldstein, one of the star graduate researchers at Scripps, discovered a hundred-fold increase in the population of those aquatic insects over the last forty years. Miriam applied the "theory of island biogeography," originally conceived by E. O. Wilson and R. H. MacArthur in 1967, to explain the relationship between floating plastic and species diversity.[24] Among questions she considered: When a new island forms (like a giant tangled mass of fishing nets and trash), who colonizes first? How many species are there and how diverse is it? It's a new twist on the theory.

In 2012, I led the 5 Gyres Institute expedition to study floating debris, fifteen months after the 2011 tsunami. Hank Carson, a marine biologist from the Washington Department of Fish and Wildlife, and I collected floating plastic objects for Miriam's diversity study. Eight hundred miles east of Tokyo we hauled a 500 kilogram tangled mass of net and line up the mast, shook it like a piñata and watched thirty-six different species fall to the deck. Three dead fish, decomposed, were entangled, demonstrating how nets are persistent killers even when lost. After studying this net and 241 other pieces of floating trash, Miriam counted ninety-five different colonizers. The bigger the piece of plastic, the greater the diversity. Among hitchhikers discovered in her analysis was a dangerous invader, the folliculinid ciliate *Halofolliculina* spp. Thought to be limited to the Indian Ocean and South Pacific, it erodes coral and kills its polyps, leaving a black band that slowly marches across the coral head as it dies, a condition called "skeletal eroding band disease," which is now wreaking havoc on remote reefs across the North Pacific.

Back on the ORV *Alguita*, Joel yelled, "Buoy two o'clock, five hundred meters!" I scooped it with the net and hauled it aboard. It was heavy, with a healthy colony of gooseneck barnacles. Little pelagic crabs scurried about the deck, and bristle worms and little isopods nestled deep in the bouquet of barnacles stretched into the air their fan-like feet—which they use as nets to snatch plankton—and gasped for breath. With a filet knife, I shaved them off. Charlie walked up with a kitchen pot.

"Fill this half full of barnacles for me, will ya?" When lunch rolled around, he announced, "Barnacle rice is served." It turned out to be tolerable. The novelty wore off quickly, and the next day the leftovers reeked of rotten seafood and were stealthily tossed overboard. (Years later Miriam would dissect 385 of the same barnacles from the same area and find that 33.5 percent had plastic in their gut.)[25]

There's sufficient evidence now, from published work and personal experience, to say our trash is dynamic in this environment and has an impact on marine life, ranging from chemical contamination to introduction of invasive species via plastic highways. Although media representations often depict charismatic megafauna, like whales, birds, and turtles, as the victims of pollution, the reality is that impacts are pervasive at the bottom of the food chain and come back to us in what we harvest from the sea to feed much of the world. This knowledge will continue to build over time, prompting policy decisions that will be matched by industry counteroffensives. Anna and I will log thousands of miles at sea and share our experiences with hundreds of colleagues, collectively contributing to a movement with the common core values of love for the ocean and the desire to right a wrong, couched in the seemingly emotionless rigor of science methods and writing.

Joel and Jeff, both eager to get in the water, pulled scuba gear from the storage locker after Charlie cut the engine and gave the go-ahead. We had been trawling since 5 a.m. in flat seas, having reached the doldrums, where in absolute stillness the sea surface took on an oily appearance, and every piece of plastic was apparent. Fibers from fishing gear, which are near neutral buoyancy, gently rose to the surface. Fuel economy demanded that we called it quits until wind arrived. The sun, at zenith, weighed heavy on us. We sat motionless, like the garbage. Underwater there was eternal depth and clarity and no reference, so we let the anchor hang deep. After a gear check all around, Joel and Jeff went under. Charlie was in next to inspect the pinholes in the hull that we had patched with putty a week ago in the lee of Necker Island, near Oahu.

Anna and I sat on the back steps to do a gear check and calculate our dive time. After that, we were in. The surface quickly faded as we sank deeper, her hand in mine. The clarity was immaculate. I could see

Charlie hovering below, the anchor hanging dead vertical behind him. My weight belt wasn't fitting quite right, so I took a few minutes to adjust it, and we separated. Anna was above me doing the same, it seemed.

Too much lead weight on my belt, I thought. I looked for my dive meter, which I couldn't find easily. When finally I looked at it, I paused for a second to reread as a wave of fear passed through my entire body like a tsunami. I realized I was way too deep. At 150 feet, I'd gone sixty feet deeper than I'd ever dove before, and did so in seconds. The ORV *Alguita* was a small silhouette above me. I didn't see Jeff, Joel, or anyone. I frantically looked for Anna as I made my way upward. *Where is she?* I thought. I paused for a second in a panic to look for her above me. Then I looked down.

She was deep. Maybe fifty feet below me and sinking deeper fast. My chest felt as if the volume of my lungs had been cut by half. With all of my effort, I raced to her, pressurizing my ears the best I could as I descended. In my head I was screaming to her, *No! No! No! Come back! Look up!* She was descending into the darkness below. "Breathe slow," I told myself, to ward off hyperventilation as I reached down.

I grabbed her by her vest. She was doing the same thing I was doing, looking for her dive meter on a scuba rig she'd never used before. I was holding on tight as I began to inflate her buoyancy compensation (BC) vest. We rocketed to the surface. I don't know how deep we were, but our BC's inflated quickly as the air inside expanded. This also happens in human blood; divers who get the "bends" from rising too fast can be killed as CO_2 bubbles form in their veins.

Another fear set in. "We've got to get back down!" I yelled and pointed. She trusted me. We dove down to the bottom of the anchor chain, where we hovered for a while, then went twenty feet, ten feet, then to the surface. Without a reference for depth, in truly unfamiliar territory with unfamiliar gear, we had set the stage for what could easily have been pierced eardrums, the bends, or narcosis, a kind of intoxicated ride three miles to the benthos below. We experienced the kind of fear that comes from knowing you've done something really stupid while you're in the middle of doing it. It was something I hadn't felt since jumping into buried bunkers in Kuwait back in 1991.

For the rest of the day and all night, all I could think about was our vulnerability and how quickly something so beautiful could be extinguished, I could have lost the one person I know who feels the same urgency to live the changes we want to see in the world. Anna grew up in Santa Monica, California, chasing wildlife upstream in a creek next to her house; attended a school her father founded; finished college at Stanford University; and then went to the Monterey Institute of International Studies for graduate school in environmental policy. Her journey through West Coast progressive culture couldn't have been more different from my Deep South military upbringing, but we converged on a strong conservation ethic, rich in science and in the recognition of the inherent value of all life. I had found my partner in life. I could not fathom losing her. I felt the urgency not to lose any more time. There is no dependable tomorrow, only now.

The next day was February 14, Valentine's Day. The sails hung lazily in the middle of the North Pacific Subtropical Gyre. By 10 a.m. it was already eighty-five degrees on deck. Charlie shut off the engine and turned on the blender, serving up piña coladas. Bob Marley reigned. On every expedition, Charlie chose one day to chill. We were likely the only party a thousand miles in all directions.

Hours passed and we all succumbed to laziness: sleeping, reading, headphones plugged in, watching calm nothingness on a glassy sea. Anna was hiding somewhere. I found her on top of the ship, sleeping on a bed made up of the sails cradled on the boom. I left and returned with something I'd been thinking about.

A few days before, I had netted a piece of green fishing line that drifted by. I had woven it into a ring, roughly the size of my pinky finger. I climbed back up to the sails and lay next to her.

OK, you ready? I thought to myself. I was actually not sure if I had said that aloud.

"What's up?" she asked, reading my nervousness.

"Nothing," I replied.

"Tell me. I know you're up to something."

"Okay, you know that I love you," I said, which is a weird way to start a conversation. I was nervous as hell and she knew it. She was smiling, amused, wondering why the silly antics.

I reached into my pocket while we embraced, and when we separated I filled the space between us with my hand holding the entwined fishing-line ring.

"Will you marry me?" I asked, pausing for less than a second before adding, "but, but you don't have to answer now. You know I want to build another raft. You can think about it till we get to land. . . . You can think about it as long as you like—about the raft and getting married."

She smiled big, the edge of her lip curling to one side like it does.

"Yes." And I felt her arms wrap tightly around me.

The hourly logbook for the ORV *Alguita* lists the usual latitude, longitude, date, time, and boat speed. Under "comments," it reads, "Valentine's Day in the Garbage Patch, Marcus and Anna were engaged."

CHAPTER 3

IMUA

I was struck by the vast and seemingly unbridgeable dissonance between sailors and drifters. The former wait for favorable wind; the latter must out of necessity journey wherever the wind blows. In another sense, one uses nature, one submits to it. The sailor is heroic, the drifter romantic. Even though the drifter often raises a sail, he does so only with the wind directly—or very nearly so—at his back.

—P. J. Capelotti
Sea Drift, 2001

The *Junk* would be my eighth raft. In my journal, I sketched elongated pontoons of plastic bottles wrapped in fishing nets, poles lashed across the deck, a cabin that looks like a giant doghouse, and a square sail billowing in the wind. Plastic bottles are an ideal boat-building material. Seemingly unsinkable, they're tough, UV-resistant, and designed to last on store shelves for decades. Having been sold the idea that bottled water is better than tap water, consumers bought more of it than milk and beer by the 1990s, and by the turn of the twenty-first century, they paid more for it than gasoline. Today, water packaged in plastics that may contain leached plasticizers and microplastic fibers is likely bottled locally, despite pictures of mountains and waterfalls on the labels, and the industry has complete freedom from any standard of quality, unlike free water from your tap. Plastic bottles are plentiful on roadsides and beaches. They're floating down rivers and bobbing across oceans. If you puncture one on your raft, there's likely another one floating by.

Soon after coming off the Mississippi River in 2004, I built the Los Angeles River *Cola Kayak* with students of the Environmental Charter

High School in Lawndale. We launched during "first flush," the first heavy rain in Los Angeles after a long dry season, which sends the contents of trash-filled storm drains, roadsides, and homeless encampments out to sea. The rain picks up millions of plastic bags, bottles, caps, cup lids, Styrofoam cups, straws, forks and knives, tennis balls, tampon applicators, coffee stir sticks, ketchup packs, chip and candy wrappers, and every brand of fast-food packaging in Los Angeles. All of it leaves the land, traveling the Los Angeles River in a rapid deluge along a concrete-covered riverbank and bottom, doing exactly what the US Corps of Engineers designed it to do—leave land quickly. Ours was a rapid, three-day trip, interrupted three times by local police. ("Let me hop on that," two officers said, posing for photos rather than escorting me off the river like others did.)[1]

Bottle-boat building became a hobby, a habit, and an obsession. By 2006, I had drifted 2,300 miles down the Mississippi River on the *Bottle Rocket*, fifty-two miles on the Los Angeles River in the aforementioned *Cola Kayak*, eight miles down the Chattahoochee River in Georgia on *Spastic Plastic*, and a mile on the *Plastic Poison* in Juneau, Alaska. There was a half-mile crossing of the Potomac River in the shadow of the White House on the *Potomac Attack*, and a 226-mile sail along the California coast on *Fluke*, totaling 2,587.5 miles on plastic-bottle boats. I was eager to sail across the ocean next.

Fluke was the test of an oceangoing bottle boat. At the time, I hadn't met Joel or Anna yet, and the name *Junk* didn't exist. The first choice for a name was *Plastiki*, which I announced during a lecture at the 2006 California Science Education Association Conference at Pepperdine University. "We're paying homage to Heyerdahl's *Kon-Tiki*," I said. It would be a perfect name. Or so I thought.

A few weeks later, I was on a conference call with members of the Clean Seas Coalition to discuss municipal plastic-bag bans. I mentioned the project.

"And we're calling it *Plastiki*." The words hung in the air for a moment, until Leslie Tamminen said, "But some guy from National Geographic is doing the same thing, and he's calling it *Plastiki* too." Same catamaran design, same route to Hawaii for 2008, same mission and name. My jaw hit the floor.

There's no way, I said to myself. The only things that came up in a web search were East African plastic industry sites (plastic is "plastiki" in Swahili) and the availability of the domain name. I bought "plastiki.org" and built a website with an animated picture of the bottle raft *Fluke* bouncing across the Pacific Ocean. On June 19, I got an e-mail from Susan Reeve, director of the Explorers Program at the National Geographic Society, demanding we end our *Plastiki* project. According to Reeve, David de Rothschild had thought of it first. I dug in my heels, determined not to give up the name or my plan to raft across the ocean. I was a fool, missing the big picture. I learned that I wasn't the first to do so.

There are nearly fifty highly publicized rafting adventures on record since Thor Heyerdahl's *Kon-Tiki*. Despite lofty goals and tales of high-seas adventure, these rafting expeditions were often plagued by rivalries fueled by colossal egos. They were rife with public and professional shaming, and with sabotage of rafts and careers.

The golden age of rafting began with *Kon-Tiki* in 1947, that is if you ignore the centuries of interisland Polynesian sailing technologies, or the thousands of rafts used to escape to a new life. As Torgeir Sæverud Higraff, aboard the *Kon-Tiki II*, explained in January 2016 after rafting to Easter Island: "In ancient times, the rafts were also used to escape wars, poverty, or politics. After a disaster like El Niño, earthquake, volcano eruptions or drought, rafters were able to find new land and start a new life. Today the rafters only find more politics."[2]

Seven decades ago, Heyerdahl, a cultural anthropologist, had argued that Polynesia-to-South America cultural exchange was not one-way. How else would tomatoes or the South American sweet potato (*Ipomœa batatas*) have reached Easter Island? He launched the balsa-log *Kon-Tiki* from Callao, Peru, in 1947, reaching the Tuamotu Islands of French Polynesia 4,300 miles and 101 days later. His crew of five Norwegians and one Swede enjoyed a long drift in good weather on a sinking raft, sailing faster than the worms could bore holes. They were instant celebrities, winning an Oscar at the 1951 Academy Awards for their documentary film.

Next, in 1952, Alain Bombard, a trained physician frustrated by the piles of bodies that washed along the French coast after wrecks of wayward ships, set about to prove that survival at sea can be had indefinitely with a small raft, a few hooks, and a fruit press for squeezing fresh water from fish guts. He left the Canary Islands on an inflatable dinghy named *L'Hérétique*, drifting westward toward the Americas and away from his wife and one-month-old child. After sixty-five days, he landed at Barbados fifty pounds lighter, covered with open sores. His fish press is found in ocean survival kits today.

In 1954, William Willis built *Seven Little Sisters*, a near replica of *Kon-Tiki*, and solo-navigated Heyerdahl's same route, but kept going 2,200 additional miles to American Samoa. He survived on salt water and a paste made from rye flour. Ten years later, in 1964, he built *Age Unlimited*, and rafted alone from Peru to New Guinea, 11,000 miles in 204 days. He then turned his eyes to the North Atlantic. On May 2, 1968, Willis, aged seventy-four, left Long Island, New York, to raft to Europe. Two months later, a Soviet trawler spotted his submerged boat four hundred miles off the Irish coast, without its captain. Willis held the record for the longest solo voyage adrift, until Salvador Alvarenga arrived in the Marshall Islands 438 days after the engine on his fishing boat died near the coast of Mexico in November 2012.

One of the more eclectic rafting voyages, and perhaps the closest to that of the *Junk*, was the journey of *Lehi IV*, a nine-ton wooden box that drifted from the California coast to Hawaii in 1958 with four men aboard—the same route we would take exactly half a century later, almost to the day.

DeVere Baker, a California shipyard owner and devout Mormon, theorized that white men had originally populated Hawaii, and he aimed to prove it. He derived his ideas from the Book of Mormon as he read of the prophet Lehi: "The voice of the Lord came unto my father, that we should arise and go down into the ship."[3] Baker was sure that Polynesians could not have populated Hawaii. He believed that fair-skinned people of the Americas had been sailing along the West Coast of North America and occasionally a voyager lost at sea would drift unwittingly to Hawaii. "Soon, very soon, the warm sun and exposure would have turned their fair skins to a golden bronze, and the genes of each succeeding generation prepared the one to follow with the added pigment—nature's coloring—until at the advent of birth, the tiny, warm infant was ready to bask in the tropical sun, his protective skin coloring having already been taken care of by a Wise Providence."[4]

He invited Don McFarland, who was looking for a project to write about for a college term paper. McFarland was content to read books and catch fish all day, while Baker preached and sang "Jesus Wants Me for a Sunbeam." As they neared Guadalupe Island on day eight, they had to decide whether to go east or west of the rocky coast. They chose west, wisely or not, and spent the next two days on twenty-four-hour watch, all emergency gear packed and ready to be flung overboard, in the event waves pushed them ashore. (Exactly fifty years later, Joel and I chose east, and got stuck for three days in a giant eddy behind the island.)

Don followed our journey and became our mentor. He told us over and over to bring an extra harpoon in case we lose one, like he did. "Don't jump in without looking for sharks first," he said, adding, "and use a T-shirt to catch a plankton soup." On *Junk*, we saw no big sharks and no tuna, and caught only sixteen fish in a voyage that was twenty days longer. Every time we put a net in the water to catch plankton, there was always more microplastic trash.

In 1968, Heyerdahl was at it again with the papyrus-reed *Ra I*, leaving Safi, Morocco, to demonstrate that the Phoenicians could have brought technology to South America long before the Spaniards or Portuguese ever did, either intentionally or as lost vessels set adrift. That didn't sit well with Brazil. Skeptics lined up offering dire predictions that the *Ra* would sink. They were right. Eight weeks later a fishing boat rescued Heyerdahl and his international crew of seven flying under the UN flag. They were grasping remnants of their submerged raft. He built *Ra II* two years later and made it 3,270 miles to Barbados in fifty-seven days. Heyerdahl and crew reported finding globs of tar along the way, samples of which they brought to the United Nations. Their report was one of the first public discussions of marine pollution.

Santiago Genovés, one of the crew members on *Ra II*, had rafting ideas of his own and built *Acali*, a giant Styrofoam box colored with psychedelic swirls akin to the animated skies in *Yellow Submarine.* Genovés explained, "The Acali Experiment is neither exclusively science nor exclusively the story of a raft at sea. It was a bold experiment of human behavior aboard an isolated floating laboratory, a real sea adventure in which volunteers agreed to participate with the consequent risks, to obtain firsthand data about aggression, conflict, misunderstandings, and possibilities for harmony in a world of violence."[5]

There were six women and five men aboard, and Genovés had three rules: (1) take care of your own sexual needs, (2) don't expect monogamy, (3) no orgies. Halfway across the North Atlantic, Genovés wrote: "The intellectual atmosphere of the raft is scraping bottom."

Genovés described a "disgusting, foul and polluted sea" within three hundred miles of the Yucatán. Tar balls ranging from the size of a grain of rice to a five-pound melon were ever present. On July 16, 1973, the crew hauled aboard a 220-pound shark with black petroleum chunks between all of his teeth. (In the 1970s, it was common practice for oil tankers to clean sludge out of empty hulls as the ships returned to their home countries.)

Only a year earlier, the first research paper on plastic pollution in the ocean was published by E. J. Carpenter and K. L. Smith Jr., who reported finding lentil-shaped polyethylene spheres, known as preproduction pellets, or "nurdles."[6] The pellets are the feedstock of all things plastic, and are easily lost as they are transported around the world from train to truck to ship. They are also the perfect design for ocean persistence—solid and spherical, often coated with UV inhibitors.

In 1973, the Ocean Affairs Board of the National Academy of Sciences (NAS) convened to discuss sources, sinks, and solutions to petroleum in the oceans, including those pesky tar balls Genovés found aboard the *Acali.* The NAS estimated that 6,713,000 metric tons of petroleum entered the marine environment to date: half lost on land and half from at-sea shipping discharges of all sorts, including catastrophic spills, hull cleaning activities, and even intentional unloading of excess oil in high seas.[7] In response, the Intergovernmental Maritime Consultative Organization (IMCO) created MARPOL 73/78, aimed primarily at stopping ship discharges of oil into the sea.[8] In the decade following the implementation of the new restrictions, evidence of tar balls significantly declined.[9] It was not until 1988 that MARPOL was amended with Annex V, which banned maritime discharge of any plastic anywhere in the ocean. As of 2013, Annex V bans dumping of all forms of trash at sea.

Back on the *Acali*, which landed on August 20, 1973, 101 days after launch, Genovés had a long list of maritime stories of plastic pollution to tell, as well as sociocultural observations of life at sea. But the press wanted to know only one thing: "Who screwed who?" Many other rafts, with misunderstood grandiose goals and outsize drama, have followed.

Viracocha, a reed raft built by Phil Buck, successfully sailed from Chile to Easter Island in 1998, completing a voyage that Kitin Muñoz, a Spanish anthropologist, had tried and failed to make years earlier with the much larger raft *Mata Rangi* (it sank after breaking in half). A feud had ensued, putatively over the authenticity of primitive boatbuilding but more realistically about who would be first to prove the voyage could be done on a reed boat. "The ship was built in Bolivia with plastic cord in its interior and natural fiber on the exterior," Muñoz said, pointing out to the media that Buck had used synthetic string to hold reeds together. "Personally, I consider the project a fraud," he added. Though Buck had used the plastic, his was still a primitive raft. Buck went to Heyerdahl himself, who agreed and said, recognizing that the two sailors were missing the bigger picture, "Experience is not as important as a good sense of humor."

Now came the two *Plastiki*s, both with lofty missions to alert the world to a growing environmental disaster, and both with the same design and route. It would be an exercise in self-deception to think my idea to float an airplane across the Great Pacific Garbage Patch on plastic bottles was any less ridiculous or more adventurous than any of the other rafting adventures of the past. Not in my wildest imagination did I think someone else would want to do the same journey in the same year on a plastic bottle catamaran named *Plastiki*. Though I'd used the name *Plastiki* hundreds of times to discuss my next rafting voyage, it wasn't documented in print or film. I sent David de Rothschild a note in June 2007.

Five days later, I received a response from his management firm asking when I had first used the name, and whether I could prove it. After a long e-mail exchange, the firm pointed me to an interview in early 2007 in which David mentions *Plastiki*. It's the only reference to a *Plastiki* bottle boat that preceded my website. "Great minds think alike or idiots seldom differ," as a friend said.

I wanted to think I could absorb this and respond in a way that reflected my core values. That was the pretty story I told myself, but in reality my emotions went nuclear. This was an embarrassingly stupid quarrel, a struggle to come to terms with who was going to sail across the Pacific Ocean on plastic bottles. Superbly stupid. De Rothschild's boat, with more funding than I could ever muster, would probably reach more people, so leaving it to him was better in the big picture. But it was *my* idea, I insisted.

Over the next days, my ego slowly began to soften. "Let it go," I said to myself, watching the tentacles of ego and competition lose grip. Hovering above myself, recognizing the nature of my emotions and what triggered them, I let go . . . for now.

With a deep sigh, I said, "To hell with it all." With a little more objectivity and sensibility, I replied to de Rothschild in early spring with, "It's a bittersweet coincidence that we both independently thought of the same name for the same voyage, rather strange I think. I see no point in using a name you used first."

In all the drifters and vagabonds who have dared to raft across the seas, we can see a microcosm of society: religious fervor on *Lehi IV*, social dynamics on the sex raft *Acali*, and Norwegian heroes and Easter Island egos on *Kon-Tiki* and *Viracocha*. Each expedition reveals the challenges we face on land and reflects the distractions and social dramas that plague both scientists and social movements and take us away from the task at hand. As an old Korean War vet I met protesting the Iraq War liked to remind me: "Keep your eyes on the prize!"

What these rafting adventures have in common, which is instructive for the future, is the nature of seclusion on a floating island, where there's limited space, food and fresh water reserves are easily exhaustible, and entropy is accelerated when maintenance is ignored. This microcosm of overpopulation, resource scarcity, and pollution reflects the same challenges the earth's biosphere faces today. Our biosphere, in essence, is a raft adrift. We have not kept our eyes on the prize.

Plastiki was out, so we needed a new name. I mentioned *Pacific Ocean Rover* to Anna, and she rolled her eyes. She came back with a few crew suggestions: *Patchy*, *Freedom from Debris*, *Net Baller*, and *Garbagio*, which sounded more like a Las Vegas casino than a raft. Had I come from the plastics industry, I might have chosen a name like *Recycler*, or *Dandy Polymer*.

Our words, after all, reflect our politics. In *Don't Think of an Elephant*, George Lakoff, a cognitive linguist from University of California, Berkeley, described messaging in the context of divisive American politics: conservatives embrace the authoritarian father figure who must discipline children for their behavior; when they grow up, the father must be hands-off to give the adults the freedom to do what they know best.[10] This perspective plays into the values of conservatives, and the messaging that follows decries the evils of big government and expensive social programs. In the world of plastic pollution, this translates into an industry emphasis on bad behavior by people who litter and who need to be punished, instead of on plastic products, which, according to this view, are made by responsible businesses that know what they are doing and need no oversight. Conservatives call plastic waste "litter."

Progressives, on the other hand, embracing the nurturing values of equality and community and appealing to social and environmental justice, point out the inequity of corporate influence over domestic and foreign policy. In the world of plastic pollution, this translates into an emphasis on product stewardship on equal par with personal responsibility, placing government in the role of enforcing laws that protect people and the environment, rather than guarding the special interests of a few corporations. Progressives call plastic waste "pollution."

When the plastic pollution problem began to register in the public consciousness in the early 2000s it was "marine debris," a benign term used for decades to describe mostly natural material that washed out to sea and the occasional shipwreck that washed ashore.

But because 90 percent of foreign matter catalogued from the ocean is petroleum-based plastic, the terms "marine debris" and "marine litter" are inappropriate. Some scientists, hoping to feign objectivity, continue to use "marine debris," and falsely argue that using the term "plastic pollution" is a form of advocacy. What those scientists don't realize is that using the term "marine debris" bolsters the industry position of refusing to call plastic in the environment a pollutant.

The American Chemistry Council fights to define language by leveraging its funding of organizations, or by supporting conferences, such as the 2011 Fifth Annual International Marine Debris Conference in Honolulu, where participating NGOs with progressive views were intentionally excluded from meetings. In the 2011 meeting, council members drafted the conference's position on solutions to plastic pollution, titled *The Honolulu Strategy*.[11] In Washington, DC, on December 9, 2014, UNEP, the United Nations Development Programme (UNDP), EPA, and the Ocean Conservancy sat on a panel together to discuss plastic pollution solutions. Judith Enck, regional administrator of EPA region 2, a fiery speaker with a take-no-prisoners persona, referred to the Ocean Conservancy as the "cleanup people," and the Ocean Conservancy fired back with the label "activist NGOs" for any group that stood in opposition to their and the plastic industry's viewpoints, the same way Republicans use the term "activist judge" when confronted with any judicial decision they don't happen to agree with.

So is it litter, debris, or pollution? Imagine if headlines from the 1989 *Exxon Valdez* oil spill, which wreaked havoc along the Alaskan coastline, read: "Oil debris from ship needs recycling." Plastic in the ocean is pollution. Our words matter.

"What then do we call our raft?" I asked Anna, back aboard the ORV *Alguita* days after getting engaged.

Before we made landfall, I asked Joel if he wanted to join me on the journey across the Pacific. Anna explained what we had in mind. I breathed a sigh of relief when a week later he said, "I'm in." I realized I would not have done the voyage without him.

We talked about details that needed to happen first, like fund-raising. I insisted on a June 1 departure date, which left us only three months to do everything before cyclone season began. The three of us talked through logistics, funding, and messaging. We agreed to build the raft with trash. As soon as we returned home, Anna contacted Burbank Recycling and a dozen schools to get bottles, and Joel scoured junkyards for old sailboat masts and fishing nets.

"How about *Junk*?" Anna said. "That's what it is." Joel liked it, agreeing that it defined ocean trash—how, once plastic is out there, it's too toxic to recycle because of all the persistent pollutants that stick to it. To me, it was encompassing, short and simple.

Junk it was.

"You'll be shark bait!" roared Geoff Folsom, finding our project hilarious. "I'll give you all the bottles you need, and a pork-chop necklace!" The CEO of Burbank Recycling, Geoff gave us the hard-hat tour of his operation, which sorts city trash as it rolls along on Rube Goldbergian conveyor belts. Magnets pulled iron off quickly. Newspaper was blown out of the mix, while glass dropped into another bin. An optical sorter then identified plastic by polymer type and shot a blast of air to launch PET (polyethylene terephthalate) into one hole and HDPE (high density polyethylene) into another. Finally, a row of men and women with thick gloves hovered over a conveyor belt picking off their assigned material. One worker grabbed only milk jugs, another only aluminum cans. What was missed tumbled over a giant rotor with stubby teeth, separating cardboard. "This is where plastic bags get stuck and clog the system," Geoff said. "The damn things blow around. They're usually full of other junk, like dog poop. They're a pain to deal with."

Anna, Joel, and I stood outside when Geoff overturned a Dumpster of plastic bottles at our feet. He drove a forklift like a kid on a BMX bike, popping wheelies in and out of his factory. He has more fun playing with trash than I do.

To build a boat, you want PET soda bottles. With thicker walls, and caps with a gasket to seal in pressurized CO_2, they are perfect. Your typical water bottles, on the other hand, are useless. They are thin, crack easily, and their caps pop off if you give them a good stomp. To estimate the number of soda bottles necessary for rafting, we tied weights to a single two-liter bottle, threw it into a neighbor's pool, and found the neutral buoyancy at 5.5 pounds. You can't sink a bottle boat. In the following weeks, we returned to Burbank Recycling half a dozen times to fill my van with thousands of bottles. Geoff reminded me every visit: "Don't forget to come back for the pork-chop necklace!"

The day after meeting Geoff at Burbank Recycling, Anna and I met Mark Capellano. "Ten thousand [dollars] should get you going," Mark said, offering a gift from the Skyscrape Foundation, a family foundation he had a seat on. He's a modest man from Spokane, Washington, the sixth kid of six, son of a postman, with humble blue-collar roots. He understood the power of the grassroots efforts of a passionate few, and we unnecessarily assured him that every penny would go a long way.

A few days later, Jerry Schubel, CEO of the Aquarium of the Pacific in Long Beach, met us in his office. He's known about us ever since the mythical Garbage Patch off the California coast made headlines. We chatted about the *Junk* and casually mentioned the large grassy lawn next to the aquarium's front entrance. "Okay, you can build it here," he said.

Less than a month after returning from the North Pacific Subtropical Gyre, we'd secured all the bottles we needed, along with starter funds and a place to build *Junk*. There were less than two months to go before we launched on June 1.

"Turn here," I say to Joel. He pulls into the aircraft boneyard in La Mirage, California. A fighter plane is half-buried in sand as we approach, as if it landed that way, like a dart. The center cabin of a 747, sliced horizontally just below the windows, creates a structure akin to a Quonset hut, leading to the yard's office. "Just go pick the one you want and I'll get a crane out to ya," the manager says, barely lifting his eyes off his desk. There are a few acres of airplanes, mostly fuselages with wings detached, lying haphazardly near each other, like tadpoles trapped in a puddle. Joel and I jump from the top of one to another; otherwise there's no clear way to get around. Deep in the middle of a nestled group of fuselages, we find one with intact windows and doors. Soon after, a crane lifts it high above the others, setting it gently on the trailer behind my van. Sand was pouring out.

In front of the aquarium, we've barricaded a small plot of grass where our mountain of trash begins to grow. Visitors stroll over with the same questions—most notably, and understandably: "Are you crazy?"

"Aren't you gonna glue the caps on?" says an eleven-year-old girl, walking away from her school group.

"Nah, hand-tight is fine," I reply. "I've done it before." Words I'd come to regret.

Over the past few weeks, Joel had stripped a dozen masts, a few rudders, and some scrap sails from junked sailboats, and he scavenged fishing docks for trashed fishing nets. *Junk is what it is*, I think, standing over our outdoor workshop.

Jerry, the aquarium director, comes outside and asks, "Are you guys getting close to having something to show? My board is wondering why we have a pile of junk out here." I understand that he may have promised something with a bit more aesthetic value than the junkyard we've created. By May 1—one month to go—we'd complete much of the raft. Half of the fishing-net pontoons were filled with thousands of bottles, thanks to two high school groups, the Green Ambassadors from Environmental Charter High School and Team Marine at Santa Monica High School. We build thirty-foot-long wooden troughs in their classrooms, lay the net in, rinse out the bottles, and stuff them inside. Joel's success in the boat junkyard produces all the masts we need for the deck. Without using any nails, screws, or bolts, we tie the mast in a grid using Polynesian raft-building techniques. I spend many hours in my workshop welding supports for the two recycled rudders, and base plates for two masts to create an A-frame. A Y-shaped plate on top holds the two masts at a specific angle, with room on top for our radar equipment. Finally, we take a grinding wheel and remove every unnecessary nut or bolt from the airplane fuselage, thus bringing its weight under three hundred pounds. Cargo straps hold it to the deck.

In the final weeks we're scrambling. Sponsors donate solar panels and a wind generator, to power our new communication and navigation electronics, along with satellite phones. We get thousands of free minutes from Explorer Satellite, and a thousand-dollar shopping spree is donated by Whole Foods. In the end, *Junk* is a functional boat, even registered at the California Department of Motor Vehicles. Our total budget for the entire project is under $40,000, which covers new navigation and communication equipment, airfare, shipping, food, insurance, tools, lights, wiring, fishing gear including spear gun, medical kit, life raft, and a meager salary for us during the build. By late May, our budget has dwindled and we continue fund-raising to pay for additional satellite minutes. At that point our principal sponsor is my Visa card.

The week before departure, in late May 2008, Anna and I give a few lectures around town, and we appear before the Pasadena City Council to speak in favor of a proposed plastic-bag-ban ordinance. These plastic-bag ordinances are popping up across the United States and represent the front line in efforts to address the plastic pollution issue. The Pasadena mayor's veto of the council's decision was met with a roar of discontent from the packed city hall. (Years later, under persistent public pressure, he'd reverse himself.) We're quiet on the drive home.

"There's a chance things could go wrong," I say, breaking the silence, beginning a conversation we've both avoided till now, about the journey ahead.

"I don't want to think about it," Anna replies. The raft could fail. Our departure in a few days could be the end of it all.

"Love or justice?" I ask. The risk of what we're doing confronts us with greater clarity, now that there's no time to spare. What is the value of love if there's a crime before your eyes—the inequity of unleashing our trash on people and the planet, causing families to live on landfills and leaving a wasted sea, while the polluters manipulate public perception and policy and evade responsibility?

"It just feels selfish that we should be putting so much time in our relationship, when we could focus on doing more work," I add, referring to the many weekends and evenings we've spent together, when we could have been working harder on bag bans and planning expeditions.

"They are the same," Anna says. "We love what we care about. What I feel for you is like what I feel for my family, maybe our future family. It's everything. Love creates justice."

Our love for each other drives our compassion, provides context for our work. The work is also a kind of self-preservation. It can best be described as reciprocal altruism—I take care of me by taking care of you. It's what Joel and I will experience in the weeks ahead on *Junk*. This logic extends to everyone, where there is a causal relationship between someone's suffering and your own state of being. We must care for others so they are prepared to give to the community.

Love and justice: there's no need to differentiate.

JUNE 1, 2008, MILE 0

Launch Day, Rainbow Harbor, Long Beach, California
(Latitude 33°45', Longitude 118°11')

Don McFarland, one of the four sailors aboard the *Lehi IV* in 1958, walks down the dock to us. Now in his seventies, he carefully climbs aboard *Junk*. "I hope you brought an extra harpoon like I told ya," he says.

After reminiscing about DeVere Baker, he grabs a permanent marker off the airplane dashboard and writes "IMUA" outside, above the windshield. "It means 'forward,'" he says of the native Hawaiian word. "We wrote it on *Lehi IV*."

David de Rothschild had contacted me only two days earlier. I had been foolish to be suspicious of him. I'm reminded for a moment that there's an underlying camaraderie among seafarers, perhaps born of a recognition of the common friend and foe we share beyond the shore. He sends a note in stoic fashion on May 29, just two days before our departure.

> Marcus, I have no doubt you will make it and continue to bring much needed awareness to the issue. God speed and calm seas.
>
> —David

CHAPTER 4

JUNK-O-PHILIA

Our Obsession with Stuff

That's all you need in life, a little place for your stuff. That's all your house is: a place to keep your stuff. If you didn't have so much stuff, you wouldn't need a house. You could just walk around all the time.

—George Carlin, 1986

We have an inglorious knack for accumulating stuff. In a 1955 article in *Life* magazine titled "Throwaway Living," a mom, dad, and daughter stand beneath a shower of disposable cups, bags, plates, and utensils falling from the sky.[1] The article begins: "The objects flying through the air in this picture would take 40 hours to clean—except that no housewife need bother. They are all meant to be thrown away after use." A clear sign of the cultural times, the article foreshadowed an economic model of mass production and planned obsolescence that continues to hold sway.

Whether it's because fashions change or because products are manufactured to fail, we're primed to buy as often as possible. The psychology of advertising has optimized the selling of stuff to every demographic. Eighteen-month-old children have an average repertoire of two hundred brands they recognize before first grade.[2] Sadly, there's a strong correlation between higher body mass indexes, known as BMIs, and recognition of "golden arches and silly rabbits."[3] Plastics Europe, the second largest trade lobby for plastic next to the ACC, reported production of just over three hundred million metric tons of new consumer plastic globally in the year 2013, up from almost zero in the mid-twentieth century. What we don't burn, bury, or feebly recycle is either stuffed in our attics or floating in the ocean. It doesn't go away.

Two months before Anna and I sailed with Charles Moore in 2008, I filmed a Weather Channel skit, titled "Hitting the Bottle," that began in the middle of the Puente Hills Landfill. As the repeat character Commando Weather, I was in the largest dump west of the Mississippi River to see what "away" really meant for our junk. House-size bulldozers caused the ground to rumble beneath my feet as they climbed over and flattened a mound of residential waste, delivered here from the homes of ten million Angelenos, while fireworks exploded over my head. Seagulls unloaded a volley of creamy white feces that spattered around the film crew. "They drop chicken bones in neighborhood swimming pools," an amateur pyrotechnician explained. "The fireworks shoo them away."

Until it closed in 2013, Puente Hills Landfill buried half the residential waste of Los Angeles—1,300 tons per day, entombed in a five-hundred-foot-tall layer cake of trash, sand, and dried human waste from sewage treatment plants. It's a literal shit sandwich, the largest terrestrial dump in the United States.

William Rathje, an anthropologist from the University of Arizona, coined the term "garbology," meaning the study of human artifacts left in landfills, a kind of contemporary archeology. He began the Garbage Project, a multiyear survey of a quarter million pounds of garbage destined for US landfills. He and his students meticulously sorted and characterized the waste. They estimated 20 to 24 percent of what we bury is plastic and 40 percent is paper, a third of which is newsprint. That same distribution seems to apply at Puente Hills, where I climbed over stacks of wet magazines and newspapers, construction lumber, a swing set, broken flowerpots, black and white bags, Styrofoam, and random colorful broken toys. I reached down and picked up a dirty action figure, pocketing it for my own collection.

The World Bank estimates the amount of global municipal solid waste produced annually at 1.3 billion tons, a number that is expected to double by 2025.[4] The EPA tracks our trash, too, estimating that in 2013 alone Americans generated about 254 million tons of municipal solid waste, and composted or recycled about 87 million tons of it.[5] That's a 34.3 percent diversion rate, leaving almost two-thirds of our trash to be buried, burned, or lost to the environment. We've found it floating in the middle of the ocean as far from land as possible, and there's even more buried in our lakes and rivers.

In Los Angeles County, I've surveyed these sunken plastics in the watersheds of the Los Angeles and San Gabriel Rivers and Ballona Creek, which collectively cover roughly 4,130 square kilometers of urban, suburban, rural, and industrial space—a region inhabited by 3.7 million people. Water from infrequent winter rains, overwatered lawns, car washes, and treated sewage from half a dozen plants in the city, flow into three concrete-lined rivers (the ones you saw in the movies *Grease* and *Terminator 2*). A kilometer from the ocean, the flat concrete walls and floor of each river give way to natural sediment, where I collected buckets of mud laden with the sunken evidence of urbanity: bike locks, keys, nuts, bolts, utensils, wrenches, a handful of bullets, and plastics—lots of plastics.

Pieces of car taillights, broken CDs and DVDs, bicycle reflectors, soda bottles, fragments of cigarette lighters, and polycarbonate pre-production pellets account for a density of 474 grams per cubic meter of sediment, roughly a pound of plastic for each cubic yard, potentially amounting to more than forty-five tons of plastic buried in Los Angeles County rivers alone. The majority of plastics produced today are polymers that sink in seawater, such as PET soda bottles, vinyl toys, and PVC pipes; polystyrene salad clamshells; all polycarbonate; as well as all thermoset plastics, such as fiberglass, resins, and epoxies. It's as if the newest layers of sediment in all lakes and rivers globally are collectively the largest landfill on the planet.

I've still got that Puente Hills action figure somewhere, in some box. I've always been a bit of a hoarder. In the early 1980s, back in Louisiana, my neighborhood crew of gangly teens would Dumpster-dive behind local stores, using shopping carts to carry our treasures home. Once I waited patiently while a store manager smashed the faces of fifty new Texas Instruments calculators. (When the model was discontinued the store was ordered to destroy the ones that remained rather than donate them.) I retrieved them all from the Dumpster and brought them to my science class for a week of tech dissection.

We once hauled home thirty boxes of toy car racetracks from the same store, linking them down our block the length of a football field. Broken bikes, a lawnmower, and busted power tools made it home with me.

On July 9, 1982, the skies near my home filled with smoke: Pan Am Flight 759 took off from Louis Armstrong New Orleans International Airport, circled over my neighborhood in Metairie, and crashed eight blocks from my house, killing all 145 people aboard. We ran to see it. I grabbed a piece of acrylic window that was stuck in a cypress tree. I still have it somewhere. I've always wondered who was looking through it in those last seconds.

During the 1991 Gulf War, I arrived in Saudi Arabia with one bag and left Kuwait City seven months later with three duffel bags filled with souvenirs. I have Iraqi uniforms and helmets, a camel tooth, two dead scorpions, and a camel spider I smuggled home. The Iraqi gas mask I brought home has eerily decomposed into an amorphous blob of rubbery goo.

In a small safe I bought when I was twelve I still have a coin collection, a Mardi Gras doubloon collection, a stamp collection, stacks of foreign currency, and comic books from the seventies. In dozens of plastic milk crates I keep dinosaur bones I excavated from the badlands of Wyoming—around ten thousand pounds by now. All of it has real or perceived value according to manufactured standards of rarity, quality, and history. Everything has a story, and perhaps that's the essence of it . . . of what draws me to all of this stuff. I'm not alone.

By 2007, one in ten US households rented storage units, and the self-storage industry earns over $6 billion in annual revenue. Waste management is equally lucrative. What doesn't fit in attics, closets, and garages cycles through yard sales until it reaches the inevitable dump. No species hangs on to its trash like ours does, and now thanks to the resilience of its chemistry, trash exceeds our lifespans. Before plastic, nearly all waste was biodegradable, or would oxidize and rust away, or was inert like glass and ceramics. Metal, wood, and glass are the material culture of all archeological sites predating the last half century. Today, plastic dominates our material landscape.

A long line of chemistry innovators emerged on the coattails of the Industrial Revolution. In 1824, Charles Goodyear, a young American inventor in and out of jail for debt, discovered that sulfur mixed with raw rubber made it durable and pliable, even when cold. Goodyear invented vulcanization and created the Vulcanite Court, a collection complete with inflatable rubber furniture, which he displayed at the Great Exhibition in 1851.

The Englishman Alexander Parkes invented the first plastic as Parkesine, a liquefied cellulose nitrate that air-hardened into moldable sheets. Parkes displayed his wares at the International Exhibition in London in 1862, presenting examples of Parkesine buttons, combs, knife handles, and pen- and pencil-holders. Parkes figured that Parkesine could do what vulcanization could not do because of vulcanization's reliance on raw rubber: be purely synthetic, thus freeing the Industrial Revolution from dependency on nature.

That dependence on nature was a limit to production. Take, for example, demand for real elephant ivory for billiard balls. A precipitous drop in supply in the 1860s fueled a $10,000 prize for non-ivory billiard balls. This motivated John W. Hyatt to invent collodion (a variety of Parkesine) and incorporate it into a series of patents, resulting in collodion-coated billiard balls with explosive effects if hit just right. Tinkering in his chemistry lab, Hyatt stumbled upon a recipe that used camphor and turned cellulose nitrate into the more stable celluloid, patented in 1870, a material used for knife handles, combs, photographic plates, and toys, despite its potential for spontaneous combustion. It is still used today for ping-pong balls, which remain highly flammable.

By 1907, other chemists were picking up where the early inventors left off. Leo Baekeland experimented with formaldehyde and phenol to create Bakelite, which was perfect for electrical components in a growing technological age. Ideal for insulating wires, electrical sockets, and anything else that might rust, Bakelite resisted heat and chemicals, and it held its shape over time. You can see it in those old black telephones in movies of the 1950s, and in molded and polished translucent jewelry beginning in the Art Deco era.

Soon two giants emerged: DuPont and Dow. The DuPont chemical company, which began a quarter century after the American Revolution producing gunpowder, pioneered the synthetic revolution, with materials such as Teflon, neoprene, Kevlar, Mylar, Lycra, and nylon.[6] Nylon stockings debuted in the United States in 1939, and became the admiration of World War II servicemen with their pin-up posters. Production of nylon stopped two years later, when DuPont switched to making parachutes instead. A shortage of stockings led to post–World War II "nylon riots" that plagued stores nationwide. But with one rip the stockings were trash, prompting consumers to buy more. They were the first throwaway synthetic domestic product.

From changing how we preserve foods to prolonging the lives of soldiers who wear bulletproof Kevlar vests, DuPont's innovations have improved Americans' quality of life, but we bear the burden of the products' toxic legacy. DuPont invented Freon, the chemical responsible for depleting the ozone layer above Antarctica. Following public pressure and a successful movement to end CFC production in the mid-1970s, DuPont completely phased them out by 1995. Less than a decade later, the hole in the ozone layer began to shrink. It took the hard work of raising public awareness and implementing environmental policy change to solve this environmental problem. DuPont, with a fiduciary responsibility to its shareholders to sustain profits, could not begin to do it on its own.

The other American giant, Dow, is the predominant producer of polyethylene and polypropylene, two plastic polymers that comprise the majority of single-use throwaway products and packaging, as well as nearly 80 percent of plastics floating in our oceans.[7] Founded in 1897, Dow was the chief US producer of bleach, but it soon gained fat World War I contracts to make metals and incendiary materials for flares and explosives. In 1937, Dow invented polystyrene, branded as Styrofoam (Dow frequently chastises journalists who use the trademarked name without permission), and that same year cofounded the Society of Plastics Industries with DuPont in an effort to collectively position plastics as the replacement material for metals and natural textiles, and to defer competition from bio-based polymers and fuels and win big World War II contracts.

In 2016, Dow and DuPont merged into the so-called Double D, creating a $120 billion chemical and agricultural giant and reducing their corporate tax burdens. This would also allow the merged companies to shed less-profitable product lines, such as Saran Wrap and Teflon, to other companies, and to dominate emerging markets for new materials, like bioplastic.

Bioplastic has been around a while. In the early 1940s, Henry Ford demonstrated the resilience of a "Soybean Car" with bioplastic fenders and door panels, made from a soy-based phenolic resin. But petroleum plastics, cheaper and readily available during those war years, edged bioplastic out, sending the world down a rabbit hole of fossil-fuel dependence that we're trying to climb out of.

With today's inconsistent oil prices, companies including Procter & Gamble and Coca-Cola are exploring plant-based plastics as a means of creating a more reliable and consistently valued resource decoupled from fossil fuels. Along with Unilever, Danone, Ford, Heinz, and Nike, they created the Bioplastic Feedstock Alliance. With strong support from the World Wildlife Fund, the alliance's intent is to replace fossil fuels with renewable carbon from plants. Envisioning a "bioeconomy," these companies see bioplastics "reducing the carbon intensity of materials such as those used in packaging, textiles, automotive, sports equipment and other industrial and consumer goods."[8] In September 2015, the Brazilian company Braskem began production of plant-based polyethylene, which has the same chemical structure as the polyethylene in your typical plastic bag made from fossil fuels but is derived entirely from sugarcane fiber. These are the same plastics, causing the same plastic-pollution problem—only they're not sourced from fossil fuels. That's it. Plant-based plastics are completely different from the biodegradables.

Polylactic acid (PLA), however, is a biodegradable polymer, found in products you see advertised as "corn cups" or in utensils called "spud ware." Another is polyhydroxyalkanoate (PHA), made from bacteria. They biodegrade differently: PLA requires an industrial compost facility, with lots of heat and rich microbes, to degrade, whereas PHA will degrade in the marine environment.

In advertising, there's plenty of confusion and greenwashing when it comes to the use of the terms "bioplastic," "plant-based," and "bio-based." Only the label "biodegradable" in advertising is subject to strict guidelines. "Bioplastic" is a loosely defined catchall term that describes plastic from recent biological materials, including truly biodegradable materials and nonbiodegradable polymers that are plant-based. These definitions leave a lot of room for advertisers to manipulate public perception.

When Coca-Cola unveiled the PET PlantBottle, with green leaves and circular arrows on its label, a week before the 2009 Copenhagen Climate Change Conference (COP15), many NGOs and government agencies, including the Danish consumer ombudsman, took the company to court for greenwashing, prompting label modifications. Even though it's "plant-based," and despite all the leafy greenery, it's the same PET bottle you'll find floating across the ocean.

Looking back at last century, we can see that the Depression-era ethic of conservation, where nothing was wasted, gave way to ad-driven consumerism and planned obsolescence, where throwaway living reflected a culture that valued convenience and leisure time, and being germ-free. But the environmental movement of the late 1960s through the 1970s took note of the destructive consequences of the trash blowing across fields and highways.

In 1971, Iron Eyes Cody was on TV across the United States as the "Crying Indian" (he was actually an Italian American actor) standing next to one of America's new interstate highways shedding a tear as plastic trash tumbled by. The slogan "People cause pollution, people can stop it" accompanied the print ad version, and ad campaigns urging "Don't be a litterbug" and "Give a hoot, don't pollute," collectively and effectively put the blame for plastic pollution on the consumer. The ads were created by the organization Keep America Beautiful and were funded largely by Anheuser-Busch, PepsiCo, Coca-Cola, and Philip Morris. The strategy deflected attention away from producer responsibility and product design, and we bought it hook, line, and sinker.

In 1973, the first PET soda bottles hit store shelves, replacing heavy, breakable glass with durable, disposable plastic. I remember as a kid scouring roadsides in southern Louisiana for glass bottles and returning them for a nickel each to the local Texaco station, which stored them in a chain-link cage behind the shop. My skinny hands could fit through the fence to steal bottles I had just returned. I returned the same bottle a few times until the manager caught on. One month, an excavator dredging local drainage ditches unearthed hundreds of glass bottles. I hit the jackpot.

Early bottle-redemption programs were expensive for companies like Coca-Cola and PepsiCo, considering that every local bottler had to collect, store, transport, wash, refill, and redistribute soda bottles back to the retailer. Single-use, throwaway plastic changed everything. Production could be centralized, so bottling factories could be shut down. Dealing with plastic bottles became taxpayers' municipal waste-management problem, thanks to intense industry lobbying efforts to defer responsibility. Beverage bottlers shifted all costs of negative externalities to the public.

Oregon passed the first bottle bill in the United States in 1971, creating a deposit system that allowed consumers to return empty bottles for a cash refund. In 1976, three more states proposed their own bottle bills: Michigan, Colorado, and Maine. The Michigan United Conservation Clubs gathered four hundred thousand signatures to make the bill a ballot measure, which won by a substantial margin. While Maine eventually succeeded, Colorado didn't, and has yet to try again. Today only ten states have bottle bills. Meanwhile, Michigan has reached a 94.2 percent recovery rate for bottles sold versus bottles recovered.[9] In most cases, however, public interests are outspent and lawmakers are inundated with industry lobbyists. Dwight Reed, president of the National Soft Drink Association (now the American Beverage Association), in 1980 admitted the strategy for evading producer responsibility:

> Society is telling us in unmistakable terms that we share equally with the public the responsibility for package retrieval and disposal. This industry has spent hundreds of millions of dollars in the attempt to dispute, deflect, or evade that message.[10]

By 1992, the United States made more plastic than steel. The industries that make plastic and manufacture stuff from it had successfully deflected claims that they shared any responsibility for the endgame of their material, leaving the public with the myth that recycling was our savior.

CHAPTER 5

THROWN AWAY

Sigh no more, ladies, sigh no more.
Men were deceivers ever,
One foot in sea, and one on shore,
To one thing constant never.
Then sigh not so, but let them go,
And be you blithe and bonny,
Converting all your sounds of woe,
Into hey nonny nonny.

—William Shakespeare
Much Ado About Nothing, 1612

DAY 1: JUNE 1, 2008, MILE 0

Launch Day, Rainbow Harbor, Long Beach, California
(Latitude 33°45', Longitude 118°11')

Next to the Aquarium of the Pacific in Long Beach harbor, before a swarm of television cameras and after dozens of interviews and farewells and floral leis from family and friends, we untie *Junk* from its moorings. The chaos of the morning leaves tasks still undone. I'm welding brackets for the solar panels, and Joel is installing electronics and wiring the wind generator. Anna is guiding volunteers who spray paint "J-U-N-K" in giant letters on the sail. Everyone is still tying knots to hold the raft together. We are determined to keep to our departure time. Any compromise would send us deeper into hurricane season.

"Charlie, we're ready," I say.

The ORV *Alguita*, with Captain Charles Moore at the helm, is standing by to tow *Junk* sixty miles offshore. After months of scrambling, we had finally built our ocean-crossing raft. Charlie checks the towline. Joel is on the bow of *Junk* with a Cheshire-cat grin. Nicole, his girlfriend and a volunteer on the raft's construction, is by his side.

With my arms around Anna, we watch a wall of waving hands and listen to the cheers. "Fair winds and following seas!" "Be safe!" "You guys are nuts!" We are deep in the harbor, where storm drainage from the city empties and circulates poorly. I reach between the pontoons and yank a plastic bag out of the water, hold it high, and say loudly: "This is why we're doing this!"

Then I whisper, "What the hell am I doing?"

Junk is moaning as the ORV *Alguita* tows the raft through swelling seas and into a coming storm. The six pontoons and their thousands of plastic bottles undulate beneath the raft, bending over the bow each time they are dragged into a wave. This is the shakedown cruise I wanted three weeks ago, when we towed *Junk* through Los Angeles Harbor for a test run, but that day was calm and sunny. Now, with real weather, we recognize points of failure.

We are much heavier than expected, with three hundred pounds of food, three solar panels, and four hundred pounds of batteries, plus new electronics and metal framework to hold it all together, a full ice chest, two giant spools of rope, and two car seats ripped from my Ford van just yesterday. The deck, fabricated from two dozen sailboat masts lashed in a square grid, sits a foot lower in the sea than I expected, with rough-cut ends jutting out from the perimeter. The outside pontoons are slipping from under the raft and riding on the sides, like the thick black rubber ring around bumper cars at an amusement park.

My mind endlessly revisits the engineering of the raft. I don't know if the combined weight will cause it to buckle. I don't know if the pontoons will rip open, or if the deck will torque and tear lashings, or if tension on the stays will bend the masts. With each wave, the cables holding the A-frame mast vertical give slack and then whip back into shape. *This isn't going to work*, I think.

At four knots of towing speed it will take until tomorrow to get sixty miles offshore. It's dark and cold, and we're still tethered to the ORV *Alguita* as Anna and I profess our love for each other under swirling gray skies and six-foot seas. Night passes slowly, sleeplessly. I'm aching with uncertainties, knowing that I cannot turn back—it's a self-imposed trap of publicly proclaimed expectations. When morning comes, Joel and I assess the outcome of the first night at sea. Wind is now gusting at thirty knots.

"Bottles! Hey, there are bottles blowing across the deck!" Joel yells.

Waves are washing over my feet. We stuff loose bottles in the airplane fuselage. The front port-side pontoon is deflated, having been pushed out and flipped over the deck, then ripped open by the sharp edges of masts that jut from all sides. The derelict netting used for that pontoon, given to us by a fisherman in Santa Cruz, had degraded from heat and sunlight and was more brittle than we thought.

"Charlie, we've got pontoon failure," Joel explains over the VHF radio. "You gotta stop for a few minutes." I don my wet suit and dive in, stuffing plastic bottles back in through the first hole I see, my fingers growing numb. Luckily, each pontoon is a tapestry of scrap netting, triple wrapped, so the majority of bottles are secured. The deflated pontoon is largely unmanageable in rolling seas. It's like wrestling a giant wriggling grub. I strangle the front of the pontoon with a piece of rope and lash it firmly to the deck. With a burgeoning sense of failure, I say to Anna, "I hope this works."

If we fail in the middle of the North Pacific Gyre, we'll surely join that list of rafting adventures since Thor Heyerdahl's *Kon-Tiki*, but as the fools who died trying. But if we succeed, the conversation will be about what we did right and why we did it. That prize is worth the risk. The prize means owning the conversation about solving the plastic pollution problem and asserting a role in defining the language we use in science, policy, and the public arena. We need a good story to rally the public around, and this adventure is the entry point for many people becoming aware of the environmental problem. But we are not the only ones with eyes on that prize.

The American Chemistry Council was on the offensive in California with a new public campaign: "Plastics: Too Valuable To Waste." The group embarked on a multipronged effort that began with a $2.5 million pledge to California public education, and involved inserting language about "recycling," rather than "reduction," into California state science standards. Then, in November 2007, the ACC hosted its own conference, titled "Tackling Marine Debris." Two years earlier, in September 2005, Algalita Marine Research and Education had held its own conference, "Plastic Debris, Rivers to Sea," which threatened the ACC by taking a strong position on policy aimed at stopping virgin plastic pellets from leaving factories and washing up on California shores. Despite an industry program known as Operation Clean Sweep, which sought to improve industry practices for keeping pellets out of rivers and the sea, conservationists and other advocacy groups won support for California Assembly Bill 258 (aka, the "nurdle bill"), which put teeth into enforcement of industry standards for preventing pellet loss. So the ACC was working overtime to define and deflect regulation.

What the hell am I doing here? I thought, as I sat on a panel at the ACC's 2007 conference, with my PhD in education, sandwiched between Miriam Doyle from the Joint Institute for the Study of Atmosphere and Ocean at the University of Washington and Seba Sheavly of Sheavly Consultants, both well published in marine science. Both, with research support from the ACC, had made a very targeted case that Charlie Moore's research was overblown. Together, they asserted that there was nothing out there to worry about.

I immediately became defensive. "If you haven't been out there, you can't really comment on it," I argued. With no one else studying the accumulation of plastic in the waters between Hawaii and California, how could they shoot the messenger? The only study in the North Pacific Gyre was between Hawaii and Japan, back in 1985, by Robert Day. It showed abundant floating plastic, but Day didn't look where Charlie did. All current modeling shows a convergence of trash where Charlie found it. What we found was clearly evidence of a global contaminant, and that's a colossal threat any way you parse the data.

In the audience was Miriam Goldstein, a graduate student at Scripps Institution of Oceanography with a driving passion for conservation and for reducing plastic pollution. She had invited me to speak at the weekly Ecology Seminar at Scripps, so just six weeks before *Junk* was set to sail, I stood before a packed room with as many faculty as students.

"Just a month ago," I explained, "we returned from another cruise through the North Pacific Gyre, from Hawaii to San Francisco, to re-sample the same sites Charlie visited back in 1999. There's a six-fold increase in plastic pollution, and preliminary results of fish guts show widespread microplastic ingestion." The audience was listening patiently, bobbing their heads in acknowledgment. Then came the Q & A and the public flogging.

"What do you know about spatial-temporal distribution of the plastic debris?"

"Do you think the fish you say ate plastic are actually ingesting plastic before or after they enter the net?"

"How can you all think your sample size of eleven net tows is representative?"

I stood my ground feebly, answering, "I'll get back to you," unknowingly confirming their assumptions about my academic credentials.

I met Chelsea Rochman for the first time there. Years later I asked about that day at Scripps. "I think people generally concluded that the science wasn't being done right. Don't take offense to this, but people thought you were presenting yourself as a marine scientist when you were not," she said. That's true, but at that time we were only counting floating pieces of plastic on the sea surface and in fish guts. This was relatively simple, descriptive science—looking under a microscope and counting: one, two, three. . . . The complexity would come later, as the science moved to ecotoxicology and human health. Interestingly, these doubts about my credentials faded when I published. But at that point there was an academic glass ceiling separating the amateur from the first floor of the academic tower, and to some degree it will always exist for those who publish from outside that tower. Like Charlie Moore had said to me once before, "It's the PhD club. They won't let you in without one, and you've got the wrong one."

Chelsea had become interested in plastic pollution during a semester-abroad program in Australia, where she saw trash on beaches and reefs. "I was initially interested in policy, but realized that there wasn't much science being done. In doing science I would earn the credibility I need to take strong policy positions," she explained.

"So, science is a means to an end?" I replied.

"Yes, but also an end in itself. You know how it is, you answer a scientific question and ten more questions pop up," she answered.

In the journal *Nature*, Chelsea argued that if countries classified the most harmful plastics as hazardous, their environmental agencies would have the power to restore affected habitats and prevent more dangerous debris from accumulating. Immediately, the ACC responded, writing on February 15, 2013: "The suggestions by the commenters in *Nature* are neither justified nor helpful," completely discrediting Chelsea and her colleagues and disavowing responsibility for the single-use, throwaway plastics that pollute the planet. The ACC argued that although plastics do absorb pollutants, we still don't know if those toxics are bioavailable. "America's plastics makers agree more research is needed," they concluded, a standard mantra to delay action of any kind.

"You're an early-career scientist looking to land a tenured position somewhere, but are you worried that your policy positions will count against you?" I asked.

"Sure, that's a concern. You're not supposed to have an opinion when you're first starting out. They say, 'Be pure. Do science for the sake of science. Don't advocate anything,'" she explained. "But things are changing. There's a greater desire for applied science, something that makes a clear difference, and if that means a policy opinion, then so be it. There is a growing recognition of doing science that matters." As Rutgers University political scientist David Guston put it, "the blurring of boundaries between science and politics, rather than the intentional separation often advocated and practiced, can lead to more productive policy making."[1] But there's still an institutional bias against advocacy, since the old guard is quick to defend the social structure of academia. It applies to scientists testifying at hearings, and to activists talking to scientists.

While Charlie Moore's initial publication awakened the public to plastic pollution, the topic as a new field of marine science was already evolving into new marine debris programs around the world. Toxicology studies emerged from Hideshige Takada of the University of Tokyo, along with a wealth of microplastics research from Richard Thompson and his students and colleagues at Plymouth University in England. Charlie soon established a research program at the University of Hawaii at Hilo, where Hank Carson was taking students routinely to "Junk Beach" at Kamilo. Scripps soon entered the game, and SEA at WHOI began poring over archived plankton samples.

The plastics industry hasn't changed. It took activism, advocacy, and media attention to turn a "difficult to verify" (few venture to the middle of the ocean to report reality) environmental catastrophe and drag science from under the thumb of industry. With public interest driving corporate and policy reaction, there's suddenly abundant public and private funding to validate unsubstantiated claims. Science is expensive, and requires much more than the virtue of the scientist. As Chelsea Rochman said, "Science happens till the funding runs out." And that's the leverage the ACC understands all too well.

DAY 2: JUNE 2, 2008

San Nicolas Island

I can see the elongated silhouette of San Nicolas Island on the horizon, illuminated by the falling sun. In the hours before sunset, I rethink the raft design, something I will do every day for the rest of the journey. The weather is fierce, forcing waves over the deck. The raft undulates, torques, and warps in unpredictable ways, yet it stays together for now. I don't know if this design can last six weeks. Each new noise or movement is a sign of engineering success or failure.

In the lee of the island we find shelter from the largest waves, but not the wind. We drop both anchors and drift along the southeast corner until the anchors set. *Junk* is motionless relative to the island for now. We'll stay here overnight and make repairs tomorrow. Joel unties the towline as Charlie gives us slack. We abandon *Junk* for a brief respite to enjoy a warm farewell dinner aboard the ORV *Alguita*; we are in the warm galley, where there is the warmth of chicken and tomato stew, and I have the warmth of Anna's hands. Viewed from the window, *Junk* appears small and insignificant, barely visible except for the green and red running lights tied hastily to the railing.

We give a toast to a success, to unspoken fears of failure. Darkness beckons Joel and me to stir. We have worked tirelessly, without rest, for three solid months, in preparation for this moment. Everyone is on the back deck as Joel gives final handshakes and hugs to Nicole and the crew. He jumps into the dinghy with Jeff for the return trip to *Junk*.

Anna and I stand on the bow together in darkness, holding each other and the rigging of the mast. She reaches into her jacket pocket to retrieve a small envelope, which she puts into my hand, gently closing my fingers around it.

"These are forty-two little notes, one for each day you'll be out there," she says. "Read one each day and hear my voice when you do." My arms melt around her.

Only one year ago I met Anna, at the apex of my personal catharsis. I was taking my future seriously for the first time in the months before we met, and was learning that there were things I didn't know that I didn't know about life and love. I was inspired by books like *Shambhala: The Sacred Path of the Warrior* by Chogyam Trungpa and *Turning the Mind into an Ally* by Sakyong Mipham, which unveiled a new path of right thinking, right speaking, and right doing, replacing the constant suffering we bestow upon ourselves and others with understanding and compassion. I had also learned the other half of being a warrior that the Marine Corps never taught me: defining my own friend and foe rather than having it determined for me. I also knew the man I wanted to be for others, and for Anna. Now, after all of that work, I feel as if I'm casting it away.

Junk comes into view. I kiss Anna gently. I love her and I don't want to leave her. My love is desperate, as if I am falling from a cliff. We approach the raft. I climb over the rail. I look at her. I give her a long-lasting embrace. "I love you," we say again and again. I'm falling. Throwing it all away. I jump to my little bottle raft. "I will chase the sun till I see you again," I say above the howl of the irreverent sea.

DAY 3: JUNE 3, 2008

Near San Nicolas Island

"I think you're right, the airplane moved," I say, pausing a few seconds. "Hey, Joel, did you feel that?" The storm hasn't let up since the ORV *Alguita* departed.

"Yup," he replies, with a deadpan monotone of calmness or resignation.

Joel is the perfect co-navigator, with red and green navigation stars tattooed on his feet. He lives on his sailboat in Ala Wai Harbor on Oahu. Anna and I first met him in Hilo, on the big island of Hawaii, when we were buying a few hundred pounds of fruits and veggies for Charlie's voyage through the center of the North Pacific Gyre back to California. On the boat, Joel takes off his shoes and moves about the rigging like a lemur, instantly comfortable on this boat (and likely any boat). Before joining NOAA, he spent many months in the Hawaii hills catching near-extinct songbirds in an effort to save them from the hungry mouths of rats, cats, and mongooses. Before that, he helped restore native habitats on the Colorado River after earning a degree in environmental science from Purdue. And before *that*, he spent many summers traveling to Belize, Ecuador, and Honduras with his parents—both scientists and educators—studying rain forest and reef ecology. His love of nature began when he would wander the fields of Indiana with his sister for half the day, until moonlight guided them home.

Joel and I endlessly compare notes on the raft, guessing what might fail next. I'll realize later that Joel's improvements on my initial drawings of *Junk* will be what saves us. But for now, I can't sleep. A wave slams against the underside of the cabin, and then another crashes over it.

Joel sits up to gaze at San Nicolas Island, checking our position relative to the one light visible on the south point. If we lose our anchor, we will be washed against the cliffs or carried out to sea. "We're not in the same place we were," Joel reports. Both anchor lines are tight. They must have jumped from one crevice to another.

By dawn, the sea is a carpet of white froth riding the pinnacle of each wave, splashing between the masts that make up our deck with every swell that passes through us. Joel and I agree this is a design advantage. We are more than a foot deeper in the water than when we began. Of the six pontoons under the raft, two have rotated outward and are riding above the deck. Each wave crunches them against the rough ends of the deck.

The bow disappears with every wave. We are listing to the starboard side. By midday, the skies let up for a couple of hours. I scramble to the edge of the raft to discover that the lids of the polycarbonate bottles are twisting off. The caps are still attached by a loop that fits over the neck of the bottle, but they are dangling. For ease of removal, the caps are designed with teeth around the edges, as on a gear. This same design is allowing the nets to grab the caps and spin them off. That little angel on my shoulder keeps chanting, "Why didn't you glue the caps on the bottles?"

I cannot fathom failure, though the raft and the plan are unraveling. I briefly think of the many people who have invested time, money, and hope, with their only reassurance an overconfident smile from me. If I don't lose my life, I will lose my job and reputation. These thoughts are distracting, so I look to the dark sky swirling above and reassess my priorities.

It begins to rain again. Joel secures the SSB radio antenna. The milk crates tied between the masts in the deck were intended to store dry gear and buckets of food above the waterline, but they are now underwater. Canned goods are floating, their the labels washed away. The aluminum aircraft doors, which we wedged between the masts on the deck to give us something to stand on, have slid under the fuselage. I tie them down. Rain pelts my hands and face. Joel pulls the anchor chain around the perimeter of the raft to spin it around, so the pummeling wind and waves don't damage the same side further. Knowing we've done all we can to secure the raft, we climb into the cabin before the next storm.

"What do you mean you're sinking?" Anna asks over the satellite phone, panic in her voice. I explain everything rapidly and hang up just as the next wave slams the fuselage.

In our rush to leave in advance of cyclone season, we neglected to leave time to test our design. It's now clear that we made shortcuts on materials and supplies. Bottles are slowly filling with water, the deck is tilted and twisted, and the airplane fuselage is threatening to slide off the raft. We'll surely join that list of ill-fated rafting adventures.

What will people think if I fail? Control and ego claw at my ankles like the sea, distracting my focus from the obvious: saving the ship.

I reach into my dry bag for the little envelope of notes Anna gave to me. They are all printed on tiny strips of folded paper. The largest note on top instructs, "READ FIRST." Anna had written,

> To mark the days, each morning as I wake, I will think about one thing I love about you. The look on your face when I walk in on you in the kitchen, sneaking a spoon into the ice cream, and then hiding it behind your back. It melts my heart.

I crack a smile, the first time since we parted. There are forty-one little notes left. If we make it that long.

CHAPTER 6

COMING UNSCREWED

The Little Fish in a Big Sea

Turning and turning in the widening gyre
The falcon cannot hear the falconer;
Things fall apart; the centre cannot hold;
Mere anarchy is loosed upon the world,
The blood-dimmed tide is loosed, and everywhere
The ceremony of innocence is drowned;
The best lack all conviction, while the worst
Are full of passionate intensity.

—William Butler Yeats
"The Second Coming," 1919

DAY 5: JUNE 5, 2008, MILE 60

San Nicolas Island

I step out of the airplane into the sea. Another night has beaten our little *Junk*. Joel and I climb and sit atop the airplane during a very brief respite. I see failure, whereas Joel sees options. *We're such amateurs*, I think.

"It's too heavy," I say.

"We can dump what we don't need," Joel responds.

"Look at the deck. It's twisted. Are you sure those lashings will hold up?" I complain.

"They'll hold up. It's the same technique the Polynesians have been doing forever," he replies.

I imagine failure, in the broadest sense, would mean needing our abandoned raft towed behind a rescue boat—returning with our tails between our legs. Even worse, I see a derelict raft contributing to the very problem that inspired our journey. I see funders asking for a refund of donations long gone. I see years of having to explain to random strangers why I'm the guy who tried to cross the ocean on that piece of junk. It's mostly a conversation in my head, where I can sulk in solitude. *It would be better if we died at sea,* I think in moments of self-pity, though Joel may differ. What I like about Joel is that while I'm in here sulking, he's out there working.

There comes a moment when you kick yourself in the ass and say: "Shut up, make some decisions, and get to work." Thoughts shift from what's wrong to what's missing, and the emotion falls away. I join Joel atop the airplane to discuss our options. It's a mental space Joel has occupied all along.

"We've got to lift the raft," Joel says.

"Maybe if we rope the pontoons we can get them back in shape," I reply.

The outside pontoons have rotated out from under the raft, and the bow is half-sunk. Those two thousand Nalgene bottles Patagonia gave us after the bisphenol A (BPA) story broke have opened. When BPA, an ingredient in polycarbonate water bottles, made headlines as an endocrine disruptor, Patagonia was the first company to get rid of the bottles. Now, more than half of ours are full, and because polycarbonate is more dense than water, the full bottles act like an anchor, causing the bow to list.

The SSB antenna is bent over the solar panels. The airplane is one foot farther astern than where we put it, but the tow straps are holding it taut against the deck. The airplane wing and the two aluminum doors that were wedged under the fuselage have shifted around and now seesaw on the deck. The three-eighths-inch galvanized cables that hold the A-frame mast vertical are loose and whip violently when the raft lunges in each wave. Above all else, we've lost buoyancy. The deck water is ankle-deep and the craft lists precariously. We need to rise.

Dark clouds burst above us. Crouched inside, we make a mental list of things that must happen: to survive another night, we need to get higher. If we lose more buoyancy and waves start crashing against the fuselage, we're sunk. We wait for the next break in the storm to scurry outside and start pulling full bottles of water out of the front pontoons, emptying them and stuffing them back in the pontoon. We work until the cold rain numbs our hands and darkness forces us into shelter. The storm is unrelenting. The sounds of the raft are different than before, because of the change from being on the water to being in it. Each new sound means a change from the known state of disrepair. That clunking I hear is from our food buckets now floating and hitting each other.

In a sleepless delirium, I imagine complete failure—not just the tragic sequence of our deaths, but also the material science chain of events: how the raft will disintegrate, sink, decompose, rust, and persist indefinitely on the sea floor.

The beginnings of catastrophe have occurred—a warning to fix or fail. The airplane, weighing well over a thousand pounds with batteries, food, and two sailors inside, is held by two thin cargo straps. If the plane were to slip into the sea, it would immediately turn tail downward, regardless of which end entered first. Joel and I would fall into the tail of the plane, covered in wet sleeping bags, mats, and blankets. Batteries and electronic supplies buried beneath the instrument panel would come crashing on top of us. The door of the airplane, held closed by only a small bolt latch, would pop open and water would rush in or the thin polycarbonate windows would implode, whichever came first. It would be a quick drowning as we hurtled to the seafloor like a spear.

"What do you mean, you're sinking?" Anna had demanded yesterday. While I was soaked on a sinking raft, she was sitting at a coffee shop in Santa Monica with her mother, Maryann, who overheard the conversation and declared, "Well, go get him." What I adore about Maryann is her immediate leap to solve a problem. The next thirty-six hours consist of satellite phone calls with resupply lists, and Anna's frantic search for a boat with a volunteer crew that could leave at dawn.

"I need fifty tubes of marine epoxy," I say.

"What for?" she responds.

"To glue the caps back on the bottles," I explain, adding, "and more food . . . chocolate and beer. Duct tape." Most of our dry goods are now wet, so a couple bags of rice, peanut butter, and granola make the list.

Six volunteers rally at 2 a.m.: Josh and Bryan, from the group Ocean Detox, who drop everything and drive in from Las Vegas; Jeff "Boat Monkey" Ernst from the recent gyre expedition with Charlie; Nicole Chatterson; Duane Laursen from AMRE's board; and Kyaa Heller and Captain Ray Arntz, owners of *Sun Diver*, the powerboat that came to the rescue. After Anna spent hours calling a dozen sail, scuba, and boat charter companies, a final call to Ann Close from USC's Wrigley Institute had led to *Sun Diver*. Ray and Kyaa chuckle at the idea of rafting to Hawaii and quickly say, "We're in!"

Anna pulls it all together, proving that a small ragtag crew with enough determination can get itself in and out of trouble, the benefit of trial by fire.

They all meet at the Long Beach Marina at 3:30 a.m. Operation *Junk*-sunk is under way.

DAY 7: JUNE 7, 2008

Operation *Junk*-sunk, San Nicolas Island

Red and green running lights on the bow of *Sun Diver* appear out of the mist at 6:30 a.m. Operation *Junk*-sunk is quite simple. The seven arriving volunteers will spend the next fourteen hours, till sundown, cutting one-third of the pontoons—the two that have rotated from under the raft—apart and transforming them into mini-pontoons, each the size of a duffel bag.

I see Anna, and before we can tie the two boats together, she's jumped aboard *Junk* and into my arms. I look back to see Nicole and Joel in a deep embrace. It's less jovial this time, with the realization that the unknown unknowns are more dangerous than we ever imagined.

"I got almost everything you asked for," Anna says. She's as nervous as I am. This isn't a rescue mission but more a chance to repair and restock for the much longer journey ahead. Maybe six weeks. Maybe much more.

We set to the task of cutting netting, emptying and refilling bottles with air. We use the cans of expanding polyurethane foam Anna has delivered to inflate them permanently.

We create eighteen mini-pontoons. Josh, Jeff, and Bryan take them under the raft, using dive weights to force them where they're needed most to add buoyancy. When it's my turn to jump in, I hesitate, looking at Joel, who rolls his eyes and jumps in instead. We work against the clock, scarcely pausing to wolf down sandwiches. "We've got to be on our way by sunset," Captain Bill explains, and with the last glimmer of the sun he starts his engines. Duane Laursen tosses over to us the food we didn't eat, including a huge salami, insisting, "You never know what might happen."

Anna is last to leave *Junk*. A final embrace and a lingering kiss. I feel apologetic for roping her into this madness. With the team all aboard, leaving Joel and me alone on the raft, the boat pulls away. I hold Anna's hand until we're pulled apart. Joel retreats to the warmth of the cabin, which he earned after working in fifty-five-degree water much too long. I stare at the horizon until Anna is gone.

"We're sailing!" Joel yells two days later. We rig the jib and mizzen sails, slip a few more mini-pontoons where we're still sinking, and get all the new provisions stowed away, including that giant salami from Duane. It hangs high above the airplane fuselage. We say goodbye to San Nicolas Island and start drifting east toward Santa Barbara. "Let's get the spinnaker up!" Joel yells. San Nicolas Island will not let us go. The cacophony of sea lions and elephant seals is drowned by the noise of crashing waves as we drift closer to the rocky shore, then suddenly a strong north wind sweeps us away, as if saying, "Be gone!"

Joel adjusts the sails for hours, checks the chart plotter, and fiddles with the electronics. I take his direction. He's laser-focused on the work, not wanting to waste an opportunity to increase efficiency.

We take alternating four-hour watches to keep track of the big ships around us. Our AIS (Automated Identification System) and radar screen show us where they are. It's the only new equipment on the raft. We drift around Catalina Island and then Cortes Bank, where a shallow rise from the ocean floor creates monstrous breaking waves in the middle of the sea. We're soon west of Baja California, Mexico, having left the sight of land.

The open ocean is workable; it's the hard stuff around the edges you've got to worry about. Joel cooks while I clean. That last storm, five days ago, submerged our canned food, dissolving the paper labels. We play mystery meal, hoping for corn or peas. It's four cans of beans in a row.

We're smiling now these first few days, knowing that we're on our way. We relax for a moment, filling the space with a great conversation about what we've accomplished to get this far.

"What's that tattoo on your arm?" I say, pointing to the garden of roses that wraps around his forearm. He tells me about the stars on his feet and his other tattoos, and the first time he showed them to his family.

"My sister would have never wanted one," he says. "She was too studious and athletic." They grew up together, chasing friends in the fields of Midwestern farmland. Joel, three years older, headed off to Purdue University and was in school when he got the news that doctors had discovered she had a brain tumor. The operation was set a week later. Soon after surgery, she died.

"Her name was Amity," he says. I can see her name, meaning "friendship," tattooed in the garden. Joel is quiet, stoic.

"She burned bright. I had a great seventeen years with her. She's still on my mind all of the time. Soon after she was gone, I went back to school, got focused, and got better grades. I knew I had to leave Indiana. I had friends who got stuck," he explained, adding, "and that wasn't gonna be me."

There's much more to this man than I know.

CHAPTER 7

"JUNK IN, JUNK OUT"

Entrenched interests need not produce "junk science"
when they have a wide selection of credentialed scien-
tists to choose from in support of their positions.

—Roger Pielke Jr.
The Honest Broker, 2003

DAY 16: JUNE 16, 2008, MILE 163

West of US–Mexico border
(Latitude 32°32', Longitude 119°04')

"Unidentified vessel, this is the Coast Guard, over," comes a loud crackle over the VHF radio.

"This is *Junk*, over," I say into the receiver. For the last thirty minutes we've watched an orange and gray C-130 aircraft circle three times in the airspace above us.

The Coast Guard replies, "Roger, Captain. We're just kinda curious about your boat because we've never seen anything like that. Wondering where you guys are heading, where you guys are out of . . . your home port."

"Our home port is Long Beach. We left there a couple of weeks ago and we're heading to Hawaii on a raft made from fifteen thousand plastic bottles, a Cessna aircraft fuselage, and about five thousand plastic bags woven into rope. We should get to Hawaii . . . we're hoping in about two months," I say. We explain why we're doing what we're doing, and the science behind the adventure.

"*Junk*, this is US Coast Guard. That's quite a feat if you guys do that. . . . Interesting boat."

"They don't believe us," I say to Joel, who's laughing at the whole thing.

"They must think we're running drugs or people across the border," Joel replies.

"*Junk*, Coast Guard aircraft here. We got a few more questions for ya real quick. As far as power goes, you only have those solar panels? Is that the only power you have? Do you have any battery backups? And a sail plan? We're just curious if you've filed a sail plan—if the US Coast Guard knows about this? And safety gear—how many life jackets and things like that?"

Joel hops on the radio this time. "In terms of gear, we have PFDs, a four-man life raft, two handheld watermakers, IPRB, handheld GPS, and a handheld VHF."

"Tell them we've got a DMV registration too," I say to Joel. The Coast Guard is asking the questions the California DMV didn't. I'm a little worried now, wondering if they'll try to stop us. They've got our safety in mind, sure, but is it the raft design or our sanity they question? Or our mission? Are we a junk raft or junk science?

With time to think, I often ask myself, *What kind of scientist am I?* Despite the circuitous route to environmental science I've taken through citizen engagement (one that perhaps invites criticism from scientists of a particular academic lineage), is there also a thread of bias stemming from my own conservation ethic? If so, does that matter? And doesn't the peer-review process weed out subjectivity?

In Roger Pielke Jr.'s *The Honest Broker: Making Sense of Science in Policy and Politics*, he describes five roles scientists take in the policymaking world. Of the first four, the Pure Scientist does science for the sake of science, finding personal interest in the subject and process, but not the utility of the product, which is left to its own interpretation. This is rare in today's world, as funding is almost always tied to expectations and relevance.

The Science Arbiter is the "scientist for hire," commonly employed when the tools of science are needed to investigate specific questions. Many government-employed scientists fill this role.

The Issue Advocate aims to narrow the available choices to a few or just one, based on research that defends a position. While other scientists find the term "advocacy" to be derogatory, they should consider that the Pure Scientist doesn't exist in the world today. Advocacy is the responsibility of a scientist in a democracy. Everyone takes a position. Even those scientists who resist participation in the policy actions that follow their work advocate for a position by their inaction. Silence is consent.

The Honest Broker aims to be as objective as possible, giving the public and policymakers a full understanding of the scope of possible actions they could take. The intent is to empower those making decisions to make the best possible choices based on all alternatives available.

In early 2007, I encountered the fifth type of scientist: the stealth advocate. I was invited to Sacramento to testify before the California senate's Environmental Quality Committee on AB 2058, a bill calling for a twenty-five-cent fee on paper or plastic bags.[1] The bill would create a funding stream to help municipalities with litter reduction, cleanup, and prevention programs. An American Chemistry Council representative also appeared. He and I provided back-to-back testimony of three minutes each.

"The density of plastic in the ocean increases as you leave the coast, and is highest in the center of the North Pacific Gyre," I explained.

"But do you see plastic bags there?" one senator asked.

"We do not, but that doesn't mean they aren't out there. In our samples," I hold up a jar of swirling plastic confetti and plankton, "you find shredded fragments of plastic film. Plastic bags shred quickly to the size of fish food."

"So you don't actually see plastic bags in the ocean," he repeated unnecessarily, betraying his political position on the proposed regulation.

"We do in coastal surveys, for sure," I replied. The three minutes I was allocated was gone before I could take a breath to say another word. The ACC scientist took the stand.

"As you well know, plastic bags employ Californians, and the last thing we need is another tax," he said immediately. Although he was presented as a scientist appearing before the committee to discuss alternative positions on plastic bags, he'd opted to push political buttons that elicit value judgments in the minds of Republican senators.

He continued a well-rehearsed tirade. "Some scientists will tell you there are chemicals in plastic, like bisphenol A, causing trouble"—a piece of information he pulls out of nowhere. He adds, with a yell and a glance in my direction, "Show me bisphenol A in plankton!" The intent of the statement was to create a bit of doubt through a deliberate injection of junk science. (Bisphenol A degrades very quickly in the environment, so it's unlikely to ever be found in plankton.)

The ACC scientist knew this, but he also knew that senators on environmental committees have limited time to learn the complexity of the issues they make decisions about, much less read through entire bills. They have other committees, media commitments, and floor votes. This committee meeting should be a hearing to allow science to inform policy, but it's also theater of political persuasion. His three minutes ended quickly. Before he could sit, papers were shuffled and senators were running for the door, dragged by their staff to the day's next agenda item. Although AB 2058 passed the committee, it died in the senate without a vote.

The role of stealth advocate is the most ruthless, because it undermines science's public image and policy role. The stealth advocate hides a political agenda, as in the case of AB 2058, to kill the bill behind a wall of junk science. Junk science is very different from bad science. In his book *Junk Science*, Dan Agin describes the practice as intentional corruption of objectivity and/or methods with the goal of achieving political or financial gains. Think of eugenics in Nazi Germany, or the inquisition that imprisoned Galileo in 1633 (the Catholic Church officially acknowledged its error in 1992); those are examples of junk science. Bad science is science done with flawed methods or sloppy procedures, or scientific conclusions based on false assumptions.

In January 2011, comments by Dr. Angelique White of Oregon State University appeared in a university press release titled "Oceanic 'Garbage Patch' Not Nearly as Big as Portrayed in the Media." The story went viral, countering the "Texas-sized garbage patch" meme and prompting a plethora of interviews. It drew accolades from other scientists for finally bringing some light to the issue, and criticism from many conservation NGOs that asserted White must be an industry shill. She had recently surveyed the coast of Chile and found no microplastic in the majority of her sea-surface samples. White's counterargument was intended to correct what she perceived as bad science and media-driven misinformation.

I asked her, "Was your intention to counter previous research?" She replied: "I had no intention to counter any one group, but yes I believe is it inaccurate and misleading to present the patch as a cohesive region twice the size of Texas with six times more plastic than plankton. My belief is that this sort of hyperbole undermines the credibility of groups aiming to reduce the amount of debris entering our ocean."

This was the blowback that we knew would come sometime, after the wave of media in the early 2000s about garbage patches and islands of trash. Interestingly, now the story in the media was about how scientists were somehow responsible for the myth and misinformation the media had created—a bad case of journalism reaping what it had sown.

A similar dialogue was happening in scientific publications in a more systematic way, as more discoveries of plastic marine pollution were reported worldwide. Methods improved, and theories were refined or abandoned. Scripps had returned from the SEAPLEX voyage and had begun to publish results. The researchers replicated Captain Moore's work on plastic ingestion by myctophid fishes, reporting 9 percent ingestion versus the 35 percent in Moore's study; the difference reflected an improvement in methodology to avoid net feeding— better science—but neither study was junk science. Science objectively improves itself, whereas dogma, political values, and financial motives are more entrenched. The self-correcting nature of science can improve bad science, without losing the credibility of the scientific enterprise, whereas junk science only creates doubt all around.

What Angelique White didn't know was that Anna and I had recently surveyed the same waters she had sampled near the coast of Chile, but we continued to the center of the South Pacific Subtropical Gyre and onward to Easter Island. While there was little plastic in the first few samples, a result similar to what White had found, the density slowly rose to four hundred thousand plastic particles per square kilometer in the center of the gyre.

With publication of these results, the 5 Gyres Institute earned credibility with other scientists. Internally, we refined our communications based on our own original literature. Herein lies a lesson for grassroots environmental movements: get in the science game. Besides gaining credibility, you also ensure you're tackling the right problems. So many NGOs fighting plastic pollution have referenced the mythical "Texas-sized garbage patch" as fact, rather than as the bad science that it is.

In the mid-2000s, I answered what seemed like monthly inquiries about possible methods of cleaning up the gyres, from plastic-to-oil conversion systems to giant nets that funnel plastic (while miraculously missing all marine life) into a giant floating waste bin, even a giant sixty-foot-diameter floating pizza that would collect plastic, which would be washed into giant bins shaped like individual slices. This waste of time and resources is the result of reliance on fictional hyperbole rather than published science or personal experience at sea. It's risky for small NGOs to base expensive campaigns on popular media. You need to make sure you're spending your resources on campaigns driven by accurate information, otherwise you waste your money and you're powerless against the larger, richer industries that dominate policy and public perception. Good science makes you an effective watchdog. Pardon the mixed metaphors, but once you find you're barking up the right tree—and in the case of plastic pollution, it's upstream design—then the little fish in the big sea can shake the tree.

Ten minutes later the Coast Guard states, "All right vessel *Junk*, it sounds like you guys are prepared," adding, "Is there a website where I can see this?" A smile instantly grows across our faces as we take turns answering a few more questions.

"You guys need anything real quick while we're overhead?" they ask.

Joel replies, "Hey, thanks a lot, and can you give us any information about the weather in the next couple of days? We heard there were some tropical storms to the south off the coast of Mexico. If that's true we'd like confirmation of coordinates and the direction the storm may be heading, and wind speed, over."

"Hey, *Junk*, if you guys will stand by on this frequency we'll climb up high. Once we get a good radio signal we'll give you a call and let you know what we find out." The aircraft climbs higher and out of sight. It returns in about twenty minutes.

"Vessel *Junk*, this is Coast Guard. We weren't able to see anything," they respond after a short visual inspection of the skies in the direction we're headed.

We talk about the weather a little more, letting the conversation linger awhile, knowing without acknowledgment that we don't really want to have another conversation. Calling on them in the future would mean that something went wrong. They give us their emergency number in case we need to call Coast Guard stations in California or Hawaii.

"Roger that, Captain. I think we've got everything we need. You guys be safe and be careful, and if you guys need anything you got the Coast Guard."

"Thank you very much, and hopefully we'll not need your assistance, but we won't hesitate to call if things take a turn for the worse, over."

"Roger that. Coast Guard aircraft on standby channel sixteen."

"Standing by on channel sixteen," Joel says. "*Junk* out!" We both crack up laughing at the conversation, the validation by the Coast Guard, and the novelty of contact with another human, maybe the last for a while.

"Well that was the highlight of the day," Joel says.

A few days later, on June 20, Anna relays a comment left on our blog: "Hey I was part of the Coast Guard crew that was talking with you guys yesterday. We were all amazed when we spotted your vessel. It's truly one of a kind!!! I hope you do not have to use the # we gave you and make it safely to Hawaii. Thanks for bringing attention to a growing problem people need to be aware of. Be safe and enjoy your float across the Pacific."

CHAPTER 8

GUADALUPE LOOP

The Recycling Myth

Once in a while you find yourself in an odd situation. You get into it by degrees and in the most natural way but, when you are right in the midst of it, you are suddenly astonished and ask yourself how in the world it all came about.

If, for example, you put to sea on a wooden raft with a parrot and five companions, it is inevitable that sooner or later you will wake up one morning out at sea, perhaps a little better rested than ordinarily, and begin to think about it.

—Thor Heyerdahl
Kon-Tiki, 1950

DAY 26: JUNE 26, 2008, MILE 295

(Latitude 28°28', Longitude 118°23')

We slip by Bishop Rock, an underwater mountain a hundred miles west of Baja California. There's one shipwreck there already. Without much fanfare, we drift over it at 4 a.m. Guadalupe Island, the size of Manhattan, juts out of the sea directly in front of us only sixty miles ahead. As much as we want to go in the direction of Hawaii, the California Current is sweeping us to Acapulco. Meanwhile, the raft can barely sail 120 degrees off the wind. In three weeks, we've drifted three hundred miles of south latitude, and not an inch of longitude.

"So, what's our speed?" I ask Joel. Without much else to do, he's constantly checking speed and bearing.

"Two knots!" he exclaims. "It's a new record." We're making roughly thirty miles per day, with the wind consistently coming out of the west, 90 degrees on our starboard beam. We're dreaming of the trade winds, with consistent twenty knot winds or better.

"Fish!" Joel yells, and soon we've got two in the pan and strips of flesh drying in the sun. It's a rudder fish, bluish-black, the size of a dinner plate. Joel whips up a mean curry with coconut milk. He cooks, I clean. Joel's a night owl, reading and monitoring the electronics and sails till 1 a.m.; then I take over for eight hours till 9 a.m. It works well. We're still a few days from the island.

In 1958, DeVere Baker and his three crewmen confronted Guadalupe Island head-on while adrift on their nine-ton wooden raft *Lehi IV*. Don McFarland, the last surviving crewman from the voyage, was at the dock weeks ago to bid farewell to our little *Junk Raft*.

"We had to deploy our pilot chute to avoid hitting Guadalupe Island," Don said. "With enough room to spare, we went west around her."

When daylight comes, Joel and I go over the plan. Going west means we battle waves pushing us against the island until we clear it.

"I think we're approaching Guadalupe too close to justify going west. We'll be fighting wind and waves pushing us ashore the whole time," I suggest. Joel plots our course, accounting for our eastward drift, and comes to the same conclusion.

"Yup, let's go around the lee of the island," he replies.

Suddenly the AIS starts beeping. Hidden from view in front of our square sail is a massive container ship from China, less than a quarter mile away.

"Yes, I see ya," says the captain from the container ship. "I saw you a mile ago." He is responding to our frantic near-emergency calls to the ship over the last twenty minutes. Our AIS system indicates a collision course. Despite the hundred-thousand-to-one size ratio, the container ship is far more maneuverable than our raft. Reluctantly, the ship changes course, then cruises at twenty knots right in front of us. Had it not seen us, it would not have noticed plowing over us.

Shipping lanes are like crowded highways, with Chinese ships in the fast lane. It's a constant fear of sailors worldwide—being run over. There's a photo circulating in sailing circles of a container ship arriving in a foreign port with the mast and rigging from an unidentified small sailboat hung up on its anchor.

*   *   *

According to the US State Department, US imports from China exceeded $440 billion in 2013, a three-to-one ratio over US exports to China ($141 billion).[1] Of the total coming in from China, the largest import categories are electrical machinery ($117.5 billion), machinery ($100.4 billion), furniture and bedding ($24.1 billion), toys and sports equipment ($21.7 billion). Footwear alone comes in fifth place, at $17 billion.

That three-to-one ratio of trade means that we return one container of three to China with our exports. What's in the other two?

"I fill them with plastics," Joe Garbarino said to me. He's the CEO of Marin County Recycling, just north of San Francisco. Anna and I sat in his office, which was lined with photos of military tanks Joe restores as a hobbyist. One large framed photo of a newspaper clipping shows Joe standing in front of a one-ton bale of plastic bags blocking the front door of a local supermarket.

Joe, a son of Italian immigrants, and his family have been hauling San Francisco Bay Area trash for nearly a century. He's the king of recycling; his company sorts everything imaginable from the industrial and residential trash he receives. He crushes metals and car parts into giant bricks, cuts trees for firewood, breaks down concrete into road aggregate, and pulverizes construction Sheetrock and the gypsum used in agriculture. He sorts plastics and paper into a dozen categories, and mountains of food scraps from restaurants feed his pigs and chickens.

"Plastic isn't easy to deal with," Garbarino said. "I've got to deal with this plastic somehow. I could send a ton of plastic bags to a landfill here in California and pay a sixty-three dollar tipping fee, but China will take it for free in empty shipping containers. Very few companies in the US want used plastic." When a local grocery store invited customers to bring plastic bags for recycling, Garbarino knew "they were full of bull." He saw an opportunity to expose misconceptions about recycling. He dropped off a ton of bags at the grocer's doorstep and alerted the media.

Garbarino's experience reflects the reality of how plastic moves through American hands. *The New Plastics Economy*, a study published

by the Ellen MacArthur Foundation in 2016, notes that the global recycling of plastic as we know it is a failure. The foundation estimates
that of the 78 million tons of plastic used for packaging in 2013, only
14 percent was recovered for recycling. Four percent of that is lost in
processing and 8 percent is downcycled into inferior products, leaving
2 percent, or 1.5 million tons of the original volume, brought back into
the loop. The other 86 percent not captured for recycling is burned,
buried, or washed out to sea. One problem is that the price of new
plastic is coupled with the price of oil, so when oil prices drop, virgin
plastic is cheaper than recycled plastic. Decoupling recycled plastics
from the commodities market is essential, so that the market for recycled materials doesn't fluctuate as wildly as the market for fossil fuels.

The diversion of valueless US plastic waste to China worked for
many West Coast recyclers, but in 2010 China raised the "Green
Fence," implementing a policy intended to control the quality of in-
coming trash. China no longer wanted our poorly designed "unrecyclable" plastic products and poorly sorted bales. While Garbarino's
bales of plastic waste are the cleanest in the industry, others are not.
China also grew tired of receiving plastic waste that occasionally had
radioactive material tucked away, or had live ammunition or rotting
human tissue inside. Of the eighty- to ninety-million tons, on average, of scrap plastic that were exported over the years to China before the Green Fence, much was processed in primitive melting pots
in family-owned workshops, where useless materials and wastewater
runoff contributed to the country's rapidly degrading environment.
Meanwhile, literal mountains of unrecycled waste are growing across
Southeast Asia, and the occasional trash slide buries workers alive.
The Green Fence sets the bar high for the quality of plastic coming
from US recyclers. China still wants plastic, but it is, in essence, enact-
ing principles of extended producer responsibility (EPR) to capture the
true costs of externalities borne by people and the environment. The
message: "Send us your trash, just not so trashy." In response, some
US recyclers improved the quality of their waste by rejecting some
products from the public, or found other countries, such as India, to
take trash—preferring anything to paying domestic landfill fees.

In 2013, I visited the Dharavi slum in Mumbai, India, a country
that imports US and European plastic waste. Walking through nar-

row pathways clouded by acrid smoke, I arrived somewhere in the center, where plastic processing happens. A plastic bag at my feet read: "NY, NY HAVE A NICE DAY." Here, a mound of sorted bales gets a final review before a row of women who give the occasional scrap the bite test to confirm its polymer type. The plastic is transferred in buckets to the shredding room, where a giant razor-edged flywheel reduces it to fragments the size of cornflakes. Then it's on to the melting room, where the plastic is fed into a red-hot cannon that melts and extrudes it like spaghetti. A young man, maybe in his late teens, used a knife to chop the strands into smaller pieces, called "preproduction pellets." After ten minutes, my eyes were tingling and the back of my throat burned. The men in this room absorb the largest dose of volatile plasticizers and pollutants, and according to a local NGO, they give up somewhere around twenty years of their lifespan for two dollars per day sorting our trash. After all that, where does this recycled plastic end up?

Both India and China reuse these plastics in new products coming back to the United States—and it shouldn't surprise us that these aren't always safe. In my hometown of New Orleans, I talked with Holly Groh, cofounder of Verdi Gras, an organization aiming to remove the toxicity from the stuff that revelers at Mardi Gras throw to the crowd. The vast majority of plastic beads and trinkets are imported from China. In Verdi Gras's recent report, titled *Healthy Stuff*, the lead toxicity of Mardi Gras beads was linked to recycled plastic pellets from China made with melted circuit boards.[2] Those lead levels exceed the regulatory standards set by the US Consumer Product Safety Commission for lead content in US products. While Louisiana may allow those imports, states such as California reject imports of trinkets and beads from companies, including Beads by the Dozen, that stock the parade clubs in New Orleans. Note to parents: don't let your kids put beads in their mouths!

Our current linear economy is failing, as evidenced by the hazards created in plastic's life cycle. In the circular economy, on the other hand, materials come back to the manufacturer through a revised value chain that creates economic incentives, or policy initiatives. Putting product designers, systems engineers, and recyclers in the same room to design in tandem is how we close the loop.

DAY 28: JUNE 28, 2008, MILE 308

(Latitude 28°14', Longitude 118°31')

"We're stuck in a loop!" I yell to Joel, as we continue on another collision course, this time with the east side of Guadalupe Island. We chose to go east around the island, the opposite of what Don McFarland and DeVere Baker did on their raft the *Lehi IV* fifty years ago. While they battled westward winds blowing them onto the island, we're stuck in a two-mile-diameter eddy of currents in the shadow of Guadalupe. We're being drawn in for the second time in two days, but closer this time.

"We've got to think about abandoning ship," Joel says. The sight of the sharp, craggy coast and the sound of waves crashing along it grow closer. There's no beach where we're headed—or anywhere in sight—just vertical rocky outcrops from which we hear the bark of sea lions. The waves climb up along the shore and then seem to drop a few meters. Guadalupe Island is known for shark-cage diving in this exact spot, where waters in the lee of the island are calmer and sea lion pups are plentiful appetizers for hungry predators.

The life raft is loose, and I clutch my ditch bag, preparing to jump overboard. The bag contains a collection of survival gear I replicated from a bag in Stephen Callahan's *Adrift: Seventy-Six Days Lost at Sea*. Within a hundred yards of the breaking waves, the current diverts southward and back out to sea—we hope.

"That's the second loop," I say, with mixed frustration, relief, and amusement. We can't seem to enter the North Pacific Gyre, into which trash seems to have no problem drifting. Joel throws up the parachute-shaped spinnaker sail, which he hopes will pull us in a new direction. The wind is erratic in the lee of the island, alternating calm and swirling gusts.

Plastics recycling in the United States is in dire need of a new direction. It is wasteful and ineffective. Despite the growth of the recycling industry and increased public education on sorting waste, economically and environmentally, nothing has changed over the last couple of decades, as John Tierney explained in a *New York Times* op-ed titled

"The Reign of Recycling."[3] China's Green Fence and the plummeting value of petroleum have reduced demand for post-consumer plastics. Meanwhile, municipalities pay more per ton for recycling than for tipping fees at most landfills. Why recycle when the dump is cheaper?

In *The Recycling Myth*, Jack Buffington cites growth trajectories over the last fifty years for waste management, incinerators, and landfills, compared with the trajectory of the recycling industry.[4] Waste management has surely changed. I remember helping neighbors haul trash to the dump on hot, balmy Saturday mornings in the late 1970s. There was a massive pit, more than fifty feet deep and as big as an Olympic-size swimming pool. You'd simply back your truck up to the edge and toss your trash in. We brought a mountain of roofing shingles one summer, tree limbs knocked down in a hurricane another time. When we brought our beloved green patent-leather sofa, a massive claw on the end of a crane, like the grab machines at amusement parks, lifted it into the open furnace doors of a fiery incinerator. These images are long gone for most Americans.

Our trash is now efficiently moved from your curbside, out of sight and out of mind. Three corporations—Waste Management, Waste Connections, and Republic Services—handle 45 percent of US trash, and they've become very good at whisking waste away from your front door to an equally tidy dump miles away.[5] Recycling centers lag behind. Buffington says, "In contrast to today's mega landfills and waste management companies, recycling operations remain small, decentralized, inefficient, and disconnected from the front-end industrial supply chain."[6] Recycling centers are still operating like your neighborhood hardware store, while waste management, incineration, and landfills are the Home Depot of waste. It's a disproportionate scale of efficiency.

Many large cities have material recovery facilities (MRFs) tasked with sorting recyclables and compostables from the residual that goes to a landfill or incinerator. Instead of demanding end-of-life design for products and packaging, which would make everything truly recyclable, the cities continue to spend tax dollars to upgrade technology to capture more complicated types of waste. Laminates of plastic, metal, and paper, such as Tetra Paks, juice boxes, and thousands of other new packaging designs, are slipping by current MRF recovery technology and going straight to the landfill.

And even if MRFs could recover and sort every bit of plastic they receive from curbside sorted plastics, comingled trash, and commercial waste, is it worth it? Thomas Kinnaman, an economist from Bucknell University, argues that the costs of energy, infrastructure, and labor needed to recycle waste is roughly double what it costs to bury it.[7] Kinnaman says, "It has been proven that mandated programs lead to higher recycling rates, but it should not be assumed that higher collection rates lead to higher secondary material reuse. In reality, collecting more of something that cannot be efficiently reused does not solve the fundamental problem but only mitigates the mess, at best."

Cheap oil and reduced market demand, along with the complexity of product and packaging design and supply-chain inefficiency, are prompting many recyclers to throw in the towel and surrender to the economic rationale of landfills and incinerators. Tierney, in the *Times*, concluded that "cities have been burying garbage for thousands of years, and it's still the easiest and cheapest solution for trash. The recycling movement is floundering, and its survival depends on continual subsidies, sermons and policing. How can you build a sustainable city with a strategy that can't even sustain itself?"

But Tierney is wrong, according to city and state leadership across the United States.

Mayor Eric Garcetti of Los Angeles, working with Zero Waste LA, Don't Waste LA, the Los Angeles Alliance for a New Economy, and many others, laid out a blueprint in 2015 to reach 90 percent recovery of solid waste by 2025. "Nothing upsets me more than to hear people say they want to recycle but are unable to," Garcetti said. "Now, we are going to expand that to businesses and apartments where we can recycle seventy percent of our trash instead of putting it in landfills."[8]

Mayor Bill de Blasio of New York City set the same goal, with a deadline of 2030, saying, "We're going to constantly drive down the amount of waste we create through composting, through better recycling. We're going to constantly drive that down to the point that nothing goes from New York City to a landfill in the future."[9]

But if you're going to hedge your bets on recycling everything, then you've got to demand that everything be recyclable. In *The Recycling Myth*, Buffington suggests that "we head in the direction of improvements based on material science innovation (e.g., green chemistry) and design and supply chain transformation."[10] Bringing product and packaging designers to the same table as MRF owners will lead to transformative change, but it will not happen voluntarily.

Policy-driven extended producer responsibility is essential. When a company is responsible for the full life cycle of its product and its packaging, innovation for recovery catches on like wildfire. Germany, where EPR laws have been in effect since 1991, has seen efficiencies in everything from waste-collection vending machines to a Green Dot system that rewards product brands with an EPR plan, resulting in a 1.1-million-ton reduction in the volume of packaging produced between 1992 and 1998, and progress continues today. In May of 2016, President Michelle Bachelet of Chile signed the Recycling and Extended Producer Liability Law, the strongest legislation of its kind in South America, requiring producers and importers to take full responsibility for recovering the stuff they make. Among its provisions is a requirement that producers and importers develop and fund a waste recovery industry to collect, sort, and transport packaging back to the companies that produced it.[11]

Other than container-deposit laws, EPR in the United States is pretty slim. We are the only country out of the thirty-five member nations of the Organisation for Economic Co-operation and Development that doesn't have EPR for plastic packaging. Beverage bottling companies have been fighting bottle-deposit programs for decades, but in the ten US states where they still stand, recycling ranges from 65 percent to 96 percent, whereas the national average hovers around 32 percent. In 2013, the California Redemption Value for PET was ten cents for two-liter bottles and five cents for smaller ones, so recovery rates soared above 70 percent. In my neighborhood in Los Angeles, not a single PET soda bottle or HDPE water bottle stays on the ground for very long. Bottle-redemption programs work as an efficient recovery system in a circular economy. Now imagine a redemption value on everything.

In response to John Tierney's rallying cry to bury and burn waste instead of recycling it, Conrad MacKerron, founder of the EPR advocacy group As You Sow, says, "If recycling doesn't make economic sense, then Tierney needs to ponder why the CEOs of Walmart, Procter & Gamble, Colgate-Palmolive, and even Goldman Sachs last year established a $100 million loan program, the Closed Loop Fund, to boost the effectiveness of recycling by improving curbside infrastructure and recovery markets."[12]

The trend in recycling is EPR in front-end design to truly close the loop. It's what we want—better design, so that recycling really means the material easily returns to the manufacture stage. Psychologically, we're primed to recycle, as demonstrated by our response to advertising that promises biodegradability and recyclability, words that tug at our ethical heartstrings. We want to do it. We only need the systems behind the scenes to practice what they preach.

"We're going to Acapulco!" I say to Joel. It's our new story, suggested by our friend and storytelling guru, Randy Olson, who suggested, "Pretend it was your plan all along. Broadcast it on the blog!" Recreate our story, instead of submitting to the fates of the sea. We're a heap of junk adrift, without much control over where we are going. We left Los Angeles three weeks ago. We're three hundred miles away . . . with two thousand to Hawaii, one thousand to Guatemala, and four hundred to Acapulco.

I dive under *Junk* to inspect mini-pontoons placed there during Anna's repair and resupply mission. All seems well, except for a little shifting. A school of palm-length fish hover below me while I add two more pontoons, tie knots, and cut loose ends. While Joel repairs the rusting stove, a fur seal swims by. Indigenous to Guadalupe Island, they can venture a hundred miles from land to hunt, or to check out *Junk*.

Two black-footed albatross gently swim for hours behind us. Every time one of us stands close to the rail, they approach, stare, and appear to be waiting for us to do something. But there's nothing to do. Life is slowing down. The chaos of building *Junk*, the emotional and physical drain of responding to a social network tied to this project, have all but vanished, except for the messages from Anna over the satellite phone. I write her a love letter. I dig into our trash bucket to find a wine bottle we kept after celebrating our departure. I stuff the letter in the bottle and jam the cork all the way inside, then throw it into the sea. Then I sit for hours. In these long intervals of time, I notice that my head becomes crowded with my own conversations, now louder than ever.

I could almost assign a personality to each. There's the conversation about defending our project: scenarios of failure and what people would think. I call it the *image manager*, and it's rooted in some insecurity, so I tell it to be quiet. There's the conversation about Anna: how much I miss everything about her, and what our future will be like. It's dreamy and sometimes jealous. The *dreamer* is sometimes fun to entertain. There's the conversation about a meaningful life: what's worth doing with the time left, and what's not. He's the *old man*. I think about strategy in the plastic pollution movement: what's the best way to fight this problem, and what science needs to be done to best facilitate activism. The *activist* has long conversations.

There are long conversations about our fate. Not only the destiny of our raft, but the path of civilization toward resource scarcity, overpopulation, and pollution—the collision course we may experience in our lifetime. I think about my youth in Metairie near the bank of the Mississippi River, where the waste of a nation—roughly 42 percent of the continental United States, all or part of thirty-one states—floats by. They call the hundred-mile stretch of the river where I grew up "cancer alley," owing to the protection Louisiana politics affords petrochemical companies that use the river as a highway to access the globe.

I spent many summers catching critters in the batture, that sliver of willow-tree woodland between the levee and the river. When I was fifteen, my brother and I, with the support of a very tolerant mother, had a collection of eleven snakes, one baby alligator, and ninety-six turtles in a giant homemade pond we dug in the backyard. It was a valuable lesson for us both, as we couldn't keep up because of overcrowding (overpopulation), feeding and watering requirements (resource scarcity), and necessary cleanup (pollution). We watched a closed system collapsing, and quickly released the animals back to the wild.

In the closed system of our planet, we have populated and polluted much of it. In a natural system, all life is in a tooth-and-claw struggle to defend and maximize reproduction, limited by all other life doing the same. Human ingenuity and culture have made us the winner among species in that very primitive race, but we've now arrived at the finish line. Can we rein in our material culture, back to a natural cycle? Can we evolve industry and technology so we are able to exist perpetually in a closed system? Do we have the capacity to replace that primitive directive to consume, populate, and pollute with collective reason and restraint?

These conversations are beginning to drift into a kind of emptiness. Nothing to do . . . nowhere to go, staring at the horizon with nothing but now to experience. It is the hardest conversation to have.

CHAPTER 9

TOO WASTEFUL TO VALUE

ChicoBag vs. Plastic-Bag Lobby

If you want to build a ship, don't herd people together to collect wood and don't assign them tasks and work, but rather teach them to long for the endless immensity of the sea.

—Antoine de Saint-Exupéry
Paraphrased from *Citadelle*, 1948

DAY 34: JULY 4, 2008, MILE 529

Patriotism in the Pacific (Latitude 24°36', Longitude 120°37')

"Shall we raise the flag?" I ask, referring to the Stars and Stripes at the bottom of my dry bag. It's a massive flag, one that covered my stepfather's coffin. It hung lazily from the mast as we were towed out of Los Angeles Harbor a month ago.

"Yeah, I was just thinking that," Joel replies, adding: "If people saw us they would think we're just nuts." Joel is busy sewing the last stitches on the "Frankensail," a patchwork of scrap sail pieces held together by duct tape and thick line. His hope is that it will improve our speed and direction.

"Is that gonna work?" I ask.

"Yeah, I think so. I can't think of a better use for all of the scrap bits of sail," Joel replies.

Another ten minutes go by in our prolonged conversation. "We are nuts," I say, "but not any crazier than anyone else. I mean, we're doing something unusual, but with a huge purpose."

Another long silence, then Joel responds: "Yeah, I know this is not a stunt. . . . Well, maybe it is, but I think knowing what we know, it seems logical that people should be concerned."

"Enough to risk dying for," I interrupt.

"We're not gonna die," Joel replies.

"Well I'm not planning on it," I say, again pausing for a minute or two to kill time.

"It's patriotic," Joel says. "It's doing something that's not about yourself. Of course there's some ego involved, but you get this feeling of duty, like an obligation."

We stew over that thought for a long while, so long that it would seem to the outside observer that the conversation was over, but out here time expands to the horizon.

Minutes later: "You know," I say, "it really feels like something much bigger than us. I mean, first, there are so many people involved in this project now, so we're doing it for the team." I pause for a stretch, then add: "And we can be proud that we're doing something to get our country to pay attention and take responsibility."

Is it a futile, idealistic trap to expect that this adventure of ours will change anything? Is this "futilidealism"—really greenwashing a private lust for a personal challenge? In these moments of self-reflection and pessimism, I question what motivates the dozens of new plastic pollution organizations, the entrepreneurs who weekly churn out new ideas to clean up the gyres, or the makers of new antiplastic products that are constantly coming on line.

We've been sailing south-southwest 190 degrees at 0.7 knots. We're going the wrong way! We want to go west, 270 degrees or better, in the direction the wind is coming from, the direction of Hawaii. Yesterday we took a section of mast from the deck, lashed it to a spare rudder, and vertically plunged it four feet below the boat. This makeshift daggerboard improved our progress to 200 degrees. It will keep our raft from sliding across the sea with the wind. Our speed climbed to 1.2 knots.

By mid-afternoon, Joel's finished the Frankensail. "Let's raise it." He rigs a couple of blocks, one at the top of the mast and the other on the port side. Together we lift it high into the air. We feel the raft accelerate, and laugh hysterically. That improvement got us up to 215 degrees at 1.8 knots.

"See, those sail scraps came in handy," Joel says.

"Too valuable to waste," I say, playing off a plastics-industry slogan plastered across California.

We're shaving off the miles and days from Hawaii. We're sailing! Every degree westward and each knot of increased speed takes us away from the storms brewing off Cabo San Lucas a thousand miles away.

The American Chemistry Council is the world's largest petrochemical trade organization, representing Dow Chemical, Monsanto, DuPont, and more than two hundred other corporations. It spent over $50 million on lobbying activities between 2011 and 2015, according to OpenSecrets.org, the website of the Center for Responsive Politics.[1] If you drive along California's beaches, you'll see fifty-five-gallon garbage drums wrapped with ACC-funded ads showing a little girl with a bike helmet drinking from a plastic bottle. The ads read: "Plastics. Too Valuable To Waste. Recycle." The campaign perpetuates consumer responsibility, while aggressively rejecting EPR.

In 2012, a good friend and graphic designer helped me duplicate the exact color and font of the ACC ad on a huge decal, but with some modification. It now read: "Plastics, Too Wasteful To Value: REFUSE." We began blasting the beach with our counter-message directly covering their ads. You've got to fight fire with fire. But plastic bags are the policy front line. When US cities began passing bans, the ACC and the plastic-bag lobby met them head-on.

Plastic bags are escape artists, blowing down streets, getting stuck in trees, and clogging storm drains. Owners of recycling centers were the first to say they wasted more time and money dealing with bags than the bags were worth. The industry mantra is simple: "Bag bans raise taxes and kill jobs." It gets plastered on bus benches and billboards in the eleventh hour leading up to a public vote. In truth, bag bans create jobs for the companies that make sustainable alternatives, while reducing overseas imports of cheap, flimsy plastic bags that pollute. Bag bans reduce taxes. Citizens across the United States suffer double taxation from plastic bags: first, we pay higher taxes to cover municipal waste-management costs for removal of plastic bags from trees, drains, fences, and public lands, an expense the San Francisco Department of the Environment calculated at a total cost of 17 cents per bag, borne by the taxpayer. Second, a grocer includes the cost of so-called "free" disposable bags in the cost of groceries, on which the customer pays sales tax. By the end of the first decade of this century, plastic-bag ordinances were popping up across the country. Nantucket, Massachusetts, was the first municipality in the United States to ban plastic bags, and in 1990 West Coast governments began instituting plastic-bag bans and fees. San Francisco became the first city in California to ban bags in March 2007. Initially, San Francisco had sought to charge a fee for plastic bags, but that was challenged by industry front groups. The Save the Plastic Bag Coalition is one such group, engaging in stealth advocacy and sowing misinformation and confusion among the public and policymakers in order to create doubt. Led by "merchant of doubt" Stephen Joseph, it argued that cities could not charge a fee without preparing an environmental impact report (EIR). EIRs are too costly for most small towns to prepare, so the requirement effectively destroys some efforts to ban plastic bags. Jennie Romer, founder of Plastic Bag Laws, said, "What these suits accomplish is delay in enactment or implementation of bans, in addition to intimidation."

On September 30, 2006, Governor Arnold Schwarzenegger of California signed AB 2449, "California Plastic Bag Recycling Act," which essentially preempted municipalities from charging a fee for plastic bags. When municipalities, such as San Jose and Oakland, tried to ban bags, they were sued by Save the Plastic Bag. "We haven't challenged anyone that's done an EIR," Stephen Joseph said.

Anna and I were confronted by Joseph in San Jose when we gave a lecture in the city library. He sat behind a dozen adolescent Latina women, whom we believe he planted in the front row and who unleashed a volley of scripted questions about the immorality of denying poor families the use of plastic bags to carry their groceries home, taxing them and taking away their jobs.

Save the Plastic Bag Coalition sued San Luis Obispo, Santa Cruz, Long Beach, and Palo Alto. It also sued Marin County. Joe Garbarino of Marin County Recycling testified that plastic bags and Styrofoam "should be outlawed, worldwide," citing how they gum up the machines in his recycling center, in addition to the lack of a market for dirty plastic bags.[2] Ultimately, the Marin County ban was upheld because it was brought to the table by citizens, rather than through the city council, therefore it had wide support from the beginning.

San Francisco went for an outright ban without an EIR. Joseph sued it too, but a San Francisco Superior Court judge upheld the city's ban, which went into effect in October 2012. Los Angeles did an EIR and won its bag ban in early 2014. In 2016, there were sixty-seven ordinances covering eighty-eight municipalities statewide.

In Edmunds, Washington, Anna and I testified in April 2009 on behalf of council member Strom Peterson's proposed plastic-bag ban, which passed unanimously. When Seattle tried to pass a twenty-cent fee on plastic bags that summer, the ACC stepped in with its front group, the Coalition to Stop the Seattle Bag Tax. It collected twenty-two thousand signatures, spending an average of eight dollars each in wages for outside signature gatherers who stormed the city, effectively forcing a ballot referendum.[3] Radio ads blasted, and print ads went up across the city, asserting those two time-tested, hot-button claims—that the bag fee is a "tax" and that it "kills jobs." Steve Russell of the ACC said, "There are ways to achieve what we all agree is the goal of more recycled material that don't punish people on fixed incomes or people less able to pay those kinds of fees."[4] Local advocacy groups, such as Green Bag Campaign, raised a total of $65,000 throughout the year to fight the referendum, but were outspent 21:1 by the ACC's $1.4-million contribution to the referendum effort.[5] The ads worked, and in late 2009 the referendum overturned the city council's decision to ban plastic bags.

Industry was now on the attack.

In 2010, Andy Keller, CEO and founder of ChicoBag, a producer of high-quality reusable bags, was served notice that he was being sued by three of the largest disposable single-use plastic-bag manufacturers on the planet: Hilex Poly Company, Superbag Operating, and Advance Polybag. They claimed that ChicoBag's "false advertising and unfair competition in interstate commerce" caused "irreparable harm."

Strategically, the lawsuit was filed in South Carolina, where there are no anti-SLAPP (strategic lawsuit against public participation) laws. A SLAPP suit is a common industry strategy intended to silence critics by overwhelming them with the cost of litigation until they give up the fight. This transparent intimidation tactic is illegal in most states. The lawsuit was about bankrupting Andy, and nothing more.

Andy founded his company in 2004 after visiting a local landfill and seeing thousands of plastic bags blowing in the wind. He was horrified by the landscape of white and beige single-use bags. Driving home he couldn't help noticing all the bags stuck in trees and blowing across the street, like urban tumbleweeds. The idea of founding a company to solve the problem guided him to a secondhand shop to buy a used sewing machine. On his kitchen table, he created the first of what would become millions of reusable bags.

In the lawsuit, Andy was accused of spearheading a misinformation campaign against plastic bags in order to sell his reusable nylon bags. An info page on his website cited EPA statements about the 1 percent recycle rate for plastic bags and the fact that you only need reuse a cloth bag eleven times to equal the carbon footprint of a plastic bag. He cited *National Geographic* statements about the half-trillion plastic bags used each year and the accumulation of plastic trash in the ocean's gyres, and quoted a *Los Angeles Times* statement about the hundreds of thousands of mammals and birds harmed by ingested plastic. While these statements have been recycled in thousands of media articles and public documents, and even cited in city ordinances banning bags, the three companies spearheading the suit zeroed in on Andy. From their perspective, he was the perfect target: an activist CEO who dressed up as the Bag Monster and danced around the city halls where bag bans were being considered.

Andy's Bag Monster is a character decked out with five hundred plastic bags, representing the average number of single-use bags an American uses annually. "It is a giant walking, talking reality check," Andy said. "Most people never think about how many bags they use, how long they use them, what they are made of, how long they last or where they go after their brief useful life. The Bag Monster evokes these questions in people and shows us how ridiculous single-use plastics can be."

I was invited to join ChicoBag's legal defense as an expert witness, providing primary-source scientific literature to back up Andy's claims. ChicoBag's statements about recycling rates and global consumption of plastic bags were easy to defend. The dispute lies in the "wiggle room" in the EPA's reporting of recovery rates for plastic film, which in 2012 was 11.5 percent.[6] Plastic bags are lumped into the recovery rate for all "bags, sacks, and wraps," which include the millions of miles of film used to wrap around pallets of boxes transported around the world. Those are the easiest to recover, since that plastic film can be collected directly from the warehouses that unpack the goods. Plastic bags are practically irrecoverable, and there's no good data on how many bags are recovered and recycled, therefore ChicoBag's 1 percent recovery rate for plastic bags is likely very generous.

The plaintiffs took aim at ChicoBag's statement estimating a hundred thousand annual deaths of marine mammals, reptiles, and seabirds due to entanglement and ingestion, and a statement asserting that the largest landfill in the world was floating somewhere between California and Hawaii, full of plastic bags. The death rate, which you can find in United Nations and NOAA reports and hundreds of popular articles and websites, goes back to published proceedings from a 1983 marine debris conference about fur seal entanglement, where "50,000–90,000 fur seals are estimated to be killed by entanglement."[7] Somehow that statistic got rounded up to a hundred thousand, representing all marine mammals. Likely, the numbers of deaths by plastic is much higher—probably in the millions annually, if you lump mammals, reptiles, and birds together—and still underestimated because most of these carcasses sink to the deep soon after they perish.[8] Meanwhile, referring to plastic in the ocean as a landfill, patch, or soup is a tricky metaphorical representation. A landfill, like a patch, has defined boundaries, while plastic in the gyres do not. Calling it a soup leaves you wondering if it's like a miso, a stew, or a gumbo. These absurd arguments were not the true targets of the lawsuit. But the industry's strategy of questioning ChicoBag's website claims backfired in the wake of new scientific discoveries that made a stronger case than had the popular articles ChicoBag referenced. The effort by the three plastic-bag manufacturers backfired on another front when Andy Keller and a wide network of supporters fought back.

The Surfrider Foundation, the Earth Resource Foundation, the Environmental Working Group, Green Cities California, Care2, Heal the Bay, Plastic Pollution Coalition, and many other organizations helped Andy amass twenty-five thousand petition signatures urging the three plastic-bag companies to drop the case. ChicoBag was winning in the court of public opinion.

Andy took the moral high ground and bet on public goodwill. CNN and *Rolling Stone* ran stories. "Sadly, this lawsuit will cost millions and is a complete waste of money. If the plastics industry spent a fraction of the money they have spent on lawyers and lobbyists, actually addressing the legitimate environmental issues, perhaps they wouldn't have to rely on desperate attacks on small business," he said. He asked the three companies to provide evidence of the true recycling rate of plastic bags, and after a long silence Superbag and Advance Polybag dropped out, leaving Hilex Poly on its own.

Hilex Poly recognized the stalemate and perhaps knew it had accomplished part of its goal by driving a small, vocal business to spend many hours and thousands of dollars defending itself and making it an example of what could happen to other vocal groups. But in a win for conservation, ChicoBag reached a settlement with Hilex Poly.

In an interesting departure from the plastic-bag lobby's mantra that "plastic bags don't litter, people do," the company publicly acknowledged that windblown litter is a product of design and not consumer behavior. In the settlement, both parties agreed to provide references with any public statements about plastic bags. Hilex Poly accepted the responsibility of informing the public properly about plastic-bag recycling rates. ChicoBag added a note to its website suggesting that people wash dirty bags (this was in response to reports of *E. coli* in unwashed cloth bags), and Hilex Poly agreed to suggest that consumers tie bags in knots so they don't blow around.

If you weigh the arguments for and against the use of plastic bags, taking into account the external costs involved, it becomes clear that the thin plastic film design is severely flawed. The plastic-bag lobby still argues that plastic has a lower carbon footprint than paper, though it uses biased life-cycle assessments (LCAs) and seldom mentions the reusable option. Those LCAs never mention environmental or social impacts either. If you take an objective look at true costs, you find a different story. Recycling centers abhor plastic bags because they tangle or damage machinery and waste workers' time. Municipalities work overtime to pull bags from trees, fences, storm drains, and beaches. All of these costs trickle down to the taxpayer. Plastic bags create urban blight and have a negative effect on tourism. They become navigational hazards as they are sucked up by boat engines. More importantly, there are costs in the suffering of life on land and sea when creatures consume plastic bags or fragments of them. And let's not forget the warning on plastic bags regarding child asphyxiation; obstruction caused by plastic bags is one of the most frequent causes of infant-suffocation deaths, second to wedging between a bed or mattress and a wall.[9] Most LCAs do not capture such difficult-to-measure externalities.

I later asked Andy, "Did you ever see it coming? Had you any clues they would come after you?" He replied: "One day, after attending a council meeting in LA County, I found myself debating the facts with the Save the Plastic Bag Coalition. After a couple minutes of sparring, they said, 'You shouldn't be talking to me . . . 'cause we'll come after you next.' That was my first clear indication that I was a possible target."

While social justice and conservation groups rallied around plastic-bag and Styrofoam bans, industry resorted to a familiar playbook in its counterattack. There's long precedent of industry fighting the will of the people. The strategy is straight out of the textbook written by tobacco, acid rain, DDT, and climate doubt groups, as documented in Oreskes and Conway's book *Merchants of Doubt*.

When smoking became linked to lung cancer, the tobacco companies set a precedent for other industries to follow their strategy of defending the sale of cigarettes. The three front lines of the fight were litigation, politics, and public opinion, with selective science informing all three. In 1954, the industry created the Tobacco Industry Research Committee, publicly stating that it was for internal oversight and self-regulation, but in reality it was set up to "put out wildfires" as other organizations, politicians, and scientists discussed threats from tobacco smoking. Tobacco companies spent millions on their own research to dispute the established links between tobacco smoke and cancer. In the famed words of one tobacco executive, "Doubt is our product, since it's the best means of competing with the 'body of fact' that exists in the mind of the general public. It's also a means of establishing a controversy."[10]

Manufacturers of DDT followed a similar path. When Rachel Carson published *Silent Spring* in 1962 (after three books about oceans), she had no idea that in less than a year she would be sitting in front of a Senate subcommittee on pesticides, having rattled the chemical industry and kick-started the environmental movement.[11] DDT was first synthesized in 1874, and in 1939 it was discovered to kill insects. It was used extensively as a powder on US soldiers during World War II to kill lice, and was unleashed on the public as a pesticide following a postwar glut of product and of out-of-work veterans turned salesmen.

Industry was quick to retaliate and attempt to crush Carson's credibility. DDT manufacturers such as Velsicol threatened lawsuits against her publisher and the *New Yorker* for defamation, sent letters accusing Carson of being a Communist sympathizer employed by the Soviet Union to undermine American business, and even called her a "spinster with a herd of cats."[12] Carson had taken the shine off postwar materialism, pointing out that unleashing our invented chemistry on natural systems would in turn hurt us. She told the Senate subcommittee: "Our heedless and destructive acts enter into the vast cycles of the earth and in time return to bring hazard to ourselves."

These industry strategies are common and apply to any environmental or social justice issue. They are simple and time-tested, and wreak havoc with progressive movements:

1. **DENY**. Label the science as inconclusive, or poke holes in the research methods and demand "we need to do more research."
2. **DELAY**. The demand for more research is often followed by a flood of voluntary actions that can later be postponed, abandoned, or negotiated endlessly.
3. **DENIGRATE**. Demonize and antagonize the scientists and NGOs, challenging the industry position in order to undermine public confidence in the data.

4. **DISTRACT.** Create campaigns that promote alternate, mis-leading, or untruthful information. Often these are created by industry-friendly organizations with catchy names like Save the Plastic Bag that use slick slogans like "Plastics. Too Valuable To Waste."

5. **DISRUPT.** This includes initiating frivolous litigation and infil-trating governmental regulatory agencies. The revolving door between industry and government agencies is common and blurs the line between public and private.

6. **DOUBT.** Use of industry-led studies and internal reports that are not subject to peer review and that frequently contradict published scientific research. They are often cited during poli-cymaking and can create confusion and doubt.

Scientists, policymakers, advocates, and CEOs of small busi-nesses that are perceived to be attacking the petrochemical industry—whether that perception is real or imagined—are subject to the same aggressive tactics. Filing SLAPP suits against Andy Keller and hiring "merchants of doubt" to spread misinformation and file frivolous lawsuits; the arrival of the Society of the Plastics Industries on the doorstep of Edward Carpenter, the first scientist to study plastic in the ocean in 1972—these are some of the tactics that often work. But we can beat them.

DAY 37: JULY 7, 2008, MILE 617

Trade winds! (Latitude 23°54', Longitude 122°00')

Junk has suddenly turned west with the wind, as if everything has spun 90 degrees on a potter's wheel. The easterly trade winds blow a consistent fifteen to twenty knots above and below the equator, form-ing the bottom of Northern Hemisphere subtropical gyres, and top of the Southern Hemisphere gyres. With the wind at our starboard stern, we lock in the rudder and set the sails.

Hurricane Boris churned off Cabo San Lucas, the first of many storms this season. It took us a month to finally cross a line of longitude, all the while heading south, into dangerous territory—and somehow we had thought we'd be finished by now? We can't stay where we are. As these waters warm with the coming summer, each new storm will be stronger, last longer, travel farther. Joel has dialed in the sailing efficiency of this raft to the best of his ability. Time is too valuable to waste, but there's nothing to do but watch time pass. I call Anna on the satellite phone to get a weather report. Hurricane Boris eroded to a tropical storm, although newly arrived Hurricane Fausto is tearing up the sea where we were a week ago, which explains the great wind we're having, averaging thirty-five miles per day for the last week.

Another twenty-four hours goes by. After another rusted can of who knows what, we sit with nothing to do and not much to say for much of the day. Then Joel yells, "One thousand nine hundred and ninety-nine!" At 4:20 p.m. on June 8, at roughly 24°N latitude, 122°W longitude, we pass the two-thousand-mile benchmark of miles left to go. It's a huge landmark in our journey and does wonders for our mental stamina. To celebrate, we're going to slice one of the few remaining cabbage cores into long strips, like fettuccine, and add half a teaspoon of pesto sauce. It looks like a little bowl of pasta, and the more we mumble words like "spaghetti," "penne," "linguine" while we eat it, the more we think it is. For our main course, we split a can of vegetable medley.

"You've got to look at the serial numbers on top," Joel says, describing how he can predict what's in the label-less rusty cans. We're both laughing at the meticulous attention we've paid to the presentation of our feast. There's an involuntary illusion created in our minds to preserve sanity, an imagined alternate reality.

"You know, we're just going to laugh at this someday," I say.

"We just got to keep ahead of the storms," Joel replies. Hurricane Fausto is still behind us, but it came much closer than the one before. It traveled farther, was stronger, and was heading straight for us.

In the months and years ahead there will be more storms, always one behind the other. Anna and I choose this life and associate with those who challenge the status quo when it exploits people and the planet. Andy Keller weathered a storm that nearly cost him his company. The community organizers who lost the 2009 plastic-bag referendum in Seattle fought on and won a citywide ban in 2012. In

September 2014, Governor Jerry Brown of California signed SB 270, the first statewide plastic-bag ban. Immediately, the plastic-bag lobby employed the same Seattle strategy of hiring outside signature gathers to challenge the law with a referendum on the California ballot. The vote to uphold the ban came in November 2016, when Proposition 67 passed with wide public support.

Rachel Carson weathered the storm that descended upon her. She called on the public to form "citizen brigades," knowing that public health and environmental groups were key to fighting industry influence. To overturn the toxic status quo, we all need to remain engaged, exert constant pressure over time, and keep fighting through the storms.

CHAPTER 10

WAVES AND WINDMILLS

A Case for the Eco-Pragmatist

"Again I say," cried Don Quixote, "and I shall say it a thousand times, that I am the most unfortunate man in the world not to have seen all this!"

Sancho Panza roused him from his reverie, saying: "Master, sadness was made for men and not for beasts, but if men let themselves give way to too much to it, they turn into beasts."

—Miguel de Cervantes Saavedra
Don Quixote, 1615

DAY 39: JULY 9, 2008, MILE 658

Dead Calm (Latitude 23°34', Longitude 122°39')

The sea is completely becalmed, flat as glass, with an oily appearance. Joel and I occupy a twenty-by-twenty-foot prison, roughly the size of a boxing ring, with braided rope made from plastic bags tied around the railing. We're in opposite corners doing our own thing. I'm reading *Don Quixote* for the second time.

Joel is my Sancho Panza. I complain about the dire consequences of things while he's the pragmatic sailor keeping us on course. As I write in my journal, he's repairing a few stitches of his Frankensail where the duct tape came loose. I decide to dive below the raft to install five more mini-pontoons fabricated from tattered fragments of old netting and a dozen bottles re-inflated and sealed with glue.

"I thought we were in the trade winds?" I ask Joel. He shakes his head. Hurricane Fausto, like Hurricane Boris, survived full force until it reached where we had been a week earlier, then degraded to a tropical storm less than a thousand miles away. Hurricane Genevieve is not far behind. Strange to be so close to tumultuous seas and yet motionless.

"This raft can't take a hurricane dead on," I say. Joel nods.

What are we doing here? I think. I can't shake the absurdity of our situation. If Hurricane Genevieve hits us dead on, we will die. I know this raft like I know the feel of car keys in my pocket. I recognize every sound it makes, how the materials behave toward each other, how they bend and tear, I know its strengths and weaknesses. I jump in, set the new pontoons and close a few holes where I see loose strands of netting. It's a cool distraction from the raft, but I can't help thinking there's nothing but open water a few miles below me and a thousand miles in all directions.

We are a floating oasis sitting above a featureless ocean beneath a featureless sky. We drift amid a spectrum of blue, from the near-white of zenith to the blue-black of the sea floor, with only gravity dictating the order of space, air, water, and abyss. This sensory monotony is ripe for promoting hallucinations. I look overboard and see two fish the size of crayons come to the raft, and that is all for the day. We haven't seen a bird or bug in a month. A green film covers the sailboat masts across the deck. And now we are frozen, paused, as if holding our breath for the coming storm.

By afternoon, Joel's Frankensail hangs lazily from the mast with a few new lengths of duct tape and stitching, and the starboard side of the raft is four inches higher, leaving us content, but we know we're in trouble.

"Joel, we have to get out of here," I say, breaking hours of silence.

"I know," he replies. "It's not good." We finished the day with onion soup and a hefty chunk of that enigmatic but well-preserved block of cheddar cheese.

Same stillness the next morning: no wind or waves to move anything, complete silence. Inside my head there's a chorus of memories and emotions passing throughout the day. Thoughts and feelings arrive, like sparrows to a tree. Some stay awhile. I think about Anna most of the time. I dig through my bag and find a couple of those little notes she scribbled on strips of paper for me to read throughout the trip. "I love our park bench picnics, wine, cheese, baguette, and tomatoes, using our fingers and getting messy." Another one reads, "I love our routines together. Coffee in the morning, Sunday at the farmers market, strolling and grazing . . . movie night with popcorn on your boat, and always—best of all—curling up together, warm and safe in your loving embrace." I smile and let my longing linger.

The same internal conversations about the raft's success and failure surface, with worry about how our allies would explain our disappearance, and how our foes would relish our demise. "I told you they would fail," they would say. "They didn't know what they were doing; they just fell apart and added more pollution to the ocean."

I think a lot about the Gulf War, perhaps too much. It was so long ago—seventeen years now—but it was a turning point in my life. There are powerful moments hardwired in our memories, like knowing where you were sitting as the attacks on 9/11 unfolded. My mind meanders through these memories. Mindfulness is tough. I recognize my thoughts, as though an objective observer were saying, "Hmm, there goes that familiar story." All of those stories—the dying Iraqis, all the bodies at the "highway of death," and the oil fires—so many of them. I can recall with clarity the first dead soldier I saw, a young man ejected from an exploding jeep, nearly torn in two, lying in the sand with his arms outstretched. He had moved his arms about in the sand in the last agonizing moments before he died, making the shape of wings, the way kids make snow angels. Twelve marines had gathered around him, speechless, as we looked at someone just like us.

Although so far from me in time, these memories return to the present. I try to focus on being here and now, and fending off the mental hamster wheel that's always in need of entertainment—always ready for a spin.

I've been in this headspace before, in the mid-1990s, when it was fresh. I needed to make sense of my experience in war, to know that I had free will over a biodeterministic fate—that I wasn't just a puppet. The Persian Gulf War was a resource war sold to the public as a charitable act, defending Kuwait against tyranny. While the latter is true, the former was the dominant rationale (keep in mind, we did nothing while eight hundred thousand people, greater than the whole population of Kuwait, were killed in four months in the Rwandan civil war in 1994). I couldn't accept the great deception and betrayal, or the suffering of many thousands on the other end of our rifles.

When I came home from Kuwait, I returned to the University of New Orleans to complete my undergraduate degree in earth science, then went on to grad school at the University of Southern California for a PhD in science education. Academia was a fine distraction, as were summer-long expeditions spent fossil hunting and rock hounding on ranches in the desert grasslands of southeastern Wyoming. I avoided idle time like a plague, resisting retrospection, not wanting to ponder the heaviness of betrayal for too long. That's what it was. I had given everything, a willingness to kill and be killed, for the sake of cheap oil and national interests. Internally, pessimism thrived, while optimism was drowning. I spiraled downward.

That was not so long ago. Now I sit in an empty airplane floating on a heap of plastic bottles reading through journals buried in my laptop: old excuses to girlfriends, parts of my dissertation on aesthetic biophilia, journals from travel, and writings in the years after 9/11. I had joined Veterans for Peace and the ANSWER Coalition (Act Now to Stop War and End Racism), organizing street protests against the looming Iraq War. We marched in the streets with more than eighty thousand people in Los Angeles on March 15, 2003, in coordination with over six million people in sixty countries worldwide. The new power of social media to fuel a movement was obvious, yet the US government continued to defend the presence of weapons of mass destruction as the rationale, and took offense at any insinuation that fossil fuels had anything to do with it.

Then, on October 5, 2006, I listened to an NPR interview with former secretary of state James Baker III, the architect of the war in Kuwait, a member of the neoconservative think tank Project for a New American Century, and an advisor to George W. Bush on the latest invasion of Iraq. When he said, "We had a written policy that we would go to war to defend secure access to the energy reserves of the Persian Gulf," I pulled over to the side of the road. I was jumping out of my seat, angry and baffled, perplexed by his casual demeanor, as if a war criminal were describing atrocities while sipping tea. He went on.

> When you formulate and implement foreign policy for the United States you have to look at principles and values, yeah, but you also have to look at national interests, and we've always had a strong national interest in preserving secure access to energy reserves in the Persian Gulf.[1]

Here was an architect of war saying that for the sake of oil, young Americans and Iraqis were expendable. No marine I knew would willingly kill or be killed for access to petroleum. We have higher moral standards.

Of a barrel of oil, roughly 8 percent is required to make plastic. In the middle of the North Pacific somewhere between Los Angeles and Hawaii, I'm getting pissed off about it, again. *Be purposeful*, I think. *Contribute something meaningful.* I want to rid the world of the exploitation of fossil fuels for energy and chemistry, and of the suffering unleashed on people and the biosphere. I could walk away, but I chose to engage, and that is the crucial decision we all have to make when the curtain drops and you're confronted with an unfolding catastrophe.

DAY 41: JULY 11, 2008, MILE 694

First mahi mahi (Latitude 23°06', Longitude 123°08')

We're still becalmed. We have at least six weeks to go, and the food inventory tells us we must catch fish. There's a walnut-sized core of the last cabbage we've been nursing carefully. I photograph it.

"Why don't we call Don?" Joel says. Don McFarland had rafted these waters in 1958 in sixty-nine days on the *Lehi IV*. On the satellite phone we catch Don at home with his wife having lunch, which I ask him to describe it in detail, while we drool.

"You guys seeing any fish?" Don asks.

"Not a single one," I reply.

"That's strange. We had fish almost every day."

I hand the phone to Joel. "How about barnacles?" Don asks, referring to the gooseneck barnacles that attach to anything floating. "You can pull those off and suck the juice out of them."

Remembering the barnacle rice we ate on Charlie's expedition a few months ago, Joel and I shake our heads. "No, Don, no barnacle eating yet," Joel replies. Don laughs, enjoying reliving his adventure.

"Hey, Joel. How's our little cabbage doin'?" I ask an hour later.

"Yeah, we've got to eat the rest today," he replies, and thinly slices it with the remaining pesto. Our six-week food plan is on its sixth week. Six weeks to go. Discipline is easier to manage than hunger. I settle into the cockpit with my bowl.

"Mahi mahi!" he yells. We put our bowls down. He stalks the fish around the deck, fishing lure in one hand, spear gun in the other. Mahi mahi are curious fish and will chase anything bouncing across the surface. After an hour of flinging the lure off the side of the boat, Joel exclaims: "You've got to see this!" The fish is almost stationary under the starboard bow, with only its head hidden. It's as if the fish is thinking, *If I can't see them, they can't see me.* But in this case, half its body is exposed, less than two feet below the surface. I see only steaks with fins.

Joel slowly cocks the spear gun, aims just below the center of the fish to compensate for light distortion. Swoosh! The spear penetrates its body, sending it wriggling across the sea, making ripples where there were none.

"We've got to get it in," he yells, and yanks it atop the pontoons. He holds it down with both hands, grabbing each end of the spear through its body. I run back for my makeshift spear, the one made from a scrap of aluminum pulled off of one of the masts on the deck, ending the ordeal. The beautiful shades of blue and gold fade rapidly to gray in Joel's hands.

While I clean the fish, chef Joel sautés a sliver of garlic with two tablespoons of oil. It takes half an hour for me to fully clean the fish, stripping skin from meat and meat from bone, then I carve fifteen pieces from one side to make jerky. The pan is overflowing with fresh fish. The skeleton is hung from the railing of the raft to dry, for nibbling on later.

When I send a message to Anna she replies, "Finally. I've been worried this whole time. I even looked into an airplane drop." We've got food security for the trip if we keep this up, but weather worries are creeping up on us.

I have become an eco-pragmatist. Not the kind who believes technology will save us, but one who recognizes the essential management role we must embrace to preserve biodiversity, ecosystem services, and earth systems that make life cozy. Early-twentieth-century concepts of nature as a wild frontier to be conquered are of legend, like the rhinoceros head I lectured under at the Explorers Club in New York City. The animal was shot by Theodore Roosevelt at a time when the Industrial Revolution had proved humankind could conquer wild, limitless nature. But we have touched every corner of the planet with our invented chemistry, which persists as it floats and flies beyond the five subtropical gyres. What was wild space a century ago is "waste space" today.

My road to eco-pragmatism began with my academic pursuit following the Persian Gulf War. I studied natural history and environmental psychology, narrowly focusing on "biophilia," a term E. O. Wilson and Stephen Kellert coined to define the human affinity for life and life-like processes. Simply: I needed to know if I, and all of civilization, have the ability to climb out of primitive motivations and plan a sustainable future. It was a study of hope, motivated by desperation to find purpose. I desperately wanted to prove that we can choose our destinies, individually and collectively—that our future isn't predetermined by our biological drives to consume and expand.

I did not find the answer I had been looking for. But as it turns out, I gained a deeper understanding of what nature meant to me. On the raft, I experienced biophilia in many ways, including a practical, utilitarian need to catch fish for sustenance, but only after I dissected it out of personal curiosity. The sea also becomes a symbolic metaphor, soothing to inject into stories. When storms brew or the sunset is ablaze, a kind of natural reverence, or worship, develops. On a torn piece of sail I sketch a mahi mahi, much like a Neolithic cave painter documenting his hunt. My relationship to nature is complex and runs deep into my primitive cortex, defining why I love it so much, and why I am so deeply affected by the ecological destruction I witness here in the middle of the ocean or in the desert of Kuwait not so long ago.

I was a naturalist as much as a marine in that war, collecting scorpions and sun spiders, pressing leaves in books, and catching spiny-tailed lizards. I once used the butt of my M16 rifle to dislodge fossil clams and snails from a quarry in Saudi Arabia just before the ground war began. I took long walks when I could, to be alone with the sun and warm wind. When I saw burning oil wells shooting hundred-foot flames into the sky and covering the ground with soot and petroleum for miles, blackening the skies to complete darkness at noon, causing dark rivers to run from my eyes and nose, I fell into deep, prolonged despair. My biophilia had been betrayed, and I believed that humanity was self-destructive. I had no control of the future, and that was the core of my sadness. I had lost all hope.

The environmental movement, like any social justice movement, can grow only when people are hopeful, when they feel effective. As we witnessed in the US war in Iraq, as soon as the first bombs dropped in Baghdad, initiating the war on March 20, 2003, the antiwar movement began to vaporize as many lost hope. Those who stayed on recognized the power of persistent pressure over time to break down walls, as was the case during the Vietnam War and civil rights movement half a century ago. Environmentalism works the same way—think of the push for corporate accountability that took lead out of paint, or removed CFCs from refrigerants, or put seat belts in cars. That belief—that our effort will lead to a positive outcome—is what gives each individual the will to join movements and commit to them for the long haul.

As an eco-pragmatist, I acknowledge what we've already lost and will still lose. We work with the hand we're dealt, and we've given the generation born in the twenty-first century a gathering storm. Habitat and species are lost daily, a fact so normalized that it barely makes the news. Human population will climb to peak density around mid-century, when there may not be sufficient arable land and clean water to meet the needs of more than ten or eleven billion of us. The rise of persistent chemicals swirling in our seas and in the air will meet the decline of finite resources somewhere around the same time. We are entering a time without precedent in human history, in which there's no other land or sea to conquer to feed our appetite for unrestricted growth.

Despite this looming catastrophe, I believe we can do better. If wild nature no longer exists, we must create it. In *Rambunctious Garden*, Emma Marris describes being "proactive and optimistic," and explains how the eco-pragmatist "creates more and more nature as it goes, rather than building walls around the nature we have left."[2] We do that with forest reserves and marine protected areas. We must build wild space, restore it and protect it from further extraction, development, and exploitation. Keep carbon in the ground! In 2016, President Obama quadrupled the size of the Papahānaumokuākea Marine National Monument, from 139,797 square miles to 582,578 square miles, making it the single-largest marine protected area on the planet; organizations like Pristine Seas, led by Dr. Enric Sala, have been the catalyst for protecting more than 4.5 million square kilometers of the ocean. We need more—not well-manicured, but wild—spaces that are deliberately abandoned to preserve the sublime for the sake of our biophilic need for it. We evolved a dependency on other life, a deep affinity and ecological need for it, so we must understand and protect wild space in the context of our own self-preservation.

In the coming storm, we have one shot.

DAY 44: JULY 14, 2008, MILE 719

Hurricane Genevieve (Latitude 23°06', Longitude 123°08')

"You must stay in cold seas!" Charlie says over the satellite phone. We had called him for a weather update, frustrated that we are still becalmed, drifting about ten miles per day without raising the sail. On the chart plotter we're moving in a figure eight, like the teacup ride at Disneyland, but over five days.

"Hey Joel!" I yell across the ocean. He's swimming around with his camera and spear gun. He's chasing a pair of four-to-five-foot ono swimming near us. He's as comfortable in the water as he is on land.

A puff of wind blows across the deck, sending the first ripples across the sea surface.

"Looks like we got some wind!" I yell again. The mizzen sail whips around with a light gust out of nowhere.

"I guess I ought to come back," Joel replies. We raise the spinnaker and head due west. Within an hour we drop the spinnaker and raise the mainsail. I move the mahi mahi jerky inside the cabin, where it hangs above our heads with an unmistakable aroma.

"It's got to be around twenty knots," I say to Joel.

"Yup, we're in the trade winds now," he replies. Waves splash against our port side. We're riding the twenty-third parallel, where the water is a comfortable sixty-five degrees. A little farther south, at latitude twenty degrees, temperatures rise to eighty, perfect bath water for a hurricane. We are literally racing hurricanes to Hawaii.

Hurricane Genevieve is southeast of us now, giving us steady wind. For the next forty-eight hours we travel ninety miles, swiftly making up for lost time. There are 1,850 miles to Hawaii, another thirty degrees of longitude to cross. If we can maintain three hundred miles a week, we'll get there by the end of August. To put it into perspective, that's driving from Los Angeles to New Orleans at two miles per hour, night and day, for six weeks.

On July 17, three days later, the seas build. Waves roll in, six to eight feet in height, with sporadic whitecaps that spill over the deck. You can recognize the ones that are going to hurt by the time and distance of the wave crest from us. A large wave peaks right beside the starboard side and dumps in my lap, knocking me to the deck. The sound reverberates throughout the raft; buckets tied into milk crates are floating about. The cooking box, an aluminum military crate with our stove, pots, and pans stored inside, crashes to the deck.

I'm on watch, while Joel is inside trying to read the last pages of *Don Quixote* under the swinging clothesline of mahi mahi jerky. I'm thinking of Charlie's words: "Stay in cold seas!" We're pushing *Junk* as close to the wind as possible, beating northward. Thirty-knot gusts of wind and rain rip through. I can feel the strain as the square sail wants to lift the raft out of the water, while the tangled mess of bottles underwater keep *Junk* anchored to the sea.

Whack! The sail backwinds, sending the metal yardarm slamming into the mast. The raft violently spins around. This happens in a fraction of a second of my distraction. The loose sheet lines that tie to the bottom of the mainsail are cracking like whips. Joel jumps out of the cockpit and scampers across the deck to push the yardarm out from between the A-frame masts.

"We're spun around!" I yell above the howling wind.

"We gotta release one side first!" he yells back. It's not moving, as the sail is now working backwards. We scramble to the bow to drop the main. We both balance on slippery algae-covered masts across the deck, which is wobbling with each wave. If either of us falls in, we're dead. We're both pulling on the sail to bring it down, tackling it and tying it to the deck.

The wind is gusting up to forty knots. We keep the sail down, as thousand-gallon waves crash on and through the deck. At 9 p.m. Joel takes over the helm, steering the raft the best he can with only the rudders and his instinctive feel for where the waves are coming from. I'm sitting in the cabin, out of the rain, ready to jump out. Joel and I, and our little raft, endure a long sleepless night. There's nothing to do but hold on and wait for the next wave to crash over us.

CHAPTER 11

WASTING AWAY

The Fate, Fallacy, and Fantasy of Ocean Cleanup

*You don't filter smokestacks or water. Instead, you put the
filter in your head and design the problem out of existence.*

—William McDonough
Cradle to Cradle, 2002

DAY 48: JULY 18, 2008, MILE 895

Entropy (Latitude 23°08', Longitude 126°29')

Under blue skies, the wind is steady between fifteen and twenty
knots. The stove is destroyed. We celebrate with pizza.

One of our remaining rusty cans turns out to be tomato paste. We
layer the bottom of a pan with wheat crackers and smear the paste
over the top. I add a few slices of rancid salami, which has patches of
fuzz, like a fat, short-haired hamster. I remember during the rescue/
restock at week one Duane Laursen said, "Just take it," and hurled the
salami at us. Joel shaves a thin layer from the cheddar cheese block on
top of it. In the bag of miscellaneous tools, there's the tip for a blow-
torch. It fits perfectly over the propane valve, so we torch the cheese
from above and call it "*Junk* pizza."

The last twenty-four hours broke a new record for miles covered in
one day: 50.2. In the following week we'll average 49.8 miles per day,
sailing more in those five days than the previous five weeks. When we
break 1,500 miles to Hawaii, we open our last box of macaroni and
cheese.

True to the sailors' mantra—"Boats have destinations, not time
schedules"—the trade winds are taking us west. It is difficult to describe

the psychological shift, now that we're outrunning the storms. But there's a new foe: entropy.

The morning routine begins with an inspection of the raft. All boats require maintenance, especially when under way, as the stress of sailing makes everything move, rub, grind, and abrade. I discover that where the aluminum airplane fuselage touches the aluminum masts, deep grooves are forming. Where a single rope or line touches another, fibers fray. The two steel mainstays on the back of the raft are frayed. Dozens of holes have worn in the netting anywhere it was loose enough to rub against anything. Nuts are spinning off bolts, and even the lashings that secure the fuselage to the deck have, unbeknownst to us, come apart on one side. Entropy is the nature of things. "Subtle is the Lord, but malicious he is not," Einstein said during his first visit to Princeton in 1921.[1] The sea is notorious for tearing boats apart, from electrolysis that rapidly oxidizes metals, to cracks that slowly open to chasms. The movements are slow and seemingly innocuous, yet in time change is inevitable. The objective is to anticipate and stay ahead of the decay.

I climb to the top of the mast to jiggle a few wires on the radar and find that the top of the mast is cracked. I climb back up to tighten a few hose clamps around the crack. The next morning I find them broken and on the deck. There's too much movement up there. Nothing holds, so we watch the crack lengthen and hope we arrive in time. When I inspect it again, I look over to the mainsail, and to my horror I notice that the thick stainless-steel eyebolt holding the yardarm high has bent open completely and is barely holding up the sail.

"Joel, do we have any more shackles?" I ask. He's got the bucket of rusty spare parts opened and splayed across the interior of the airplane. He's in the middle of adjusting the backstays to bypass the sections that are rusted through.

"Nope, we're out. Down to whatever you can scavenge from something else." I rig a piece of chain to support the mainsail between the top of the two front stays. Joel finds a couple of nuts and bolts to replace the missing ones on the backstays, then he cranks on the turnbuckles to tighten the whole thing.

"We've got everything we started with," Joel says. "Nothing got thrown away." That begins a conversation, more of a thought experiment, to play out the material science of the *Junk* if it were thrown away.

Inspired by Alan Weisman's description of decomposing cities in *The World Without Us*, I wonder how the *Junk Raft* would fare if abandoned to the sea. What would its fate be? For the next weeks or months, the raft would ride the trade winds toward Japan, then take a turn northward with the Kuroshio Current, and back across the Pacific above Hawaii to the California Current again, but I doubt it would survive that six-to-ten-year round-trip intact. The aluminum A-frame mast and sail would flap aimlessly in all directions, shredding as the friction with the forestays and backstays tore it apart. The forestays, made from three-eighths-inch galvanized cables bolted to the four corners, would wear thin and break as the metal-on-metal movement took a quick toll. The mast would then come crashing to the deck. If it fell in, it would sink to the seafloor and slowly oxidize, like the metal hull on the *Titanic*.

The solar panels and wind generator would likely still function, sending a light electric current through the steel and aluminum. Rapid oxidation would begin where different metals touch, a process called "electrolysis." The three large solar panels, held together by a steel frame, would soon drop to the deck and fall over the edge. Sinking to the deep, the photovoltaic cells, sandwiched between layers of glass and plastic, would settle into the silicious ooze on the seafloor, where cold darkness would entomb them until they were subducted under the earth's crust millions of years from now. The two polyester resin rudders, held by a single metal pin, would each quietly drop their fiberglass shells to fossilize in the deep.

The airplane fuselage, if it hasn't fallen off already, would lose its last cargo strap to friction and slide backward off the deck or, with sufficient rocking on the deck, would saw through the masts and crash between them. The four hundred pounds of batteries would drop to the back of the plane as the tail rotated downward, as would our clothing, sleeping bags, and other electronics. A trail of *Junk Raft*'s well-preserved electronics, such as circuit boards, plastic housings, and glass screens, would litter the sea floor in its path.

With the fuselage, batteries, and solar panels gone, the raft would rise another eighteen inches out of the water. The aluminum masts, which were not bolted to anything, would wear holes in the pontoons where they repeatedly touch. They would begin to hang vertically as they detached themselves unevenly, and one by one drop like darts to the seafloor.

The netting for the pontoons that was exposed above water would degrade faster owing to UV sunlight and thermal loading, causing it to tear open. Once one bottle popped out, the pontoon would go limp and other bottles would follow. The bottles, nearly 100 percent PET and polycarbonate, would float as long as inflated, but sink when the polyethylene and polypropylene caps degrade.

The tangled mass of netting, ropes, and sails would form a giant net ball, or ghost net, forming an island community of life, entangling perhaps thousands of unlucky fish, birds, marine mammals, and sea turtles, until they died and decomposed. Slowly the netting would shred into microfibers. The remaining bottle caps might be ingested by seabirds. Other bottle caps, along with buckets and crates, would form microplastic fragments. The red, yellow, and orange fragments, mimicking the size and color of food, would be eaten first, and take a ride to the seafloor in the stomachs of dying fish. A large proportion of microplastics and microfibers would eventually become nanoplastic, which would either sink to the seafloor as heavy biofilms and crusting bryozoans formed on them and weighed them down, or would wash ashore on beaches somewhere. In their descent, they would ride currents horizontally around the globe, entering other gyres, including the subpolar and circumpolar gyres. But much of what drifted on the surface would cycle through the bodies of fish and filter-feeders that passively or intentionally ingest the particles, then sink to the seafloor either in the dead bodies or as heavy fecal pellets.

One of my projects on the raft has been building a surface trawl that I can use to skim the ocean surface for plastic particles. We've got a small spare sea anchor that looks more like a large carrot. I take two metal bucket handles to make a rectangular frame, and sew the edge of the net to it. A couple of two-liter plastic bottles are tied to either side of the trawl so that it floats and forces the net opening to remain vertical when towed. I attach a towline and toss it in. It works beautifully, and in twenty-four hours I retrieve it to find a handful of microplastic confetti. Blue, white, and black fragments of microplastic swirl in a soup of zooplankton, along with the water-walking insect *Halobates sericeus* and the jellyfish *Velella velella*, also called "by-the-wind sailor," because of the thin translucent sail that sticks straight out of the water. Gone are the reds, yellows, and oranges, and the bits of plastic film or foam. The consensus is that sunlight and selective feeding eliminate these colors. Meanwhile, embrittlement caused by sunlight, along with chemical and biological degradation and ingestion by fish and other marine life, reduce fragile forms of plastic to smaller and smaller particles that are more difficult to detect. What survives are these hardened fragments. What they were originally is unknown.

We trawl every day, and each sample contains plastic. If we were able to continue west to Japan for the next four thousand miles, we would see the same. If we went south to Antarctica, or north to the Bering Sea, it wouldn't stop. It might diminish, but micro- and nanoplastic would be there. Higher concentrations occur near coastal hot spots, such as the Bay of Bengal, the Mediterranean Sea, and the South China Sea. When I tell people this, I usually hear: "Well, how do we clean this up?"

Notions of mythical plastic islands and garbage patches have elicited dozens of elaborate cleanup proposals, despite the fact that current science favors other approaches. Today, most scientists and policymakers debate upstream solutions, weighing, for example, the benefits of zero-waste strategies against incineration. Ocean cleanup is generally off the table. But in the early 2000s, industry, the public, and policymakers were asking scientists for photos of the garbage patch, and many media outlets created Photoshopped images of plastic floating in water, typically from near-shore environments. These images perpetuated the cleanup myth, which inspired intrepid entrepreneurs—"gyre cleaners"—who wanted to test their inventions in the middle of the subtropical gyres.

Many proposals focused on plastic-to-oil pyrolysis machines that could mine the plastic for fuel as they motored along, or on ways to seed the seas with GMO bacteria that thrive on PET, polyethylene, and polypropylene (and which would also eat boats, docks, fishing nets, and buoys). The most intriguing ideas have come from the Dutch, who manage their lives below sea level with marvelous technical approaches to taming the ocean using dams, docks, and dredges. Anna and I met astronaut and engineer Wubbo Johannes Ockels in 2010 aboard the *Stad Amsterdam* while we were studying plastic in the Indian Ocean Gyre. He described his invention of a giant man-made island of plastic trash in the shape of a pinwheel and the size of several soccer fields. With the aid of parachutes, the island would spin and collect more plastic along the way, perpetually adding more real estate to expand Dutch territory.

My response is always the same: "Solve the problem upstream." In time, nearly all of the cleanup ideas have faded, except one. Boyan Slat, a Dutch engineering student, founded the Ocean Cleanup Project (OCP). His original concept was a sixty-kilometer-wide net array—basically a long pair of inflated booms, like wings, that would funnel large macroplastic to a single conveyer belt that dropped trash into a container.

With the advantage of Slat's youth and idealism and the promise of a silver-bullet, technological solution, the OCP raised more than a million dollars in its first year. He and I met in Amsterdam in 2013. After dinner, we strolled around the city talking about engineering projects, including a collaboration on a vertical net design to study the distribution of microplastic near the surface to a depth of five meters in the open ocean. We met again in early 2014 in Los Angeles. By then his fund-raising effort had doubled. Meanwhile, the published science on plastic pollution had more than doubled as well, unraveling the mythology that had misled so many. Solutions-minded folks were moving upstream, because downstream is too late.

Once plastic gets to the gyres, much of the damage to marine life through ingestion and entanglement has been done. With an estimated eight million tons of plastic leaving shorelines globally each year,[2] and a quarter million tons[3] we estimated to be drifting at sea, plastic is largely not making it to the gyres, unless it's something designed to last, like fishing gear. On the ocean surface there's a hundred times less microplastic than we expected, supporting our understanding that the sea surface is not the final resting place of trash.[4] The remaining "gyre cleaners" typically underestimate how quickly plastic is torn apart, fragmenting from macroplastic to microplastic less than 5 mm in diameter, especially in the case of thin film and foam used in typical product packaging. We rarely find fragments of plastic bags far offshore, and when we do, they are riddled with fish bites. Styrofoam cups and plates are practically nonexistent in the gyres, unless they were recently lost off passing ships. Most plastic packaging simply doesn't survive the long journey to the gyres intact, so if you're hell-bent on cleaning up the gyres, the science of current movements suggests the best place to be effective is very close to shore or at river mouths.[5] Focus on gyre cleanup and you've missed the boat.

Slat had completed an Ocean Cleanup Project feasibility report by late spring 2014, just a couple of months before we were set to be on a webinar together, along with Nick Mallos from the Ocean Conservancy. The scale of the project, which featured giant tethers connected to the sea floor, invited critical review from oceanographers, engineers, and marine scientists.[6] The ocean corrodes and degrades things humans make, and its inhabitants crawl over, attach themselves to, and eat what they can. The ocean isn't friendly to our stuff.

On June 25, 2014, we held our webinar.[7] My principal concern was bycatch: tens of millions of organisms—passively floating ones like the beautiful purple janthina snail, rafting barnacles, and numerous jellies (including the by-the-wind sailor)—could be captured over a short time. The OCP was surprisingly unaware of these species. In the last minutes, I asked an economic question, about the cost-benefit of alternate options. "Of the two million dollars you've raised so far, would you consider funding a small program incentivizing recovery of the big stuff, like Fishing for Litter, to see if fishermen could collect more trash at sea, more efficiently and cheaper, than you can?"[8] I'm certain that Hawaiian fishermen would gladly collect derelict fishing gear if given a euro per kilo, which is a fraction of OCP's anticipated four-and-a-half-euro-per-kilo cost-benefit for its net array. It's worth a try.

What mostly persists out there, by weight, is fishing gear—accounting for more than 70 percent of our 270,000-ton estimate of drifting trash—so it is worthwhile for OCP to go after large tangled masses of net and line before they strangle more marine life and damage more vessels, and fragment into microplastic any further.[9] What we know is that similar recovery programs are proving successful in the North Sea and elsewhere around Scotland, and are working even without monetary incentives.[10] In the 2015 G7 meeting in Germany, plastic marine pollution solutions were on the agenda, with Fishing for Litter presented as the only viable ocean cleanup program; it was labeled "a useful last option in the hierarchy, but [one that] can only address certain types of marine litter."[11]

For there to be a long-term solution, fishing fleets must take responsibility, through efforts like net tagging or lease programs (nets, buoys, and lines would be borrowed and returned, or paid for if lost). Some commercial fleets are currently implementing net lease programs.[12] Then there's the company Bureo Skateboards, which offers fishermen contracts to sell or donate their old nylon nets to be recycled into skateboards and sunglasses.

But what of all the stuff out there now? Current science suggests that stranding on a shoreline near you or burial on the ocean floor is the endgame. Deposition of microplastic on shorelines worldwide has been documented, as has accumulation in the deep abyss.[13] Like the tar balls that plagued the oceans before MARPOL stopped oil tankers from rinsing their ships at sea, stop the source, and the ocean kicks out the junk. We'll have to live with a defining stratigraphy, a geologic layer of micro- and nanoplastic covering the planet, but the ocean can recover if we do no more harm.

A week after the webinar, I received an answer from the OCP regarding my question about testing a Fishing for Litter program in the Pacific. They said, "No."

The world needs more people like Boyan Slat, with his assertive, confident solution-oriented focus, to fix problems. He seemed to me, like most of the "gyre cleaners," to have his heart in the right place, but like others, he's a victim of misconceptions about the nature of plastic in the ocean. He's indebted to a devoted following and to funders who expect results, and receives accolades from industry for pushing the cleanup narrative. But I believe he has the wherewithal to be pragmatic and change course as the current dictates a new direction, and not be like the fabled Icarus that many have pegged him to be, chasing an idea till he falls from the sky.

DAY 55: JULY 25, 2008, MILE 1,223

Entropy (Latitude 22°37', Longitude 132°16')

After a week of steadily sailing another three hundred miles, we are becalmed again. The sails hang still, like the edge of an oversized tablecloth reaching lazily to the floor. Hurricanes are forming, but are behind and south of us. I step outside to find mahi mahi under our raft.

Joel's got the spear gun at the ready. By noon, I'm slicing inch-wide strips of flesh to bake in the sun to make jerky. It seems that twenty-four hours of sunlight achieves the optimal balance of chewy on the outside and soft on the inside. I've got salt, pepper, maple syrup, and some Cajun spice left over, allowing a range of flavored jerky. I walk around the deck conducting my ritual inspection of bottles and netting. I look for wear on lines and exposed wires on stays, and I test the integrity of the lashings and welded parts.

There are more holes and worn metal, and cracks are growing wider. All things fall apart. Everyone around me will go in time, unless I beat them to the grave this summer. Everyone suffers along the way, suffering physically until our bodies surrender, and suffering emotionally as we torture ourselves with the fantasy of rigid things. I remind myself to be okay with how things in our world fall apart.

CHAPTER 12

SYNTHETIC DRIFT

Human Health and Our Trash

There may be fates worse than extinction.

—Theo Colborn, Dianne Dumanoski,
and John Peterson Myers
Our Stolen Future, 1996

DAY 64: AUG. 3, 2008, MILE 1,605

Riding the Gyre (Latitude 23°38', Longitude 138°58')

We are riding the edge of the gyre, in the fast lane with those equatorial trade winds that take plastic from North America across to Japan, exactly opposite the currents north of here that took the debris from the 2011 Japan tsunami in the other direction. In the last week, we've traveled 382 miles in the right direction, but we're critically low on food.

The makeshift trawl continues to collect degraded microplastic that, like us, is riding these southern gyre currents in a slow vortex as it continually fragments and cycles through marine life via ingestion, regurgitation, or excretion, sometimes becoming host to heavy organisms that make it sink. Those microplastics can later be buoyed to the surface when the calcium carbonate skeletons of some of those hitchhikers dissolve, but eventually it's all settling on the seafloor or washing ashore, likely very far from where it started in distance and time. We will suffer the same fate if we miss Hawaii.

I've spotted a few bits of trash throughout the day: a one-inch-diameter plastic washer, a short length of rope, and a tangled mass of green fishing line and frayed rope as big as my fist. Joel spots a piece of a blue crate the size of a dinner plate. He hops around the raft try-ing to grab it as we pass over it, snatching it at the last second. "Ha! There's a bristle worm," he says, pointing to the three-inch prickly critter comfortably nestled among a few barnacles and fish eggs.

I relieve Joel from night watch at 1 a.m. Wind and waves are at our back. With each wave that crashes against the pontoons, a biolumines-cent greenish glow explodes. The vertical migration of zooplankton to the surface is chased by plenty of arthropods, jellies, salps, and myc-tophid fish with light-emitting photophores on their stomachs flashing nocturnal messages to their own kind. Unwittingly, they are eating our trash. In the morning I check the trawl. Among the dozens of visible white, blue, green, gray, and black fragments, there's a piece of plastic film bitten at the edges, a possible chunk of milk crate, fishing line, a preproduction plastic pellet, and a flexible, triangular fragment of what was likely a piece of a flip-flop, also with nibbled edges.

Joel calls Charlie to check in on weather, and to hear another voice besides mine. We describe the fish we're catching and our mahi mahi jerky recipes, and ask about the myctophid fish we caught during the expedition five months ago.

"We've been analyzing their stomach contents. Plenty of them are full of microplastics," Charlie says. Christiana Boerger, a marine biol-ogist working in Charlie's lab, has nearly finished all 678 dissections.

"Christiana opened one fish and pulled eighty-four pieces of plastic out of it," Charlie says, "and another had one piece that was as big as the entire stomach." With this study, we can add a few new species of fish to the list of marine life affected by plastic, which stands at 557 species today.[1]

On August 5 we celebrate another milestone. Nine hundred ninety-nine miles to go! We've got a few meals left, then it's peanut but-ter and fish. We're zero for three on fishing. Days ago Joel speared a large mahi mahi, flung it on deck, and as I wrestled its body, it got away from me and slid off the slippery deck. I watched it descend in a death-spiral. I felt horrible for the waste of a life, as well as for the three feet of lost steaks, sushi, and jerky. Joel hooked another one, but as he reeled it in, the hook got hung up on the netting around the pontoon and that mahi mahi got away. This one came back, and the next day I got close enough to spear it but missed, and it swam away for good. Fishing for sport and fishing for sustenance are two different mindsets. Now we're hungry.

Don McFarland sends a message to Anna to relay to us. His 1958 rafting adventure finished in sixty-nine days—a period we will easily surpass. "I hear from Anna you're having a tough time catching fish?" he asks. "Take a T-shirt and drag it around for a while. Cooked plankton tastes like lobster."

But when we do that now, it comes up with more and more plastic. We could remove the visible plastic, but would surely mistake some of it, and certainly all nanoplastic, which is neither appetizing nor nutritious. We stick to peanut butter. This dilemma isn't an option for the billions of fish globally that rise to the surface to feed. They are ingesting nonnutritive plastic, which gives a false sense of satiation, creates potential for intestinal blockages, and introduces a buoyant material in their bodies that forces them to expel energy they can't spare to get back down deep before the sun rises. Like that piece of foamed polyurethane from a flip-flop with chewed edges: a fragment of that in the gut of a one-ounce deep-sea fish is like you or me swallowing an empty two-liter bottle and trying to swim to the bottom of a pool. The effect of plastic ingestion on fish is not understood.

DAY 69: AUG. 8, 2008, MILE 1,863

Rainbow runner (Latitude 23°47', Longitude 143°31')

"Hunger is the best sauce in the world," I say to Joel, reading a passage from Don Quixote to Sancho Panza. Had I known we would triple our anticipated time at sea, I would have brought a library. Two months ago, soon after we looped around and around Guadalupe Island off the coast of Mexico, a little school of fish appeared—hundreds of them with their yolk sacs still attached. They followed our raft, enjoying the security of its undulating underbelly with nooks and crannies for hiding. They ride what little bow wake *Junk* creates, racing forward to forage from the sea surface, and at times racing to keep up with the raft at two knots.

Now our followers have winnowed down to a half-dozen yellow-tailed fish as big as the palm of my hand. Called "rainbow runners," they're a pelagic fish found across the North Pacific, but these are found only under our raft. We decided a couple of days ago to ration our food intake so that it lasts another month. These little fish are naïvely unaware that we are predators too.

Joel, crouching at the bow and motionless like a gargoyle, has a piece of netting in his hands, submerged next to one of the pontoons. I see him splash around in the water. "Got one!" he yells. The wriggling rainbow runner is flopping on the deck. I bait a hook with pieces of the flying fish we found this morning stranded on deck and catch another two. We're sorry to nab the same fish we watched grow before our eyes, but hunger prevails. I cut two filets from each and stick them in the pan.

The entrails and skeleton are spread over the wooden cutting board. The stomach, roughly the size of an almond, feels hard, unlike the stomachs of other fish I've dissected to examine gut contents. I touch it with the edge of the filet knife and it splits open. Seventeen fragments of plastic pour out. There's nothing else inside. It was filled to capacity.

I'm instantly disgusted. It's like finding a dead fly in the bottom of a cup of tea. There's no way this fish could have passed those fragments, at least not until the fish itself grew larger and the gastric valve widened to let the trash through. Surely, there's a long residence time for plastic inside the gut, allowing whatever chemistry is in that plastic to leach into the tissues and organs.

"I don't want plastic in my sushi," Joel says.

"I can't believe we're finding this . . . in the middle of nowhere," I reply.

We talk about the long-lasting toxins that drift in our oceans and absorb and adsorb onto plastic, and then drift into us. I take the filets out of the pan and toss them on the deck.

For marine life, plastic is inescapable. The 557 species that have been documented as eating or becoming entangled in our trash (a number that changes almost monthly) represent half of all known seabirds, marine mammals, and reptiles, as well as a growing list of fish,[2] zooplankton,[3] phytoplankton,[4] arthropods, shellfish, and worms. There is growing evidence that the toxicants that absorb and adsorb onto microplastics desorb into the marine life that ingest them, and it's not a good thing. Even in fish markets, clams[5] and fish[6] have been found with abundant micro- and nanoplastics in their guts, which we ingest if we eat them whole. The microplastic particles themselves may move up the food chain as one animal eats another.[7] The evidence is stacking up that plastic pollution causes environmental harm, including cancers in fish[8] and lower reproductive success and shorter lifespans in marine worms.[9] In one study of oysters, there's "evidence that polystyrene microspheres cause feeding modifications and reproductive disruption . . . with significant impacts on offspring."[10]

Those fragmented pieces of our packaging and products drifting on the sea surface often contain a long list of chemical plasticizers, including phthalates, triclosan, bisphenone, and organotin, that were originally added during production to change material properties, such as hardness, color, and flammability. Those particles also absorb many persistent organic pollutants (POPs), such as PCBs, a globally banned industrial chemical once used as an insulator in transformers; pesticides like DDT and its metabolite DDE; PAHs from the incomplete burning of fossil fuels; and PBDEs, a flame retardant found in curtains, carpets, and furniture cushions. These novel chemicals served society at a time when the problems of environmental persistence and ecotoxicology were not relevant to a worldview of benign dispersal in nature, but knowledge of biomagnification and health impacts—from mercury in fish to distorted sexual development in marine mammals and shortened penis size in alligators—have changed everything.[11] The hermaphroditic beluga whale named Booly, in the Saint Lawrence Seaway, bore a body burden so full of PCBs and other synthetic estrogenic compounds that he and other male whales developed enlarged mammary glands.[12] A study of toxins in human breast milk in US cities sought a clean population to use as a control, so researchers sampled Inuit women in remote villages above the Arctic Circle. To their surprise, the women had higher levels of PCBs than the women in big cities did, primarily from their diet of marine mammal meat and fat.[13] Human exposure to endocrine disruptors commonly associated with plastic debris is linked to obesity,[14] autism, and learning disabilities,[15] especially at critical windows of development. A recent study of human ingestion of yellowfin tuna from the Gulf of Mexico showed that measurable levels of PCBs in fish tissues can be transferred to humans through consumption.[16] With more than a million tons of yellowfin tuna consumed globally each year, it's essential that human health impacts be understood.[17] But there are other, perhaps easier, ways that humans internalize this chemistry.

This cocktail of twentieth-century chemistry is swirling all around us, and plastic is proving to be a significant vector, or entry point, to food webs. Microplastics, especially fibers from synthetic textiles, have been found in consumer products including honey, beer, bottled water, and salt,[18] and they can be inhaled when airborne.[19] A recent study that placed stainless-steel funnels on rooftops in Paris found synthetic microfiber fallout from the sky.[20] The plasticizers in new plastics, like phthalates added to PVC to make vinyl, flame retardants, or bisphenol A, can leach into what we eat, drink, and breathe, and out of the toys we put in the mouths of children to suckle and chew. The destruction of waste plastic can pose significant risks from inhalation and dermal absorption, especially in developing countries where waste management relies on waste pickers and burn piles. Low-temperature incineration causes some carcinogenic compounds, such as dioxins and furans, to form as by-products during cooling.[21] The long-term effect of open-pit incineration is bioaccumulation of these and other compounds in human blood and tissues,[22] resulting in cancer clusters in communities located in relative proximity to primitive incinerators.[23]

From teething rings to denture creams, the chemistry of plastic is with us from infancy to old age, but not all plastics are alike. There are a few chemicals that stand out, and despite sufficient evidence of harm to humans, regulation is slow to take hold.

Styrofoam, the stuff of insulated coffee cups and cheap coolers, is the trade name created by Dow Chemical to describe foamed polystyrene, made by linking styrene monomers into long-chain molecules. In 2006, the United States made 9.6 million pounds of styrene to make car parts, food containers, carpets, computer components, and thousands of consumer products.[24] It's used to make synthetic rubber (styrene-butadiene) and the resins and epoxies used to make fiberglass boat hulls and construction materials.

The styrene monomer is leached from these materials into whatever is nearby. It's off-gassed into the air you breathe[25] or absorbed onto a greasy slice of pizza[26] served on one of those Styrofoam lunch trays still used in public schools across the United States. If you smell that plasticky aroma inside a new polystyrene coffee cup, that's the unbonded monomer drifting into your lungs. Smokers get the greatest dose of styrene, as it's a byproduct of combustion. Recently, polystyrene on beaches was found to degrade in sunlight, leaving styrene in the sand.[27]

Styrene is a suspected human carcinogen, based on substantial animal testing, and has shown a documented increase in mortality from cancers of the lymphohematopoietic system in workers who handled styrene at chemical plants.[28] Other studies provide evidence that suggests a possible association between styrene exposure and cancers of the esophagus or pancreas. While most styrene is metabolized in the body, genotoxicity (damage to genes) and immunosuppression may be the mechanism that leads to cancer.[29]

In 2006, two years before we built the *Junk*, I got a call from Frederick vom Saal, a developmental biologist from the University of Missouri. Ten years earlier he had stumbled upon the effect of low doses of bisphenol A on the size of prostates in male lab mice. "We'd like to hear more about marine microplastics," he said. We met in Chapel Hill, North Carolina, where he gathered thirty-eight scientists to discuss bisphenol A (BPA) and related negative trends in human health.

BPA is the hard polycarbonate plastic you might have in your kitchen—that old water bottle, kids' toys, or baby milk bottles—and it's still found today in the plastic lining in metal food cans, DVDs, and thermal paper used for cash-register receipts.[30] If you were to wet a cash-register receipt and hold it in your hand for sixty seconds, you might see a white residue left behind. That is BPA. Now wipe it off because it can absorb into your skin. Plastics industries make more than five million tons of BPA each year.[31] Nearly all people on the planet have detectable amounts of BPA in their blood serum, saliva, or urine, thanks to its ubiquity in our consumer culture. Those sippy cups, teething rings, and milk bottles are "BPA lollipops," as vom Saal says. When BPA molecules are linked together, they become a hard plastic, but let them loose and they act like an estrogenic hormone. BPA was originally created in 1936 to be a hormone supplement for women, but it made a better plastic.[32]

The problem is that when polycarbonate plastic is warmed or exposed to alkaline substances, it degrades, and those broken chains of BPA mimic estrogen. A substantial body of literature on rats and mice exposed to BPA show a relationship between the substance and prostate cancer, heart disease, obesity, early sexual development, and damage to reproductive systems. Vom Saal suggests that in human populations, especially considering our constant exposure, BPA exposure may be related to rises in abnormal penile/urethra development in males and early sexual maturation in females, an increase in neurobehavioral problems such as attention deficit hyperactivity disorder (ADHD) and autism, an increase in obesity and Type 2 diabetes, a decrease in sperm count, and an increase in hormonally mediated cancers, such as prostate and breast cancers.

There are epigenetic effects as well, meaning that BPA can alter how genes are expressed. In other words, as vom Saal writes, "the external environment can trigger epigenetic change in parents that can then be passed on to the offspring in a non-random fashion. Environmental contaminants such as EDCs (endocrine disrupting chemicals) can also affect both DNA methylation and epigenetic marks creating long-lasting changes through subsequent generations."[33] While Stephen J. Gould argued that "natural selection has almost become irrelevant to us," it is increasingly evident that our exposure to synthetic compounds is ushering in a new mechanism of genetic change.[34]

Unlike toxins, whereby "the dose makes the poison," endocrine disruptors do their damage at low doses at critical windows of fetal development. Vom Saal administered BPA to mice at doses twenty-five thousand times below the EPA's threshold for toxicity in humans, and the result was enlarged prostate glands in the males. "This stuff should be considered a lot more potent than we thought," vom Saal said. News of his findings got out—and that's when Dow Chemical showed up. "Can we arrive at a mutually beneficial outcome, where you don't publish this paper?" the chemical giant representative asked, according to vom Saal. But the antagonistic move was late in the game. His paper was already accepted and beyond peer review; regardless, he was not about to cave in.

The American Chemistry Council fought back with junk science. Of the hundred scientific articles that followed vom Saal's research on the effects of BPA, 90 percent showed significant harm. Meanwhile, the ACC and the Society of Plastics Industries funded fourteen studies on BPA: two came straight out of the gate to replicate, repudiate, and invalidate vom Saal's work, and all fourteen trade publications reported that BPA showed "no harm." These pseudo-research publications, intended to serve special interests, undermine the overall credibility of science. In an interview vom Saal said, "None of the industry and corporate labs have any standing whatsoever in the scientific community. And their research is pathetic because it's so totally out of date, and uses techniques that nobody would use in an experiment."[35]

One year after our meeting in Chapel Hill, thirty-eight authors who appeared on a consensus statement published in *Reproductive Toxicology* made a strong case for regulation of BPA in all applications in contact with food.[36]

But regulation comes slowly, if at all. The inner workings of regulatory agencies such as the US Food and Drug Administration (FDA) and the EPA were criticized by vom Saal and others for their impotence and vulnerability to industry manipulation. The EPA can't regulate most of the chemicals they're tasked with overseeing, thanks to the Toxic Substance Control Act of 1976,[37] which grandfathered in sixty-two thousand chemicals,[38] including BPA, to a safe haven beyond regulation. But in 1996, the same year of vom Saal's landmark study, the EPA was charged by Congress with the task of reviewing its long list of chemicals for estrogenic effects. The resulting document downplayed effects and contradicted the work of vom Saal and others. An ensuing congressional investigation found in 2007 that the work of drafting the report had been partially subcontracted to Sciences International, an organization heavily staffed by former chemical-industry scientists and lobbyists.

Regardless of these exposed biases, the FDA contended that "based on FDA's ongoing safety review of scientific evidence, the available information continues to support the safety of BPA for the currently approved uses in food containers and packaging." While Canada banned BPA in children's toys, the ACC successfully lobbied to stop similar federal legislation in the United States.[39] Antiquated regulatory systems, self-published junk science, intimidation tactics against competing scientists, and a fiercely noncompliant industry putting pressure on policymakers collectively delayed regulation.

In a seemingly positive move in 2012, the FDA "abandoned" the application of BPA in baby bottles. As the National Resource Defense Council (NRDC) and Environmental Working Group (EWG) point out, it was not a ban of BPA or acknowledgment of harm, but rather an acknowledgment that the plastics industry had voluntarily abandoned the idea of using BPA in the product consumers were alarmed by most. To this day, federal agencies continue to deny that BPA causes harm to humans at low doses, rejecting strong evidence to the contrary.[40] "I don't understand how a chemical group would oppose taking a chemical which, at the very least, may impact the endocrine systems of infants because they want to make money on it," California Senator Dianne Feinstein said to the *New York Times* in response to the ACC's success in defeating a national bill to keep BPA out of products designed to go into children's mouths.[41]

In the case of BPA, the FDA was relying on junk science and not acting as an honest broker, which is its fundamental role through its policy advisors and public servants. The seeds of doubt had sprouted.

BPA degrades relatively quickly: within a week in warm, microbe-rich rivers and lakes, though it takes much longer in the colder sea,[42] unlike the more persistent POPs that drift everywhere. POPs, like DDT, a common insecticide still used around the world, PCBs, and flame retardants, are in all of us from the beginning due to transplacental exposure, breastfeeding, and even inhalation from floating dust.[43] We know this because we found them in Anna's body.

In 2009 Anna and I knew we would be together and have a child, just one. Knowing the toxicants that bind to plastic, we were curious what would bind to our child in utero. We were visiting her older sister Julie, a surgeon in Portland, Oregon, when Anna asked "Could you take my blood?" Despite having conducted hundreds of ER surgeries in her lifetime, Julie hesitated to take Anna's blood. There's something about possible harm to family, even the slightest perception of it, that goes deep. It was the same with our fear that synthetic chemistry might be delivered to our future daughter. Anna's blood was sent to AXYS Analytical Services. The results were surprising.

Anna has spent the majority of her life as a West Coast suburban- ite. She's vegetarian, exercises routinely, and spends a good deal of time outdoors. So it was unexpected to find DDT, PCBs, and high con- centrations of PBDEs in her blood. We all carry this body burden, re- gardless of location or lifestyle. It is a matter of existing on this planet. The surest "detox" for a woman is to give birth and breastfeed. The fats in milk, intended to help infants put on weight, are magnets for these POPs. And plenty comes through the mother's placenta during fetal development. A study of infant development found impaired psy- chomotor skills associated with the presence of PCBs.[44] Flame retar- dants are associated with thyroid hormone disruption. Some PBDE congeners are linked to cancers and neurodevelopmental deficits. In a study of 475 children with the pesticide DDT and its metabolite DDE in their umbilical-cord blood (likely through pesticide spraying that occurred when they were in their mothers' wombs), many were shown to have verbal, memory, quantitative, and perceptual-performance skills effects by the age of four due to that exposure.[45]

When the EWG surveyed the umbilical-cord blood of ten newborn US citizens, it found nearly three hundred industrial chemicals in the group. Sadly, every woman carries a legacy of synthetic chemicals, which is then given unwillingly to children. What is still unknown are the long-term effects of these POPs or the effects of their interaction with other pollutants in our bodies. In addition, we don't know if they have an impact on critical windows of development, as endocrine disruptors do. The children born this century are essentially a longitu- dinal experiment of the chemical innovations of the last century.

"What should we do?" Anna asked. She really wanted one child of her own. We thought for a long while about adoption, and still do, but decided to try for a biological child.

In early 2011, years after the *Junk* expedition, she became preg- nant and had an early miscarriage. She took it much better than I did, reacting pragmatically. I've always been impressed by her stoic nature, and later we talked about the instant parental love we felt.

But this was not the time. "It's my body reacting to something that isn't right," she said.

Our stolen future (Latitude 23°34', Longitude 144°19')

My future with Anna is many miles and weeks from here, and the idea of a family is years away. Still, I think about what world we will bring a child into, with a trail of our trash drifting to the most remote parts of the planet, into the interconnected web of this ocean and into our bodies. I've saved the little rainbow runner stomach with plastic, drying it all out on the dashboard inside the airplane fuselage. I look at it every time I move about the raft. If I ate the fish, what chemicals would stay in me?

One of the six books I have with me is *Our Stolen Future*. Written by Theo Colborn, Dianne Dumanoski, and John Peterson Myers, it is an exposé of the endocrine-disrupting contaminants that interfere with the natural signals that control the development of a fetus. It's eye-opening, and in the context of the work of vom Saal, it's clear that the industries that make BPA and the trade groups that defend the chemical, like the ACC, have used junk science plagued with errors of omission, commission, misrepresentation, and misinterpretation to destroy any attempt to keep developing children from the harm of their product.

With Anna's help, we contact coauthor Diane Dumanoski and talk via satellite phone on August 9.

"You know those rusty cans you guys are eating from? They are lined with BPA," Diane says. "I'm sure it's leaching into what's inside."

"Fortunately, or maybe unfortunately, we're out of canned food," I respond. We have a long general conversation about plastics at sea and on land, and touch on some of the plasticizers in new products.

"Do you think the fish we're eating out here are contaminated?" I ask.

She pauses for a second. "That's tough to answer, with regard to what's out there, but I can tell you that in laboratory studies, animals retain contaminants and pass them on through childbirth. Mothers unload some fraction of their contaminants that way. Or contaminants can pass to other species through predation, which includes you," she says, pointing out that Joel and I are part of the marine food web, too.

Diane continues: "All you've read in the book about endocrine-disrupting chemicals tells us that we have a big problem on our hands. We pored over four thousand research papers and had many scientists review our book to ensure accuracy. The evidence is substantial that civilization is exposed to chemicals that harm us all.

"It's a vast experiment," she adds. "We know very little about the thousands of other chemicals in commerce."

The ACC lobbies heavily in the United States to fight legislation intended to curb children's exposure to BPA and phthalates, an exposure burden that falls heavily on low-income families through poorly regulated chemicals in products in dollar stores.[46] But with moral high ground and constant public pressure over time, advocates campaigning for public health have had success. On August 14, coincidentally just days after my call with Diane Dumanoski, the Consumer Product Safety Improvement Act of 2008 passed, restricting children's toys from containing more than 0.1 percent of six different phthalates. While the law excluded other routes of exposure, such as soaps, shampoos, personal-care products, school supplies, clothing, food packaging, or building materials—and did not require testing of the chemicals used to replace those phthalates—it was still considered a sweeping victory. In 2014, additional phthalates were added to the list.[46] Although we've invented over eighty-three thousand chemicals in the last two centuries, these wins matter, tackling some of the worst offenders in terms of human health.

The weight of evidence today makes a strong case that plastic pollution causes "harm" to our biosphere. A wealth of recent publications shows that hundreds of species get tangled in or eat our trash, but establishing harm on an ecological scale is more complicated, and requires looking at smaller micro- and nanoparticles of plastic and their ecotoxicology. "Ecologically relevant" means using realistic concentrations of plastic found in nature to measure an effect on whole populations. This is different from the many lab studies that overfeed plastic to marine life and wait for an effect. The frontier of science today is to look for those ecologically relevant effects. Sadly, we're finding them.

Waiting for a catastrophe to happen before we act is asking for trouble. In a recent study, ecotoxicologist Chelsea Rochman stated: "Sufficient data exists for decision makers to begin to mitigate problematic plastic debris now to avoid risk of irreversible harm."[48] This is an ethical and political decision, not a purely scientific one. Why is it so difficult, especially for our elected decision makers, to find balance between the health of wildlife and people and the economic success of a few industries? And when, as scientists, do we have to stand by our core values and become advocates for good policy?

What the work of vom Saal, Rochman, and Dumanoski shows is that there is wide agreement that plastics in the environment and the chemistry they carry and release cause harm, and that we can't wait to act. We are obligated to each other and future generations to employ the precautionary principle: scientific certainty is not required prior to taking regulatory action.

CHAPTER 13

LITTLE FISH BITES BIG FISH

There is science, logic, reason; there is thought verified by experience. And then there is California.

Edward Abbey

DAY 71: AUG. 10, 2008, MILE 1,953

Home delivery (Latitude 23°15' Longitude 145°02')

"**W**hat the hell?" Joel yells from atop the airplane fuselage. I rush out from inside. Maybe he sees a boat, or maybe he's hurt. Perhaps I'm scrambling out of the airplane because his yell was the most novel thing I've heard in weeks.

"I was sitting on top of the airplane when a dozen of them just shot out of the water!" Joel yells excitedly. He's got five or six squid, each the size of his index finger, lying in a pool of ink in the palm of his hand.

"One of them hit me right in the chest!" A big ink splat is centered on his T-shirt. An entire squad had leapt out of a wave and pummeled the deck, sail, and fuselage. I had heard a slippery smack from inside, but Joel's yell got me to my feet.

We collect the home-delivered squid from across the deck. It's been slim pickings from the ocean lately. It's not the same fish-filled ocean that Don McFarland described from his 1958 rafting journey on *Lehi IV*. I can reasonably say that if you're lost at sea today you cannot rely on the ocean's bounty to feed you. Joel slips one of the squid into his mouth, and then another. He swallows them whole, the way you shoot a dozen oysters with hot sauce. I suck one into my mouth, not chewing, feeling the ink push through its body, out of my mouth, and down my chin. I can't stomach it, and spit it out.

Joel hasn't laughed like that this whole trip. He devours all but the one I spit out. Earlier today he saw a young mahi mahi sheltered under our pontoons, and now I have bait.

Squid are the buffet appetizer of the sea. In the plastic-filled skeletons of albatross on Midway Atoll you'll find hundreds of squid beaks among the plastic trash in their chests. Every predator swimming in the ocean goes after squid. I bury a hook in the squid's body and toss it overboard. Before I can exhale, the line goes taut. I watch the golden reflection of the mahi mahi dart side to side.

"Fish on!" Joel yells. It's smallish, less than two feet. I grip it with one hand tightly to make sure it doesn't get away this time. It's been a week since our last one. To kill it quickly, I thrust the point of the filet knife above the eye, through the bone, and cut through the top of the head. It stops wriggling almost instantly. I always notice the fading colors.

I filet the flesh off one side and hand it to Joel, who has a pan ready to sear it, serving it with a coconut curry. We eat almost all of it before sunset. The other filet is sliced into a dozen strips strung up to dry in the sun to make jerky. I feel content, knowing I won't be too hungry tomorrow.

DAY 73: AUG. 12, 2008, MILE 2,042

Meeting with Roz (Latitude 23°05′, Longitude 147°12′)

Two days later, Anna asks over the satellite phone, "Do you remember Roz, the ocean rower? She's only two hundred miles from you, and she needs water."

My first response was, "Does she have any food?" Three months earlier I'd had a quick chat with Roz Savage about our respective voyages, ending with "Good luck. See you in Hawaii." She has already crossed the Atlantic and is now on her way to New Guinea and around the world, via a few islands along the way.

One of her followers posted a message on our blog with our respective GPS coordinates. Anna responded, and soon Roz's mom called from London. "Can you please find my daughter? She's out of water," she said.

"Hello Roz, this is *Junk*," I say, after some coordination among Anna, Roz, and her mom. We speak briefly, reflecting our mutual habit of conserving pricey satellite phone minutes. Joel's eyes light up when I hand him the phone. Two months at sea with only each other to look at made the sound of another voice as welcome as finding a case of beer floating by. "We'll catch a fish for you," Joel promises, while I wonder how he will come through. Closing the two-hundred-mile gap will take time. He scribbles down her latitude and longitude and plots a sail plan. "She's making thirty miles per day at a course of two hundred and fifty degrees. We've got to drop our speed."

Both of Roz's watermakers failed, so she's relying on her ballast water for sustenance. We've got our Katydn 35 reverse-osmosis (RO) hand pump giving us an easy gallon per hour if we pump constantly. In our ditch bag there's a smaller handheld RO watermaker, still un-opened. We'll give her that one. We've still got fifteen gallons of water in three sealed buckets. We'll give her one of those and make her an additional five gallons. We talk twice a day, at 6 a.m. and 6 p.m.

"Do you think she looks more like Princess Diana or the Queen?" I ask Joel. Another squall passes, leaving orange sunlight painting the sail. The wind drops off, and she passes us. On August 12 at 6:05 a.m. we are six miles northeast of Roz, and set a course of 255 degrees, hopefully intersecting her course at noon. By 1 p.m. we're still chasing her. Roz writes in her blog, "We are two very slow-moving objects converging on each other ever so slowly, like two garden snails about to mate."

"I can see her!" Joel exclaims from the top of the mast. She's a tiny white dot reflecting on the sea, dropping in and out of visibility between the waves. For another two hours we chase her.

"*Junk Raft*, this is Roz." Her voice echoes from the radio in the fuselage. It's obvious that we'll never see her before sunset at this pace, and if we wait another night we'll likely pass her by.

"I'm not sure I can pull myself to row opposite to Hawaii," Roz reluctantly says, "but I need to." She rowed across the Atlantic Ocean, always moving west. She's spent two months in the Pacific Ocean chasing the setting sun. It's a psychological trick to reward yourself with incremental progress, but now for the first time the sun sets on her stern.

She approaches quickly, her vessel, *Brocade*, leaping over the waves. Joel tosses the sea anchor, bringing us to a halt. Roz loops once around *Junk* and drifts fifty feet away. After a couple of feeble attempts at tossing her a line, I dive overboard and swim out to her with the end of a line. "Hello, you must be Roz," I say, extending my arm over her port side for a handshake. She looks like Guinevere in pigtails, with the forearms of an Olympian and the tanned form of an ocean athlete. I haven't seen another human in two months, let alone a beautiful siren from the sea.

Joel reels her in close. *Brocade* is a carbon-fiber silver missile, tapered on both ends. The middle third is open to the sky, with a blue-cushioned seat in the center between two sets of oars. On each end there's a waterproof hatch. Flexible solar panels wrap around the exposed topside, and little antennas and other bells and whistles poke out here and there. Next to *Junk*, her vessel looks like a Ferrari parked next to a rusty sedan on cinder blocks.

"I've got a few bags of food for you guys," Roz says, as she tosses the first bag over. It's full of Larabars. My eyes widen with joy.

Joel stretches for the second bag, digs in, and exclaims, "Chicken teriyaki!"

I climb onto the edge of *Junk*'s pontoon, keeping one foot on *Brocade*, and grab the third: "Turkey jerky!" We're two kids looking into a bag of Halloween candy. Now we can stop eating fish jerky. Roz tosses over her empty jerry can and two water bags, which we fill before doing anything else. Joel hands her the watermaker.

We invite her over to our bachelor pad. All of a sudden, we're conscious of our socks and underwear tied to a rope dragged under the raft. "Our washing machine," I mumble apologetically.

We give her the grand tour of patched pontoons, broken masts, and worn lashings. We know our time will be short, so we cut through the small talk.

"So what do you do to keep your mind active?" I ask. She knows exactly what I'm talking about. In my experience thus far, there have been moments of ecstatic joy and bottom-of-the-barrel sadness, blooming randomly in a wide open field of boredom.

"I can focus on rowing, or anticipate the next tea break, and then there's audiotapes. But it's different from when I rowed the Atlantic. There were more doubts and more to think and worry about. For example, when my watermaker broke this time, I simply said, 'Oh well.'" Her blue eyes are full of experience and the patience that comes with it. You get to a point where you can choose to worry or not worry about things, because worry simply doesn't change anything outside your head.

Joel is overboard and struggling toward the raft. He had jumped after a mahi mahi.

"*Hana pa'a!*" he yells, as a three-footer thrashes onto the deck. Joel climbs out of the water, his chest puffed out proudly, having honored his word. He turns on the stove. I hand him the first filet, the muscle still twitching. In minutes we're enjoying curried fish, a gift from the sea. "You two really know how to treat a lady!" Roz says, adding: "You promised me a fish, and here we are fine dining." It was a seamless operation, as if we had rehearsed it. I could see Joel was content, as I was, having a chance to simply give. Roz felt the same way.

Joel follows the curry with sushi, then sears a large piece in rancid butter. Roz keeps eating. We quickly take the role of servants to Queen Roz: "Would you like another helping, madam?"

Roz later wrote: "After the first three batches the boys leaned back and asked if I'd had enough. I hadn't, quite. I had another two generous helpings. I'd like to claim it was my body craving protein, but more likely I was just being greedy. It was the first fresh fish I'd had in months, and I was going to make the most of the opportunity."

After dinner, I pull in the trawl to show Roz what we're collecting on the sea surface. I point to the kaleidoscope of confetti swirling in the water sample and explain: "This is the 'island' you've heard about. It doesn't exist, but this reality is much worse." We talk about what our respective voyages mean to us, and the missions we've shared with the outside world, and how it's a great communications tool. We'll later give Roz this sample of microplastic from the trawl, dried and salted.

The sun is beginning to set behind a bank of clouds. The last rays are an unspoken cue that it's time to part ways. We take a few photos together, and Roz autographs our cabin with a marker: "No doubt, you're the coolest guys I've met in the last three months. Thanks for a great dinner. Bon voyage. ROZ." We watch her drift away, and the silhouette of her oars in the air as she begins rowing another seven hundred miles to Hawaii.

Joel and I are smiling ear to ear as we lose sight of her, realizing that we three vagabonds had traded water for food, sharing these basic gifts of life in the middle of the North Pacific ocean.

Later, we would see Roz in Hawaii as she rowed into Waikiki wearing floral leis with an entourage of traditional canoes around her. Then again in Vancouver, Canada, as Anna and I began our speaking tour, cycling two thousand miles down the West Coast. We'll stay friends for many years ahead, meandering into one another's lives as the plastic pollution movement grows.

Our meeting with Roz was emblematic of how organizations find each other and share resources. As the movement grows, more organizations form and create alliances. Organizations seem to sprout daily, sporting every combination of type (Alliance, Foundation, People for . . . , Friends of . . . , Federation, Defenders, Protectors, Institute, Global, National, Union, Society, Conservancy, Trust), descriptor of the ocean (Sea, Coast, Blue, Marine, Current, Gyre, Wave, Shore, Coastal, Ocean), and finally something about plastic (Plastic, Garbage, Trash, Waste, Refuse).

Much later, after Joel and I make it to Hawaii, Anna and I cofound the 5 Gyres Institute, recognizing gaps in ocean research and feeling a need to help build a movement to end the harm plastic causes people and the environment. We begin with three goals:

1. Answer the question "How much plastic is out there?" and publish the results.
2. Create a platform, in the form of expeditions, to engage and empower the public.
3. Work on collaborative, solutions-oriented campaigns.

To do this, we would launch twenty expeditions around the world, sailing over fifty thousand miles from 2010 to 2017 with boats we charter. Our strength would be our agility, as a small organization, to rapidly organize expeditions on vessels of opportunity, for example hopping aboard the *Stad Amsterdam* a few weeks after receiving a random invitation to join their film production, leading to the first survey of plastic pollution in the Indian Ocean Gyre. Our greatest success—far greater than any of our scientific publications—has been building friendships and partnerships with the crews we invite to join us (well over two hundred people to date), each with different roles in the fast-growing plastic pollution movement.

Our allies would include Ron Ritter of Pangaea Exploration, who would lend his ship *Sea Dragon* to half of our voyages. Surfrider, Algalita, Heal the Bay, NY/NJ Baykeepers, Plastic Pollution Coalition, Trash Free Waters, Clean Seas Coalition, Plastic Soup Foundation, Plastic Change, Upstream Policy Institute, Story of Stuff, Global Alliance for Incinerator Alternatives (GAIA), and #breakfreefromplastic are just a few of the hundreds of organizations networking on this issue. An environmental movement may be defined as "a loose network of organizations of varying degrees of formality, as well as individuals and groups with no organizational affiliation, that are engaged in collective action motivated by shared identity or concern about environmental issues"—what Rachel Carson, author of *Silent Spring*, called "citizen brigades."[1]

We may be little fish compared to multibillion-dollar corporations, but little fish can swim together in the same direction. Much like the success of ChicoBag against the largest plastic-bag manufacturers, hundreds of supporting individuals and grassroots organizations demonstrate the power of collaboration. We all exist organizationally independent of each other, but it's the confluence of mission alignment and strategic networking in a unified direction that forms a movement.

In early 2011 I received an e-mail from Dr. Sam Mason that began: "I'd like to explore plastic pollution in the Great Lakes." She's a chemistry professor at SUNY Fredonia in western New York. We had been working for a couple of years on a project to survey the Saint Lawrence Seaway, and Sam was ready to move. One pillar of the 5 Gyres

Institute effort is to loan equipment to anyone willing to do the work. We've got fifty nets to loan out. In this case Sam had a ship lined up, the US Brig *Niagara*, a 198-foot replica of a ship in Commodore Perry's naval fleet, which defeated the British on Lake Erie during the War of 1812. She wanted to tow one of our nets behind it. Sam led the way.

In 2012 and 2013, we launched several expeditions together, collecting floating plastic for the first time in the Great Lakes. Sam and her students did all the work of collecting and sorting, even using scanning electron microscopy on the samples to confirm polymer type. In Lake Erie we came across something perplexing: there were more plastics by count than in any of our ocean samples. Thousands of small, round particles appeared in hues of blue, purple, and red—perfect little spheres around 0.5 mm each. We had a hunch. In Europe, the Plastic Soup Foundation had been organizing an international campaign around microbeads, little plastic balls found in facial creams and toothpastes. Sam and I each took trips to local pharmacies to investigate brands. To our surprise, the microbeads polluting the Great Lakes matched the color, shape, size, and chemical composition of the microbeads in consumer products.

We found a smoking gun. Unlike with our ocean samples, for which we could never assign responsibility to a country or company, we could now hold our hands high, full of microplastics, and leaders around the world would say: "That's a shame. Someone should do something." As mentioned earlier, plastic pollution in the middle of the ocean is the ultimate tragedy of the commons. This was different. Here we could show everyone what was directly causing the problem. In 2013 Sam and I published the Great Lakes work, a collective accomplishment with eight authors and an army of students and supporters eager to see the results.

Here on the shores of Lake Erie, we had the foundation of a campaign geared to solutions.

The fact that people across the United States were scrubbing plastic microbeads into their faces and gums hadn't reached the public, but it was about to. As we would learn from our friends at Ocean

Champions, good national policy has three elements: first, a strong national network supporting local efforts with science, strategy, media, and language; second, a strong collaborator in Washington, DC; and third, traction in California.

In January 2013 we drafted a position statement on microbeads, signed by our California partners: the Clean Seas Coalition, Surfrider Foundation, and Plastic Pollution Coalition. Stiv Wilson, our campaigns director at the time, was managing the campaign, and soon became one of the principal architects of the national effort. He's a great strategic thinker with a knack for bringing people together, and little patience for corporate bullies who dismiss the suffering their actions cause people.

We had a good story, with a "gross factor" that roused public sentiment. Dentists such as Kyle Stanley told us, "I've been finding microbeads wedged in patient's gums for years. They can cause inflammation and delay the healing of bone and tissues after surgeries."[2] We had evidence from sewage-treatment plants that microbeads were escaping in wastewater effluent and that microbeads trapped in sewage sludge were being spread across cropland as fertilizer. We counted a subsample of microbeads from a few brands of facial scrubs, such as Johnson & Johnson's Clean & Clear and Neutrogena's Deep Clean, and determined that the average microbead count was over 350,000 in an average tube. All of it was destined to wash off your face and brush off your teeth and go down the drain and out to rivers and lakes. Wildlife is exposed to potentially billions of microplastic particles daily.

We also had European precedent on our side. Maria Westerbos, founder of the Plastic Soup Foundation in the Netherlands, had successfully launched an international campaign to "Beat the Bead" and convinced Unilever, the largest manufacturer of consumer products in Europe, to commit to removing microbeads in all products by 2015. They were proving that this fight was winnable.

At the same time, Lisa Boyle, a fiery lawyer, activist, and our legal advisor, negotiated with Tulane Law School, her alma mater, to host the 2014 Tulane Summit on Environmental Law and Policy focused on plastic pollution. The *Tulane Environmental Law Journal* published

"The Case for a Ban on Microplastics in Personal Care Products," in collaboration with Greenfire Law, creating a template for what legal language regulating such products might look like.

With this, the 5 Gyres Institute team found a collaborator in the California Senate, Richard Bloom, and worked closely with his team and other organizations across the state to rally support for AB 1699, banning products containing microbeads of any kind from store shelves by 2019. It was a good, conservation-friendly bill with no loopholes. The New York Assembly was discussing a microbead ban as well. The network was growing.

Meanwhile, Procter & Gamble and Johnson & Johnson were making plenty of noise publicly about ridding their products of microbeads. Years earlier, Anna and I brought our concerns to the CEO of P&G and its director of sustainability, Len Sauers, who said, "When you find our product out there in the environment, come back to us." We did. We had a brief conversation with Johnson & Johnson in early 2014, and it responded with a plan for multiyear phase-outs, a common bait-and-switch tactic that appeases the concerned public and buys time. Regardless, the legislative wheels were in motion. What we didn't know was that the company had an alternate plan: in anticipation of a federal policy, the Personal Care Products Council (PCPC), which represents over six hundred companies, got the jump on all of us by promoting an industry-friendly bill in statehouses across the United States, at the behest of Johnson & Johnson.

It did so through a group called the American Legislative Exchange Council (ALEC), a conservative nonprofit organization that drafts and shares model state-level legislation for distribution to its members, which in 2013 included eighty-five members of Congress, fourteen past and present governors, and one quarter of all state legislators, according to the website ALEC Exposed.[3] ALEC membership also includes three hundred corporate, foundation, and other private-sector representatives. ALEC's elected leaders and corporate interests get together to create "model bills" that legislators take home and introduce in their statehouses as their "own" ideas, without disclosing the names of corporations that crafted the bills for them. (ALEC has done this on municipal plastic-bag bans as well, distributing model state legislation that essentially bans bans. In Florida and Wisconsin, it is now against state law for any city to ban plastic bags.)

What made the ALEC microbead bill bad were an extended time-line and a giant loophole for bioplastic alternatives. Polymers like polylactic acid (PLA) do not degrade in aquatic environments, despite confusing ecofriendly labeling. The loophole would allow all such bio-plastic alternatives, most of which likewise don't degrade in the ocean, so the bill wouldn't change a thing for the environment. Suddenly, there were two bills out there, good and bad, and on June 8, 2014, Illinois rushed to pass the first bill banning microbeads. It was the bad bill, which defined plastic microbeads as "any intentionally added non-biodegradable solid plastic particle measured less than 5 millime-ters in size [that] is used to exfoliate or cleanse in a rinse-off product," leaving the door wide open for all bioplastic alternatives.

By the end of 2014 several other states, including Vermont, Wis-consin, Colorado, Rhode Island, Indiana, and New Jersey, had passed or were considering passing one bill or the other. But the California bill—a good bill—had failed in the state senate that August by one vote. Similarly, the good bill in New York passed the assembly, but failed in the senate. The industry was winning, so far, with its bad bill.

Why do those microbeads exist in products in the first place? It's a marketing ploy. Plastic let customers experience the exfoliant in vivid hues of purple, blue, red, and orange, and feel the freshness of clean skin as the beads gently roll across, supposedly removing blemishes along the way. Keep in mind that sand, salt, and every other natural alternative used by companies are far superior exfoliants, which is another reason microbeads are used: you need to buy more product with plastic microbeads to do the same scrubbing job that natural alternatives can do in one go.

Also, with plastic, manufacturers can control the buoyancy of the exfoliant so the particles float in the clear product, which is visible through the clear plastic packaging—another advertising ploy.

In 2015 California got organized. Californians Against Waste, Clean Water Action, Breast Cancer Fund, California League of Conservation

Voters, Surfrider, Campaign for Safe Cosmetics, the Center for Biological Diversity, Defenders of Wildlife, Environment California, Heal the Bay, Los Angeles Waterkeeper, the Natural Resources Defense Council, Ocean Conservancy, Sierra Club, Story of Stuff, and the 5 Gyres Institute were on the offense. The Personal Care Products Council knew it needed to win California, a state that contributes to 7 percent of the global economy and often leads on national policy.

Richard Bloom introduced California AB 888, the new good bill to ban microbeads. It focused only on "rinse-off" cosmetics (a shortcoming, though a necessary compromise), but the coalition held its ground on not allowing bioplastics into the bill. Our new campaign manager, Blake Kopcho, led the 5 Gyres Institute's effort, stating "AB 888 closes the so-called 'bioplastic loophole' that we've seen passed in numerous other states, and it provides the strongest protection against plastic microbead pollution in the country."

Industry wanted polyhydroxyalkanoate (PHA), a type of biodegradable plastic, to be allowed as a replacement, since ASTM standard 7801 had determined it was degradable in aquatic environments, but by sheer luck, that ASTM standard expired in 2014. Industry had failed to renew it, leaving it in a pinch and allowing us to state: "There's no biodegradable plastic alternative."

The PCPC introduced the bad bill anyway, and it spread lies to California legislators about AB 888, saying that the science was faulty or weak, that the first bill in Illinois set precedent, and that we planned to ban all natural alternatives. Another PCPC and J&J strategy was to reach out to small PHA manufacturers in California, such as Mango Materials, to turn them against AB 888 by convincing them it would be bad for business. Initially, Mango Materials CEO Molly Morse rallied against the good bill, but she flipped when campaigners appealed to her conservation ethic by showing her the wide NGO support for it. Morse said, "There is a way to ban microbeads made with highly persistent plastics and to encourage green materials innovation at the same time."

The PCPC kept arguing that AB 888 would "have the perverse effect of stifling innovation," a point that was being reiterated word for word by some legislators, proving that they were being fed by industry in an attempt to rally them against the good bill.[4]

But the PCPC was losing ground. Customers overwhelmingly said, "Stop putting plastic in these products." There was no standard for a biodegradable PHA alternative, and advocates for the good bill had strategically negotiated a "pathway for innovation" that some law-makers demanded, so that industry could invent an alternative if it wanted to. Scientists, including Chelsea Rochman, were putting out policy briefs and articles estimating eight billion microbeads entered the environment daily.[5] The PCPC eventually dropped its opposition to the bill. Strangely, Johnson & Johnson still opposed the bill. "Why would J&J continue to oppose a bill that simply required them to do what they publicly had committed to doing already?" 5 Gyres' Kop-cho often chided, pointing out the true colors of an industry willing to fight this policy to the death.

A month later, on July 17, 2015, the California Senate passed the strongest bill in the nation, in a state that makes up the country's larg-est market for microbeads.

All eyes focused on a national bill, H.R. 1321, "Microbead-Free Waters Act of 2015," introduced by New Jersey representative Frank Pallone Jr. and Michigan representative Fred Upton. It was a stronger bill than California's, with a shorter timeline, banning production by January 1, 2017, and requiring removal from store shelves a year later. On December 7, 2015, the bill passed the House, and on December 28 it passed the Senate. It reached President Obama's desk and was signed into law before the year ended. We went from science to solutions, exactly four years and two months after Sam Mason's e-mail.

But why did a stronger bill win nationally? Why did it move so fast, and why did industry support it? In March 2016, I spoke at Duke University alongside Keith Christman from the ACC. He said, "We made this happen. Do you really think the microbead bill would have sailed through a Republican Congress if it didn't have our support?" After California passed the good bill, the PCPC and ACC saw a lack of uniformity across the country; twenty-two states had passed or were passing microbead bills, with varied timelines. The groups recognized that the usual recycle story wasn't applicable to billions of microbeads in the environment. Concessions had been made for "rinse-off"–only products, keeping microbeads in detergents, cosmetics, and sandblast-ing abrasives.[6] The ASTM standard had expired, our science was solid, and a strong national coalition had found allies on Capitol Hill, with a strong unified message that the bad bill was unsatisfactory. But the truth is, industry wanted to look like winners. California was the tipping point. It didn't get the bill it wanted, so it wanted to own the bill that won.

As our friend Mark Gold, associate vice chancellor for environment and sustainability at UCLA, said of the collective effort of the movement, "You caught the perfect wave."

CHAPTER 14

A PLASTIC SMOG

We don't actually have to shoot songbirds to remove them from the sky. Take away enough of their home or sustenance, and they fall dead on their own.

—Alan Weisman
The World Without Us, 2007

DAY 76: AUG. 15, 2008, MILE 2,170

Big moon (Latitude 22°56', Longitude 148°44')

At 1 a.m. I take the helm. Joel looks like a drowned rat. That squall got me up, largely because of the twenty minutes of strong winds and choppy waves. I step out into rain as we exchange our ritual well-wishes, followed by a joke or two about who will see land first, where Roz might be, and whether I'll keep us on track in the eight hours ahead. In minutes he's sound asleep.

There's no moon. I can see flashes coming from a storm far away, and a brilliant blanket of stars rising in front of me. Painted in long brushstrokes across the sky, the cross section of our galaxy, the Milky Way, unveils itself. Then a glow begins to peek above the horizon as the moon rises. It's directly in front of the raft, and becomes my reference to steer by. By 3 a.m. it's hiding behind the top of the sail. When it appears on the left side, it means I've gone too far north. If it appears on the right side, I'm too far south. I steer with one hand to chase the moon.

But my gut is churning. Two days ago Roz left us with more food than I could have imagined. Impulsively, primitively, I stood over the cache of food while Joel was sleeping and devoured three bags of dried turkey. It's still in my gut.

I followed the turkey jerky with two expedition meals of some kind, not waiting for the full absorption of water to reconstitute the rice and dried meat before devouring it. For dessert, I slowly consumed a few Larabars. The mahi mahi jerky strung up days before now hangs sadly on the rail tied with a shoestring, having dried solid since abandonment. Now, Joel sleeps, the moon rises, and my gut continues churning forcefully. It was a dull ache most of yesterday. I couldn't drink enough water and couldn't pass anything. I really didn't drink much at all. Now it feels as if I've been punched squarely in the belly.

Should I wake up Joel? I'll wait. It's an old sailor's trick to drink salt water to stimulate the bowels. At first, the gag reflex prevents me from keeping it down, but then I get five cups past my lips. Nothing. By the time the sun rises, I've consumed three water bottles full and vomited each time. Then come waves of pain that drop me to my knees.

The sun is glowing to the east behind me and I'm lying naked on the airplane wing. Joel is still sleeping. The wind has died down, so I can lock the rudder in place for about fifteen minutes at a time. I'm sweating bricks. I try a yoga trick someone once showed me years ago, which involves squatting like a sumo wrestler and flicking your wrists rapidly, as if you're violently snapping your fingers. If Joel wakes up now he'll be horrified and perplexed at the sight of this. Nothing is working, as my mind races to the worst possible scenario. *What if it's food poisoning? Could I hemorrhage my gut lining this way? What if it doesn't pass at all and becomes infectious?* Overwhelmed with worry, I suddenly recall something similar that happened years ago. I had eaten three square meals on a heavy workday without drinking water, the result being the same ache. A trip to the VA hospital ended with a barrage of enemas to pass the mass. We don't have any of those here in the middle of the ocean.

Then I think to myself, *I'm sitting on fifteen thousand bottles!* I only need to sit on one. I tear an opening in the portside pontoon and take out a green two-liter bottle with a white cap. I rinse it a few times, then fill it to the top with seawater. Assuming the sumo position again, I resort to screwing the bottle into my backside, with the first thought, *That's really cold*, and the second thought, *I hope Joel stays asleep*. With sufficient intake, I wait, and soon it's a success. Imagine

"The 1812 Overture" with cannonfire across the bow. A moment of euphoria and a quick salt water shower, then back to the helm. "What are you so happy about?" Joel says as he emerges to take over the watch at 9 a.m.

. . . And that story reminds me of my meeting with the American Chemistry Council.

"We're interested in talking about whether/how we could work together where our interests do intersect," came a message from the vice president of the plastics division of the American Chemistry Council, Steve Russell. It's February 15, 2015, right in the middle of our plastic microbead campaign and two months after we published our paper on plastics in the global ocean. If you've seen the movie *Thank You for Smoking*, a political satire about a well-dressed, friendly front man lobbying on Capitol Hill for Big Tobacco, well, Steve's that guy: good-looking young man, pearly whites, pressed suit—but for Big Plastic. And to be honest, I like him.

We got their attention. Like many other organizations that criticize the status quo, we're usually an annoying fly on the wall of big corporations, but this time we stung. The microbead campaign hits the bottom line—because it would reduce demand for plastic in society, and the public is paying attention. Our published research becomes a widely used communications and campaign tool, adding another nail in the coffin of public tolerance for single-use throwaway plastics. The tide is shifting, and industry lobbying groups want to get ahead of their perceived enemies. So they call us in to "have a little chat."

Less than two months earlier, on the day before the December 10, 2014, release of our global paper, I had walked into a conference near Union Station in Washington, DC, just down the street from the ACC's main office next to the Capitol. The big marine-policy organizations (EPA, NOAA, UNDP, and UNEP) were there to discuss where they stood on plastic pollution, but the fast-paced frontier of science on this issue creates a huge gap between the published science and policy. I said, "The scientific community agrees microplastics at sea are hazardous waste. Do you agree, and if not, why not?" Only UNEP and EPA responded; both agreed that not enough is known.

Twelve hours later, we would announce how much was known when we published the first global estimate of all plastics of all sizes in all oceans—the collective work of nine scientists from twenty-four expeditions. It was the culmination of all 5 Gyres Institute expeditions. The publication made media headlines worldwide, and was well worth the long road to get there.

In 2010 nothing was known about plastic in three subtropical gyres south of the equator, or in the eastern North Atlantic or Western Pacific, leading to wild estimates about what was drifting in the world's oceans. Anna and I saw an opportunity, and found ourselves sailing across the North Atlantic Subtropical Gyre aboard the *Sea Dragon*, owned by Ron Ritter and his organization, Pangaea Exploration. This would turn out to be the first of a dozen expeditions around the globe. We were studying in the same waters that Edward Carpenter had surveyed thirty-eight years earlier, but heading east into unknown territory.

Over the next five years, we crossed the equator and sailed through the Indian Ocean Gyre, and the South Pacific and South Atlantic Gyres, island-hopping along the way and witnessing the same burn-and-bury strategy everywhere we looked. In the shadow of the monolithic moai of Easter Island, fragmented bits of plastic are wedged between basalt boulders, just like at Kamilo Beach, Hawaii, or at Ascension Island in the South Atlantic. On March 11, 2011, in the most costly natural disaster in human history, a magnitude 9.0 deep-sea earthquake rocked Japan, followed by a tsunami that killed nearly sixteen thousand people. Fifteen months later we sailed from Tokyo to Hawaii through the subsurface debris field to learn more about plastics persistence and fragmentation, and the transport of invasive species on plastics.

During our voyages, the trickle of science became an avalanche torrent of studies, coming out of universities worldwide. We began to understand how rapidly plastic at sea is shredded and pulverized into microplastics. Plastic in the ocean is always moving, sometimes violently, and turning brittle. It is attacked by curious fish, seabirds, marine mammals, and reptiles; colonized by microbes in the millions per particle; and ingested by zooplankton and other filter-feeders, such as barnacles and jellyfish. What remains is likely driven below the ocean surface, beneath the shallow wind-driven currents that make up the gyres, to be captured by deep ocean currents and carried far and wide around the world. We are now finding microplastics in ice cores, on remote shores, and on the ocean floor. After three weeks sailing north along Greenland's coastline to Iceland, battling a few frigid storms and nursing one crew member with a broken arm after she fell in the cockpit, we were able to transect the subpolar gyre. We found microplastics in nearly all samples, in places where we were expecting nothing. Where there's seawater, there's plastic.

We amassed an enormous data set composed of Charlie Moore and Hank Carson's North Pacific data, Francois Galgani's from the Mediterranean, Peter Ryan's from the South Atlantic and the Bay of Bengal, Martin Thiel's from the South Pacific, and that of Julia Reisser, who circumnavigated Australia. The combined data sets were given to ocean-current modelers Laurent Lebreton and Jose Borrero, who made maps of estimated weights and counts worldwide. We had an estimate, a baseline to hopefully work backward from in the years ahead, along with a global total of 269,000 metric tons of plastic pollution from 5.25 trillion individual pieces.

We made some startling discoveries in the process. We divided our plastics into four size classes: small microplastics (0.33 to 0.99 mm), large microplastics (1 to 4.99 mm), mesoplastics (5 to 200 mm), and macroplastics (greater than 200 mm). Interestingly, 92 percent of the 5.25-trillion particle count comes from microplastic smaller than a grain of rice, whereas 93 percent of the weight comes from meso- and macroplastic. Fifty-eight percent of the total weight comes from fishing buoys. (It could be argued their design wins the prize for ocean persistence—a perfectly round ball made of thick plastic, covered with a biofilm, can last almost forever.) Another 20 percent comes from derelict fishing nets and line.

When we compared the four size categories, we expected a pyramid-shaped distribution of size by count, with macroplastic on top and trillions of small microplastics on the bottom, but something counterintuitive happened. There were a hundred times fewer small microplastics particles than large microplastics. For some reason, the smallest particles of plastic pollution are leaving the surface of the sea, which poses the question "Where is it all going?"

We know from fluid dynamics that really small particles are more affected by their surface tension with water than their material buoyancy, which means that even if the polymer usually floats, a slight current can push particles deep, far below the surface where we collect our samples. Also, with smaller size, the volume-to-surface ratio decreases, so just a few colonizing microbes can make a particle heavy and sink.[1] At the same time these mechanical processes are pushing plastic dust to the depths, biological processes are at work. The top hundred meters of the global ocean surface cycles through the bodies of billions of filter-feeding organisms every few months, and that alone might be the greatest means by which the ocean spits out plastic trash. We now think that the most biologically productive regions of the ocean, where phytoplankton and zooplankton blooms may be seen from space, may serve as a sort of "black hole" that sucks floating plastic particles from the surface and sends them to the depths as fecal pellets. Particles also may be entombed in sinking bodies after they die. This vertical migration of the smallest fragmented bits of plastic trash, coupled with deep-sea currents that move under the gyres and around the globe, have diffused our waste everywhere.

We need a new metaphor to describe plastic in the ocean. The old ideas of "garbage patches" or that mythical "Texas-sized island" are inappropriate. They don't capture the distribution, toxicity, or widespread harm to marine life. Imagine if you could stand on the ocean floor and look up and see only the plastic. You would see five massive clouds of microplastic in the subtropical gyres and dark clouds of larger plastic pieces coming from the world's largest rivers and densely populated coastlines. The Bay of Bengal, the Mediterranean Sea, and the South China Sea would have the darkest clouds on the planet. All around you would be a mist of dust-like microplastic fragments slowly settling on the seafloor. These estimated 5.25 trillion particles constitute a kind of "plastic smog."

In 2015 we sailed the North Atlantic a third time, now aboard the 270-foot tall ship *Mystic*, from Miami to New York via the Bahamas and Bermuda. After collecting thirty-seven sea-surface samples, we dropped our net for one more sample in the Hudson River, in the shadow of the Manhattan skyline. We collected more plastic in that sample than the previous thirty-seven combined. The material we gathered included over four hundred plastic pellets, as well as cigar filters, colored sticks from earbuds, plastic toothpicks, condoms, a bright-pink tampon applicator, and a few candy wrappers. In our plastic smog metaphor, the pipes and streams that drain city streets are horizontal smokestacks that feed the smog of the sea.

It all begins far upstream, and what lives on land is not immune either.

The Kuwaiti desert, differentiated only by a stratum of blue, gray, and beige hues, was as I remembered it from the Persian Gulf War. I returned twenty-five years later, in 2015, with a small team on a very different mission: to preserve rather than destroy, surveying the Gulf of Arabia for microplastics near the shores of Kuwait, Dubai, Oman, and Qatar. There were millions of new pellets covering beaches, indicating unregulated pellet loss from local plastic producers. Plastic bags tumbled across highways.

In Dubai we met Dr. Ulli Werner, a veterinarian and cofounder of the Central Veterinary Research Laboratory. He arrived twenty-eight years ago to help Sheik Mohammed build the best clinic in the world for camels, one of the sheik's passions. Werner now has 160 employees, a huge hospital, fifty camels that live onsite, and a taxidermy clinic. We walked into the necropsy room to watch one of his veterinarians slice open a dead camel. "I want to show you something," he said, "but it's an hour from here."

We drove east of Dubai, away from the madness of a modern city celebrating unprecedented wealth. The new highway took us past the tallest skyscraper on the planet, past new homes and factories, and deep into the dunes where powdery red sand piles in static cresting waves, rippled by the wind. We stood in the shadow of a three-story dune, in what could best be described as a camel graveyard.

"Take your pick," Werner said, pointing to the eight or ten scattered piles of half-buried white bones. We knelt next to one. He handed me a rib.

"Start digging," he said, joining me in excavating the rib cage down to the center vertebral column.

There was some degraded plant material. *Must be its last meal*, I thought, then came the trash. Tattered plastic bags came one after the other. They were all stuck together, calcified into a solid mass. Hundreds of bags creating a huge wad of garbage. It was an oblong mass the size of a garbage can lid, and half as tall.

"I began seeing these inside camels in the hospital fifteen years ago," he explained. "Now they're everywhere."

"Is this what killed these camels?" I asked.

"I don't know, but I do know that some of the sick camels I see are dying from eating trash," he answered. He showed me a photo of a young camel that came into his clinic severely malnourished and died soon after. An autopsy found large sheets of plastic and wadded plastic bags inside it.

"These plastics kill them in three ways," he explained. "They create blockages, or give the camel a false sense of satiation when they're actually starving for nutrients, so they become malnourished and dehydrated. Lastly, they become intoxicated from the chemicals leaching off the plastic, or the gut becomes septic from all of the bacteria living inside the garbage in their gut."

Contamination from plastic pollution is a terrestrial problem as much as it is a marine problem. Humans have altered the earth with roads, mines, buildings, ditches, dams, and dumps to the degree that our era deserves a name—the Anthropocene. Natural history is punctuated by changes in life, due either to rapid evolution or catastrophic extinction, and evidence of change is sometimes marked by well-preserved, widely distributed fossils. What is our fossil equivalent? Some suggest it's black carbon from the Industrial Revolution, which shows up in the seafloor and ice caps, or it's radioactive isotopes from the mid-twentieth-century nuclear tests. Now, with evidence of plastic, transported by wind and waves, blanketing Earth from the seafloor to the tops of mountains, it is arguable that plastic is the best index fossil that represents us. Even if we stop polluting the planet with plastic today, we will have to live with a layer of microplastic that will represent this moment in natural history, when a single species so deeply affected the planet for a short while.

We drove across the desert, airborne plastic bags blowing around us. In each country it was the same scene: plastic trash completely covering fences, stuck in trees, with goats and camels foraging on trash for the soiled food inside.

Kuwait was my last stop. The Kuwaiti Dive Club met us at the Kuwaiti Ministry of Environment to talk about all of the plastic they see on the beaches and under the sea. I described what the beaches looked like years ago, when the Iraqi Army had placed thousands of steel barricades and mines to prevent a beach landing by the US Marines. I was one of the other marines out in the desert waiting to storm the city.

Later, we take the highway toward Basra, the same "highway of death" the remaining Iraqi Army used to retreat on February 23, 1991. The Iraqis were considered a target by the US Air Force, which bombed tanks, along with at least three hundred cars, buses, limos, motorcycles, taxis, and any other vehicle the Iraqis could muster. Some of them had fanned out into the desert; a hundred more were incinerated in rows along the highway.

"Stop the car," I said. I stood in the same place where I had climbed onto a bus full of incinerated passengers. I opened my eyes and there was nothing but road, streetlights, and power lines, just as I remembered. I brought a photo to match the location exactly. I closed my eyes and remembered the marine who found gold bars, surely looted from Kuwait. I remembered the dead man lying in the desert. I had robbed him of his dog tags for a foolish souvenir. I took away the possibility of his family ever knowing what I knew about his fate. I opened my eyes and the desert was empty. I took those dog tags out of my pocket and handed them to Hamida and Arawa, the two Arab women who were responsible for helping me to return.

Arawa read his name. "He was a medic. He had A-positive blood," she said. "I can have them brought back to Iraq. My uncle goes there often." I gave them to her. It was that simple. A few months later she would send me an e-mail explaining that her uncle placed them in the lost and found office in the largest mosque in Najaf.

Cars were streaming by. A flood of emotions followed my memories. So much suffering happened here, and continues in Iraq today, with the longest war in US history still raging on. The people I've met here have been wonderful: the bedouin family who took me into their tent for tea, the filmmaker I met who walked me through his entire experience during the occupation, and the young artist deep in the desert who made flowerpots from melted bottle caps.

Remnants of sorrow became reconciliation and atonement, and a new mission emerged. I returned to the Gulf with a deeper understanding of what's worth fighting for. Fighting for social and environmental justice is how we best preserve ourselves, our communities and others' lives. A warrior is well-trained, defends deep moral convictions, and follows his or her own lead, taking direction from others only when the mission calls for it. A uniform is unnecessary.

The American Chemistry Council building is a stone monolith within a short walk of the US Capitol. Steve Russell met us outside the conference room, where we could see two other people waiting.

"So what are we going to talk about today?" Steve said about how to kick off the meeting. It was cordial, inquisitive, probing.

"Let's talk about design. You guys say you represent plastic producers only and not products, but you defend products, like bags, and spend a lot to do it," I said.

"Well, they produce the plastic products," he responded, then jumped to another topic. "So, when is your next expedition?"

This conversation was starting to have the feeling of a bad first date, when you know in the first five minutes that you haven't got much in common, but you have just seated yourself to have dinner together for the next two hours.

"We've got a big one on the horizon. Want to come along?" I asked. It was a genuine invitation. I would want nothing more than to have anyone from the ACC on a boat in the middle of the ocean for a few weeks. I'm certain—and I mean this—we would arrive at a place of shared core values about how we treat the planet. I've had too many "off the record" conversations about what industry folks really think, which comes after they know that I know that they have a fiduciary responsibility to make money for their shareholders. When you eliminate the legal responsibility to be profitable that goes with the traditional corporate model, an underlying humanness emerges.

"While I might personally agree with you on some points about plastic bags, we really need to focus on"—and here was the party line—"recycling opportunities and not taxing consumers." The conversation seemed guarded; it wasn't the inquisition or the subtle threatening I expected. Perhaps the constant risk of social media leaks had made people cautious. This was nothing like Edward Carpenter's date with the Society of the Plastics Industry in 1972 at Woods Hole. But it was clear what the underlying motivations are.

The ACC wanted to know if we were a threat. Did we have a plan for future campaigns, or research that they could prepare for, fund and influence, or disrupt if it was threatening? Would we take the golden carrot?

When the conversation meandered to extended producer responsibility (EPR), the tone shifted, as though the term were heresy. How dare we come in there and mention those words? With a focused stare, he said clearly: "We would never support an EPR bill." End of story. End of our meeting.

This is the cornerstone of industry strategy since World War II— eliminate the burden of costs for negative externalities. It was throwaway living in the 1950s. It was crying Indian ads in the 1970s that made consumers feel guilty about littering, distracting them from the more meaningful issue of product design. It was crushing bottle bills across the United States in the 1990s and shifting responsibility for bottle waste from industry to taxpayer-funded recycling programs. Today it's World Bank loans to small countries, so they can buy waste-to-energy incinerators to burn it all and keep new plastic production alive.

This is the Great Divide, between the linear and circular economies. This is the battleground. The zero-waste movement is growing. It is organized, and it's winning.

CHAPTER 15

THE GREAT DIVIDE

The Linear vs. the Circular Economy

*The linear, mechanistic view of the world which
pervades orthodox economics is simply not capable of
capturing the richness and complexity of the rhythms
and fluctuations of developed economies.*

—Paul Ormerod
The Death of Economics, 1994

DAY 85: AUG. 25, 2008, MILE 2,540

1:45 p.m. (Latitude 21°19', Longitude 156°42')

"Land!" Joel yells.

He sees the flanks of Mount Haleakala above the clouds on
East Maui, and soon the northern cliffs of Molokai come into view.
We're grinning widely in awe, looking at each other with unspoken
gratitude, as the reality of our success sinks in. If all goes well, we are
going to whip around the north side of the island and shoot the Kaiwi
Channel between Molokai and Oahu straight into Waikiki. There are
at least another four days ahead. We stop fishing and rationing our
food. Neither of us writes in the logbook or does maintenance checks.
We could swim to land if we had to, maybe.

The challenge of living within the boundaries of our raft now
seems lifted. While the mast is cracked, the raft has corroded, and
the sails are tattered, we begin to feel secure upon sighting land. It's
a dramatic psychological shift, a false security perhaps, much like
the false security we all share when we look at a seemingly endless
land and sea. On *Junk* we witnessed entropy unfold in real time, but

society seldom sees ecological change, like the analogy of the frog in a warming pot of water that doesn't notice that it is coming to a boil. Civilization has reached the edges of a closed system—akin to the twenty-by-twenty-four-foot boundary of our raft—where population, resource scarcity, and pollution are pushing the system to its limits. The industries, technologies, and economic structures that drove this excess must reinvent themselves rapidly. In just my lifetime (I was born in 1967) I've watched the number of people on the planet double from four billion to nearly eight billion. No one born today will witness a doubling like that again.

"What are you going to do when you land?" Joel asks.

"Find a salad," I say. "And you?"

"A beer."

"What shall we do with this pile of junk?" Joel asks. He knows we'll keep it, but I play along.

"We could turn in those fifteen thousand bottles and recycle them for all the beer and salad you want," I say.

"Nah, that's not going to happen, the local incinerator will take them first," he says, only half joking.

Hawaii's H-Power waste-to-energy plant was built in 1990 for a few dollars shy of $150 million to reduce Oahu's landfill reliance and generate power. It burns everything but hazardous and radioactive waste, anatomical remains, and the deceased. In 2003 it vaporized 111 tons of fishing nets, enough to power forty-two homes in Oahu for a year.[1] But this comes with a "put or pay" quota; eight hundred thousand tons of municipal solid waste must be delivered each year to Covanta, the corporation that runs the plant. If that waste quota isn't met, the city must pay for the lost revenue the company would have earned selling energy from burning waste.

So there's the rub. This quota ends up undermining zero-waste strategies such as recycling and municipal composting, and it hinders efforts to ban the most polluting products, like bags and Styrofoam plate lunch containers. No one wants to pay the fine for not reaching the quota. The ocean loses.

"There must be a recycling center in town," I say.

"It would likely all get burned," Joel continues, adding: "You've got to feed the beast."

．　　　．　　　．

All of the dialogue on the raft—between me and Joel, and in satellite phone calls and e-mails from my peers and critics, both naturalists and industrialists—has illuminated some unique differences, which one would expect, but in essence our outlooks appear to fall into two divergent economic camps.

Plastic producers have enjoyed a linear economic model for the last half century, whereby plastic products and packaging are manufactured, consumed, collected, and burned or buried, securing demand for new stuff. The preferred circular economic model challenges the status quo, with end-of-life design, recovery, and remanufacture systems that keep synthetic materials like plastic in a closed loop. When that's impossible, an environmentally benign biological material steps in. It decreases demand for new stuff, and that is essentially the Great Divide.

This Great Divide, between the linear and circular economy, plastic and incinerator industries versus everyone else, influences the types of solutions one advocates for on a range of issues:

End-of-Life Design vs. Unregulated Design. When designing for the end-of-life, manufacturers and designers talk with recyclers to make a plan for product repair and reuse, and for eventual material recovery. Such approaches may include using the same materials throughout a product, as in a bottle whose label, bottle, and cap are all composed of the same polymer. End-of-life design is about slowing down waste generation—it's the opposite of planned obsolescence.

Waste Diversion vs. Waste Cleanup. When recyclables and compostables are sorted at the point of generation in your home or office, a cleaner and more valuable waste stream is created. What goes to landfills or incinerators drops sharply, reducing the need for these centralized and expensive waste management systems. Industry favors postconsumer cleanup strategies because they take the heat off product design and regulation and shift the focus to consumer litter campaigns, waste management, and production of energy through waste incineration.

Zero Waste vs. Waste-to-Energy. This is the front line between industry and environmental and social justice advocates. Zero waste embraces community engagement in waste sorting, recycling, and composting, and it holds producers responsible for the products that don't fit the system, while waste-to-energy is the plastic industry's answer to all waste—burn it all—which as an added bonus perpetuates demand for new plastic. Waste-to-energy is the obsolescence plan. But it is expensive and highly polluting, and undermines upstream zero-waste efforts.

Extended Producer Responsibility vs. Taxpayer Funding. Finally, "Who pays?" Industry has successfully deflected onto the public the costs of negative externalities such as waste management and recycling, and environmental and human health impacts. When the producer is responsible for the complete life cycle of its product and its chemistry, designing for recovery and reuse are optimized. But EPR initiatives are fought tooth and nail by industry to avoid establishing a precedent that the rest of the world could follow.

These four examples of the Great Divide reflect how entrenched industry is in defending the status quo. In 2014, Plastics Europe released its annual report outlining the forecast for plastic supply and demand, and the challenges in the years ahead.[2] Plastic production has enjoyed a 4 percent annual growth rate since the 1950s, with slight dips during the OPEC embargo in the 1970s and the 2008 economic crash, exceeding three hundred million tons of new plastic produced in 2013. If this growth rate continues, and the report anticipates it will, there will be nearly 600 million tons of plastic produced annually by 2030, and over a billion tons a year by 2050. This trajectory is betting on a growing middle class in China, Russia, India, and Brazil, as well as rising global population. But even that demand will flatline over time.

The only way to secure demand for new plastic indefinitely is to destroy the supply of old plastic (recycled and recyclable plastic) through incineration, gasification, or pyrolysis, essentially making last year's plastic material noncompetitive. It's planned obsolescence on steroids.

It's been happening for decades. Recycling has always been the stepchild of the plastics industry. Recycling rates have been dismal for

decades. US EPA recycling statistics for 2013 show that PET soda bottles, the most valuable postconsumer polymer and the most recycled
packaging form, had a 31.3 percent recycling rate, with 28.2 percent
for milk jugs; the national average for all plastic combined was 9.2
percent.[3] If your child had these scores for reading, writing, and arith-
metic, you would be dumbfounded. Zero to 9.2 percent in fifty-three
years is an abysmal failure. Industry has succeeded in perpetuating
the myth of recycling, not investing in it but rather investing heavily
in optimizing new production. Industry wants you to feel good about
recycling more than they want you to recycle.

In "Zero Plastics to Landfill by 2020," Plastics Europe advocated
banning all landfills and increasing reliance on waste-to-energy incinerators across EU states.[4] This is the plan being sold globally, but
it will not work. The linear economic model thrived under the false
assumption of unlimited resources and environmental absorption of
waste through diffusion and dilution, but now we feel the stress of
overpopulation, pollution, and resource scarcity, and the people sorting our trash in developing countries are telling the rest of the world
to fix it upstream. Can the plastics industries transform to a circular
economy? Maybe, but what if we don't react quickly and correctly?
What could we lose, and who would suffer the most if we fail?

In 2013 I met Minar, a teenager in Delhi, India, living in the Viveka-
nanda Camp with his grandfather, mother, and siblings, sustaining
his family on income from collecting, sorting, and selling plastic waste
to a middleman who makes rounds of slums collecting recyclables. I
borrowed a rickety bicycle to follow Minar around the city for a day.
I wanted to find out what plastic products and packaging are considered worthless to the last pair of eyes to see them before they head to
the ocean via the Yamuna River. What I got was a brief inside view
of Minar's ambitions and vulnerabilities, and of how the culture of
waste affects people. Minar was born just before the millennium. His
father disappeared after one of the local construction projects ended,
leaving his family to live in a tent in the camp. They've upgraded to
a plywood-walled room and tapped into the grid through what looks
like a spiderweb of hundreds of thin black wires you duck under as

you walk into the camp. Three thousand people live on one square block, with one city-managed restroom facility and a biweekly water delivery via tank truck. The side streets form an obstacle course of human and other wastes.

Local waste is dumped and sorted in a corner of the camp before it is taken to one of the main landfills. As Minar and I mounted our bicycles, a group of children gathered behind us, laughing and soon tearing into new bags of trash. When I looked back, the children were wearing blue and purple gloves on their hands and standing atop a pile of soiled gauze and bandages from a bag of medical waste they found.

Under a boiling sun, Minar stopped to pick up every PET soda bottle he saw, but never plastic bags. He explained: "Bags are dirty, and I don't have time to stop for them or I'll miss the bottle worth ten times as much. Besides, a little sand can double the weight of a bag, and my buyers will think I'm a cheat if I try to sell it to them." We stopped for any pile of trash or open dumpster. A pile of purple chai cups littered the side of the highway, so we stopped to gather cups and straws. "Only when they are all together and I can quickly collect a lot of them is it worth stopping," Minar said. By the time the day ended we'd filled a sack with bottles that stands taller than he does. He dumped the bottles at his mother's feet for label removal and further sorting. Before I left, he showed me with bursting pride his new ID card. In the eyes of Delhi, he's officially a waste manager, a citizen with an important contribution to make. I would consider Minar a sanitation engineer, not a rag picker or waste picker. He showed me a reality I never imagined, and I'm grateful for that. (Years later I would invite Minar to lead local students and educators from an affluent school in Delhi on a walk around campus to see what he will and will not pick up—a lesson about "end-of-life design" and a powerful insight into his life.) When we sat on the curb for a snack, he laughed at my incompetence in keeping up with him on the bike. When we shook hands at the end of the day, I was humbled and found it unfathomable that his essential contribution to society should be overlooked. ID cards are just a start.

Bharati Chaturvedi is director of Chintan, an organization committed to equality and human rights for the 1.5 million people in India who rely on collecting waste as their livelihood. "Without identification cards, waste pickers continue to be invisible, existing without health care, contamination from wastes, and violent abuse from middlemen, police, and each other, with women and children suffering terribly," she said from her office in New Delhi. Chaturvedi recently joined GAIA's efforts to shut down a substandard waste-to-energy plant in Southeast Delhi, where brown ash and throat-searing fumes rained down on local residents.[5]

"In Delhi we now have waste collection at six thousand door-steps," she explained, adding, "We've started e-waste dismantling and composting of kitchen scraps." The life cycle of trash is fraught with many inequities, partially stemming from the caste system that under-values the service of dealing with waste. But to really understand this, Bharati suggests we take a trip to the largest landfill in India, and soon we're driving up the spiraling road that winds its way to the summit of a mountain of trash that's more than a kilometer wide and twelve stories tall. Dogs and cows wander among smoldering burn piles and waste recyclers scavenge for the remnants of plastic film that nobody wants. A slum community at the bottom of this mountain is built on wood platforms and walkways that bridge the trickle of leachate flowing into nearby tributaries heading directly to the Yamuna River, and onward to the Ganges.

Delhi generates an estimated nine thousand tons of trash daily—nearly all of it piled in substandard landfills—and produces an alkaline leachate filled with heavy metals, nitrates, chlorine, iron, and sulfates.[6] Nearby, we visit a dairy, where the landfill cows live, and it's near the school. We walk into a dark room illuminated by a single open window, where a teacher is reading to eight to ten children from the slum as they sit on the floor. Almost all of them are coughing continuously.

"Most of these children are anemic. They suffer respiratory ailments from the constant presence of smoke from burning plastic in the landfill. They have stomach problems and suffer injuries from helping their parents in the landfill to pick trash," Bharati explains. Chintan has a program called No Child in Trash, which covers the costs of keeping kids in school, giving them the resources and materials they need to stay through graduation.[7] Otherwise, their likely destiny is a life of physical and sexual abuse and infection, and a constant threat of injury or death from roaming roadsides for plastic waste. "Chintan is creating a way to end the cycle," she explains.

What I learned from Minar and Bharati was the complex but clear relationship between social and environmental justice when linear economic systems fail. You've got to fight for the environment and for the rights of the most vulnerable simultaneously. To work on one leaves the other to persist unchecked. Imagine two leaks in a dam. Put your finger in one to stop the flow and the pressure builds against the other.

On October 5, 2015, a week before Secretary of State John Kerry gave the opening remarks at the Our Ocean conference in Chile, the Ocean Conservancy (OC) and McKinsey Center for Business Development, with support from the ACC, Coca-Cola, and Dow Chemical, strategically released a document called *Stemming the Tide*.[8] The conference was on global marine conservation policy, and three big topics were its focus: overfishing, ocean acidification and climate change, and plastic marine pollution. Weeks before, the US Embassy invited me, along with Charlie Moore and Jenna Jambeck, an environmental engineer from the University of Georgia, to visit three cities in Chile to deliver lectures before academic, public, and industry groups on the science of plastic pollution in anticipation of the meeting.

The OC document laid out a plan to target Southeast Asia with large-scale waste-to-energy incinerators, among other waste-management strategies, at an investment of $5 billion annually in five countries to achieve a goal of 50 percent reduction of plastic flowing into the sea by 2050.

It based this plan largely on a study by Jambeck that listed twenty countries as the biggest plastic polluters, leaking an estimated 4.8 to 12.7 million tons of plastic into the ocean worldwide, with five Asian countries (China, Vietnam, Thailand, the Philippines, and Indonesia) responsible for 49.5 percent of the waste.[9] Jambeck based her conclusions on data from 192 countries, including information relating to their waste management strategies and per capita waste generation, with a focus on populations living within fifty kilometers of the ocean. Her study did not include the significant contribution of waste pickers in recovering recyclables, and did not discuss the design failures in the unrecyclables they don't pick up. In fairness to Jambeck, whose work made a huge contribution to our understanding of where plastic marine pollution comes from, she used only data common to the 192 countries in her analysis. But because the available data focused on consumer behavior and waste management, her work became an industry favorite, allowing it to resurrect the theme from the crying Indian ads of the 1970s, with the slogan "People cause pollution."

Straight out of John Perkins's *Confessions of an Economic Hitman*, the plastics-industry strategy, funneled through NGOs such as the Ocean Conservancy, is to push developing nations to take on huge loans to subsidize US and European firms that build waste-to-energy incinerators that those countries don't really need. "It's part of an unholy alliance between the plastics industry and the waste incineration industry," said Matt Prindiville of Upstream Policy Institute. They will lock in waste-volume quotas to make power to sell and to assure investor returns, and in the process obliterate zero-waste strategies already working on the ground.

They argue that we need waste-to-energy incinerators to deal with the volume of waste piled up in developing countries, and that they will remove those incinerators as the countries transition to a circular economy. But this argument is seen as a Trojan horse: companies will firmly plant expensive infrastructure that would become the status quo for waste management and would be nearly impossible to uproot. Instead, argue zero-waste advocates, current waste volumes should be contained and remediated while long-term strategies are set in place.

Within days, 218 organizations and individual leaders signed an open letter to challenge the Ocean Conservancy's proposal, laying out the social and environmental injustices that would result if its ideas were put forth.[10] Despite the rhetoric of "clean technology," modern incinerators in Europe and North America consistently fail emissions standards, and in China, 40 percent of incinerators are not even monitored.[11] Health concerns continue to plague communities, as cancer clusters occur in populations near incinerators.[12] The open letter asked, "Was it even considered at all in the making of this report that in the countries mentioned, citizens are working hard to promote solutions that do not rely on incineration, and that they may not want polluting and toxic technologies in their communities in the first place? There are hundreds of solutions being implemented in these countries that rely on community-based approaches of decentralized waste separation and collection, increased resource recovery, composting, recycling and waste reduction, that have opened economic opportunities for millions of waste workers and are being sustained at costs that are a fraction of what it would take to build an incinerator."

Anna represented the 5 Gyres Institute at the Our Ocean conference. "The rapid NGO response to the OC's *Stemming the Tide* was the topic of conversation," she said. Plastic pollution groups were now aligned with the zero-waste and social justice organizations.

Months after the 2015 Our Ocean conference, Anna and I sat in our backyard with Christie Keith and Monica Wilson from GAIA and Frolian Grate, president of Mother Earth Foundation, leaders in the growing movement, to learn about zero waste in the Philippines, a working alternative to the linear system of waste generation, consumption, landfill disposal, and incineration.

At the turn of this century, an estimated 60 percent of Philippine households burned their waste and 43 percent dumped it illegally in rivers, leaving what was collected to be piled high in massive landfills, until an avalanche of landfill trash buried hundreds of waste pickers and their kids. The Republic Act 9003 followed in 2001, outlining a more circular waste-management strategy, including plans for reducing, sorting, recycling, and composting waste. The Philippines was the first country to ban incineration nationwide, and it is now on the road to zero waste by decentralizing waste management and creating local material recovery facilities (MRFs). With zero-waste MRFs now in 275 villages and 15 cities, and an average 92 percent diversion rate of generated waste away from landfills, the Philippines doesn't want incinerators to return. The social impact couldn't be more rewarding: jobs are created as former waste pickers take charge of door-to-door education and sorting and collecting. Fuel costs to transport waste plummet. In the city of San Fernando, the local waste-to-energy plant closed, citing "not enough trash to burn." These zero-waste strategies are globally scalable.

Around the world, GAIA works alongside hundreds of grassroots organizations revolutionizing how waste is managed—and how the people who manage waste are treated.[13] In Pune, India, waste pickers were predominantly women (a third of them abandoned or divorced by their husbands), and they typically worked ten hours a day or more to earn just over a dollar from recyclables collected in the regional dump. Under constant threat of disease and injury from needles in medical waste, they finally unionized in 1993 and won protection from corrupt police and waste handlers who had bribed and raped them. They got identification cards, doubled their wages, and, before the end of the century, received government medical care, transforming themselves from rag pickers to waste managers.

In La Pintana, Chile, a new approach to waste began with kitchen scraps and yard trimmings, which made up 55 percent of municipal waste by volume. Under the previous system, comingled waste of all kinds went directly to one landfill twenty-two kilometers away, and the city was spending almost 80 percent of its environmental budget on waste management. Overnight, with public education and local collection schemes, it diverted more than 20 percent of the waste stream to composting, eventually producing fertilizer for city parks and farms. One thousand liters per day of waste fryer grease is transformed into biodiesel, saving the city an average of $754 per day in 2010; add to this the savings from having fewer trucks on the road to the landfill.

When Taiwan faced a crisis in 2003 over limited landfill space, it embarked on a new waste management strategy, choosing effective recovery, recycling, source reduction, and composting over the previously planned incinerator development.[14] It rid schools of disposable cutlery and reduced use of disposable cups and bags. It created extended producer responsibility (EPR) for electronic waste, implemented fees for waste generation (called "pay as you throw"), and even campaigned for reusable and "upon request" chopsticks in restaurants, removing 350 tons of sticks per year from waste. It reduced its annual waste production by 750,000 tons in the first decade of this century, while national GDP rose nearly 50 percent.[15] This shows that equating per-capita waste generation to GDP is no longer an appropriate correlation.

Collectively, these examples from GAIA show that incineration is largely unnecessary. Alternative zero-waste strategies offer a more strategic, economically viable, long-term approach, given incineration's burden of financial debt, waste quotas, and a waste debt. There are smarter ways than burning plastic to get the energy we need. Reliance on incineration in the short term undermines future efforts to achieve zero-waste, sustainable cities.

It must be noted that not all waste-to-energy technologies are the same, and there could be a limited place for them at the very end of the waste stream. Techniques like gasification and pyrolysis are vastly different than setting a match to trash, which is what incineration does.[16] In 2010 I visited Pyrogenesis, an engineering firm in Montreal that uses plasma gasification, a process in which a plasma arc, like a lightning bolt, zaps trash at five thousand degrees Celsius. The kiln looks like a large garbage can with two carbon rods inside; the arc forms between the rods. The company has put these systems on Carnival Cruise Lines ships to end the expensive practice of dumping waste on islands or bringing stinky trash back to the mainland. Also, the US Air Force and the US Navy have purchased these systems to destroy sensitive materials and waste during overseas operations. When I asked the manager on duty what the gasifier can take, he replied: "Almost anything; all plastics, tires, computers, even dead housecats." Nearly all molecular bonds are broken, leaving mostly carbon monoxide and hydrogen. This elemental mix may recombine to form toxic dioxins and furans if it cools slowly, so the system has a quenching bath that drops the temperature almost instantly to two hundred degrees Celsius. The gaseous mix, called "syngas," can be used secondarily in conventional generators for power. The folks at Pyrogenesis claim: "If you put enough plastics in, basically high Btu organic compounds, your net energy production from syngas can be greater than the original input to the gasifier." What's left over in the bottom of the kiln looks like black glass—literally glass mixed with ash, metals, and other impurities—which can be crushed and legally used as road aggregate.

Pyrolysis is a completely different process in which plastic is melted into a vapor that is condensed and collected as liquid fuel, similar to kerosene. When I toured the grounds at Vadxx Energy in Akron, Ohio, I thought the thermal depolymerization unit looked like a NASA rocket test engine. It is the first of what they hope will be many plastic-to-fuel stations across the United States. "The cleaner the plastic, the better," CEO Jim Garrett explained, adding, "but we can take virtually all plastics that are not being recycled, which would include the bales of plastic waste headed to China or India, where plastic products and packaging, 'unrecyclable' by design, can be converted to fuel here instead."

What all these waste-to-energy schemes have in common is that they are more polluting than zero waste, and very expensive, and each has a financial model that requires substantial investment and steady streams of plastic waste to make them operational and profitable against the fluctuating cost of fossil fuels. When a financial debt is coupled with high waste quotas, who pays? What are the impacts on communities, people's health and livelihood? What other opportunities for upstream strategies are lost now and into the future?

If these technologies have a place in waste management, it's long after zero-waste strategies have pulled recyclables out and all natural organics have been composted. Waste-to-energy systems must not be employed if they undermine current source-reduction efforts, or hamper EPR initiatives. They must be sized according to need and not come packaged with waste quotas. Waste-to-energy must set high worker safety standards and meet environmental and social justice concerns, and it must have both of these evaluated by an objective third party. First, build the infrastructure for organic composting and build the market for recyclables, which would mean setting policies that require postconsumer content in products and end-of-life design for recyclability. These are huge challenges to overcome, but they are cheaper and healthier for everyone.

This must be done long before we begin a conversation about waste-to-energy, and it is no easy task. Many cities are exploring scenarios where they can reasonably reach a 70- to 80-percent diversion rate away from a landfill, and may employ a restricted use of technology to extract energy from the remaining 20 to 30 percent, called "residuals." Some city officials have said, "It makes no sense to bury Btus."

But those residuals can also be stored indefinitely. In most cases, if we employ zero-waste strategies in our cities and get good at alternative energy production, we'll likely find burning waste for energy to be more "cost" than "benefit."

Therefore, if we are to make the transition to a circular economy, we must organize resistance to industry tactics through policy and public pressure, and simultaneously support the corporate models that pave the way.

The 2016 Ellen MacArthur Foundation (EMF) report, *The New Plastics Economy*, proposed to implement an after-use economy for plastic packaging globally.[17] It contrasts with the OC's *Stemming the Tide*, but the foundation limited its engagement with environmental advocacy organizations. I sat on a panel with Andrew Morlet, executive director of EMF, during the PolyTalk 2016 conference in Brussels, hosted by Plastics Europe. "We believe in order to drive a systemic change, at pace, it is important to put the plastics material flows, system loss, [and] pollution issues in a broader economic context," Andrew said. That context includes three things, according to Andrew: improving waste management, promoting end-of-life design in products and packaging, and decoupling plastic from fossil fuels. So I asked, "How will better products compete if we don't use legislative policy to get rid of the polluting products that dominate the market?"

"We see this as absolutely critical, and we're working specifically on aspects of this as part of our plastics-economy agenda, but it's not our core focus or topic that we lead with," he replied, adding: "That's the role organizations like yours can fill." If EMF leads with policy, industry walks away.

While EMF is an ally, its approach is different. *The New Plastics Economy* is about industry making the transition to other business models that can operate along the value chain by managing materials through the consumer to a reverse value chain such as systems of "leasing" products rather than owning them, and selling more product upgrades and offering repairs rather than emphasizing planned obsolescence. It's about making a business case for managing the circular flow of plastic. When EMF reported that at least a quarter of plastic packaging globally cannot be economically recycled, reused, or easily recovered—such as small plastic items, laminated materials, and food-contaminated containers—they suggested that industry must completely reinvent how these goods are delivered to customers. Compostable, single-polymer, nonlaminate packaging with incentivized recovery offers a market-tested alternative.

But the status quo must be challenged head-on. We must make less stuff. In a circular economy, how big can the circle be? Even the most efficient waste-management system on the planet cannot handle one billion tons of new plastic by 2050. Recognizing that industry will always promote more, we must fight for making less.

The plastic marine pollution movement now joins the zero-waste and waste-picker advocacy groups, and they are aligned philosophically with climate change groups and those working on reducing toxics in our products. The movement operates far upstream, away from those who think we can solve the problem with nets in the middle of the ocean. It's what E. O. Wilson calls "consilience," whereby "the goal is to achieve progressive unification of all strands of knowledge in service to the indefinite betterment of the human condition." Creating a dignified existence for all life within the constraints of a closed system is the essence of a true circular economy.

Industry understands the threat of an organized movement and mass mobilization, having watched grassroots activism succeed in communities around the world. In the United States alone, Hawaii, in 2012, became the first state to ban plastic bags, one island at a time. In 2014, San Francisco banned the sale of water bottles on government property. New York City banned Styrofoam food containers in 2016, and later that same year, as noted previously, California upheld a statewide plastic-bag ban, after industry had forced a referendum. Industry is getting smarter. The plastics industry is pushing "ban on bans" legislation crafted by the American Legislative Exchange Council (ALEC). But the grassroots movement is organized and fighting back.

In 2016, the Upstream Policy Institute convened eighteen North American NGOs, including the 5 Gyres Institute, to seek alignment around unified and scalable strategies.[18] The coalition coordinates corporate campaigns targeting the biggest polluters. At the same time, the Plastic Movement Alignment Project (PMAP) organized a meeting in Manila, Philippines, bringing more than fifty organizations from the zero-waste, anti-incineration, and plastic-pollution communities together with social justice organizations to respond strategically to stop aggressive efforts to build incinerators throughout Southeast Asia and to promote zero-waste alternatives. Organizations including GAIA and Story of Stuff have spearheaded movement-building across the globe. The Plastic Pollution Coalition, one of the first to bring groups together, has created online forums to share strategies. Other forums also exist for sharing and engaging citizens, including Marine Debris.info, Trash-Free Waters, Be Waste Wise—each providing a clearinghouse of research, webinars, information, and activism.

On September 15, 2016, the Our Ocean conference convened again. This time, a coalition of hundreds of NGOs strategically released a vision statement under the banner "Break Free from Plastic." Frolian Grate and others shared the stage to discuss zero-waste strategies. The conversation is shifting. The science says "We know enough to act." The dominant industry narrative, which blames the public for pollution, is changing to a new narrative, in which industry must take responsibility for the lion's share of pollution. The movement is here.

We are a civilization in transition, as social, ecological, political, and economic stressors from the constraints of a closed system become impossible to ignore. Counter to the setbacks from fossil-fuel industries influencing policy and the boon to lobbyists of the Trump years, the environmental movement is well established, is growing, and will overcome.

Sure, what we want is a circular economy, one in which toxic materials have no place in the things we touch, eat, and drink, and cause no harm to anyone through their long return to remanufacture. Promoting the circular economy means fighting for democracy and demanding corporate responsibility toward those ends. How we solve the Great Divide in the next ten years will probably determine how we manage waste for the rest of the century.

CHAPTER 16

A REVOLUTION
BY DESIGN

"Comply" is not a vision.

—Ray Anderson
*Business Lessons from
a Radical Industrialist,* 2009

On the table were familiar objects from Kamilo Beach, Hawaii: degraded toys, bottles and caps, glow sticks, small net floats, and pieces of crates with Chinese characters on them, arranged in glass cases like museum artifacts. "Do you know this place?" Sophie asked.

"Yeah, we've been there a few times," I replied, taking a moment to look at the broken toys encrusted with byrozoans from months or years at sea. Sophie Thomas is a circular-economy design engineer and former director of the Great Recovery, based in the United Kingdom. She's brought these plastics here to spark conversations about design.

We were in Brussels at PolyTalk 2016, sponsored by Plastics Europe, the largest trade group of plastic producers in the European Union, akin to the American Chemistry Council in the United States. Surprisingly, the group invited its critics to the table to talk trash.

Earlier that day, when I was on a panel, I had walked center stage and unveiled the forty-five-pound camel gastrolith from Dubai, announcing, "Here's the result of poor design." I heard gasps as I lifted it above my head. "And without good legislative policy to eliminate these design failures, we're not giving smarter alternatives a level playing field to compete," I added.

Sophie was in the audience. Later, I asked, "So, how do you suppose you would solve this issue?"

"Plastic pollution is really the result of an upstream design problem," she replied. While managing the Great Recovery, she took students to London's landfill and to old Cornish tin mines, and hosted "tear-down" events, deconstructing everyday items from washing machines to radios, bras, pens, and oil rigs to see how they're made and how they could be made better. One shoe may include metal, wood, leather, cardboard, PVC, textile, and rubber, all fused with an indestructible glue; a laptop may have more than a hundred chemical components sourced from more than ten countries. "We're not designing for material recovery after its second or third life," she said.

I think back to when I was in the Marines and we learned to disassemble an M16 in sixty seconds, an ability drilled into our heads with daily repetition. How long would it take to disassemble an iPhone?

Sophie explained how her team of design students had salvaged from a landfill a perfectly good sofa that couldn't be legally resold by charity organizations because the fire-safety tag had been ripped off. "That's a design problem," she said. "Just stamp it on the fabric." They deconstructed that sofa in two hours, separating the poly-cotton cover from the foam stuffing, the plastic webbing from the felt padding, the polyester wadding from the cardboard support, the metal clips from the steel springs, and the burlap underlayer from the plywood frame and staples. "The labor alone cost more than the value of materials that could be salvaged," she said, "so unwittingly, it's designed for waste."

I looked down at her Kamilo Beach display. "So, you would design each of these differently?" I said. She'd set up her exhibit in the foyer outside the conference hall. She's smartly dressed, wears her blond hair pulled back, and has blue eyes. I could imagine her scrambling across the beach collecting junk washed ashore, as Anna and I have done, or knee-deep in a landfill with her students, excavating appliances and pointing out design flaws.

"Design for longevity and fixability, leasing over ownership, reuse before recycling, and make things easy to dismantle. That's good design," she replied. "We urgently need all designers to visit end-of-life facilities so they can see for themselves how their design choice is the difference between 'waste' or 'material resource.' You've got to plan for the endgame."

"But don't those ideas fly in the face of planned obsolescence?" I asked.

"The problem now is that you have other kinds of planned obsolescence: technological as new software and upgrades overwhelm old hardware, psychological obsolescence due to fashion ('pink is the new blue'), and conventional design weakness, to perpetuate needing the newest, latest model," she replied.

Planned obsolescence drives cheap-as-possible chemistry and design, deflecting responsibility for material management and waste to the public sector. When waste-to-energy seems to be the collective corporate end-of-life plan, incentives to achieve a circular economy are undermined.

Months after PolyTalk, I asked Rob Boogaard of Interface, Inc., about planned obsolescence. He explained that Interface's carpet squares last fifteen years, after which the company takes them back, but it's the fashion sense of architects that shortens their life considerably (same for clothing, as "transitional fashion" creates mountain of microfiber waste from synthetic textiles). "Our carpet square concept allows customers to replace the worn-out places, rather than tear up the whole room," he said, suggesting that service can replace sales, lengthening the life and deferring the obsolescence of products.

Boogaard went on to explain the importance of understanding the entire process, such as the methods of raw-material extraction, the environmental persistence and health effects of the chemistry used, the carbon footprint of transporting parts for assembly and sale, and the social justice implications along the way, such as providing workers fair wages and health care. To reduce these life-cycle impacts, Interface sources some nylon from recovered fishing nets and has a take-back program for its old carpet squares. One Interface factory in the Netherlands is operating with 100 percent renewable energy, uses virtually zero water in manufacturing processes, and has attained zero waste to landfill.

Sophie noted, "I would pass one piece of legislation that would require all product-design plans to include a second- and third-life use. In the second-life plan, you're asking yourself, 'How can I make it last a long while and set up a system of reuse and recovery to get it back?' In the third life you design for maximum material value, keeping it as high as possible because if you downgrade (like mixed or inseparable materials, or complicated disassembly) you make trash," she said. "It's not about being more sustainable, it's about focusing on what the product does and how can this service be delivered more effectively." Instead of focusing on selling light bulbs, cars, and mattresses, thinking must shift to how better to provide light, transportation, and comfortable sleep. The profit comes from meeting a customer's need over time, instead of putting all of your effort and profit into the sale of stuff that's designed for uselessness over time. In this way, the producer manages the material flow, planning for recovery, whether leasing cars or carpet tiles.

To end the Great Divide between linear and circular economic thinking, we've got to change design upstream and move "beyond the baseline engineering quality and safety specifications to consider the environmental, economic, and social factors," as Paul Anastas and Julie Zimmerman explain in the article "Design Through the 12 Principles of Green Engineering."[1] It's a thoughtful approach that considers the chemistry of materials, the design of products, the processes required to make things, and finally the systems that manage how materials flow back into the production cycle, all in the context of causing no harm to people and the environment—benign by design in its totality.

Andrew Winston, author of *The Big Pivot*, suggests an alternate model of doing business: the benefit corporation, or "B Corp," whereby corporations take on a mission statement of social or environmental justice that is on equal standing with the profit motive.[2] A rapidly changing consumer base that is more connected through communication is forcing corporations to be transparent and accountable, and to behave ethically. The B Corp is the bridge across the divide.

In 2010, Anna and I met Michael Brown, CEO of Packaging 2.0, a man in his late fifties who is an avid sailor and a design and systems thinker with a dazzling wit and more energy than Anna and me combined. His company is the first B Corp in Rhode Island, offering 100 percent postconsumer recycled PET. In 2013 alone he recycled a million pounds of PET into ten million recyclable packages, such as the salad containers you might see at Whole Foods Market. His company put ocean conservation at the top of its charter, supporting organizations like ours. Twice he joined us sailing through the gyres.

"You've got to give something back," Michael said as we sifted through bits of plastic we had just pulled out of the North Atlantic Gyre. "It doesn't add up if you're making a profit at the expense of the environment." His company's goals are to double PET recycling nationwide by designing better products and better labels, and systems to sort it. He's a model CEO.

Then there are companies like Ecovative that have taken on the chemistry of products and packaging. One of the first decisions any designer makes is about chemistry, including what is mined, drilled, and harvested to provide raw materials, and how these materials affect workers. That's the beginning of understanding "true cost." Ecovative began in 2006 harvesting packaging material from mycelium, the building blocks of mushrooms. It quickly locked in contracts with Dell and Crate and Barrel, offering a biological material you can compost in your garden as an alternative to traditional Styrofoam. Ecovative has since invented mycelium-infused wood pulp to create floor and wall tiles (mycelium being "nature's glue"), eliminating the industry-wide practice of using formaldehyde to bind sawdust into boards. They're taking toxics out of the process.

Polyhydroxyalkanoate (PHA) is a promising biodegradable plastic in some applications. Johan van Walsem at Metabolix, the largest US-based company making PHA, explained where the polymer can be useful. "PHA is ideal to be used where you need functional biodegradation—where a part has a job to do in the environment, but it would be either impractical or very costly to recover. We have customers in horticulture, aquaculture, etc., that use PHA in this way in soil and fresh water," he explained. He described how PHA could replace polyethylene as the thin film inside paper coffee cups, or as the agricultural films used on farms to keep weeds out and water in.

Chemistry is just the start. "Get people along the entire value chain weighing in on the full life of the product," Sophie explained. A recycler might say to a product designer, "Can you use screws instead of staples or glue, so I can take it apart? Can you use only one type of plastic throughout the whole product, instead of multimaterials or fused layers of paper, metal, and plastic that are impossible to separate?" Use one type of plastic and the whole thing is more valuable. For example, designing thinner walls in plastic bottles might be a great marketing ploy, but as Richard Thompson, a leading researcher on microplastics says, "Who cares about 'thin-walling' if you don't collect it? It's better to recover one hundred percent of a hundred-gram bottle than fifty percent of a fifty-gram bottle."

All costs of the processes that bring products to market, including everything and everyone impacted to create a product and eventually dismantle it, need to be weighed against the benefit of the product itself. Who cares if you make an energy-efficient LED flashlight if in the process you create a massive carbon footprint and leave a toxic legacy?

In addition to process, we have to look at systems: What happens to the flow of materials after the consumer is done with them? Are there systems in place, like bottle bills, corporate take-back programs, and other zero-waste strategies? Who is at the other end of that plastic bottle?

Chemistry, product, process, and system are the four intervention points where the utility of plastic in society needs to be reinvented.

The drivers of the change we want to see in the world will be the smart minds that design the smarter alternatives, the companies that lead by example, and the organizers who campaign for the legislative policies that eliminate the polluters and level the playing field. Without these, planned obsolescence and the burn-and-bury linear economy will prevail. The ACC works incessantly to thrust responsibility for the negative externalities of waste and toxics onto the consumer, who isn't capable of driving change alone.

It's not that consumers don't care; it's that short-term needs usually prevail. In 2011, Anna and I met with Bob McDonald, CEO of Procter & Gamble, and Len Sauers, vice president for global product stewardship and sustainability, in downtown Cincinnati at the P&G building, a monolithic gray skyscraper appropriately representing the global giant, which sells $80 billion worth of consumer goods each year, much of it in packaging without an end-of-life plan. According to P&G's extensive marketing analysis, Sauers said, "What the green generation and millennials say doesn't gibe with how they spend their money."

Procter & Gamble, like many large twentieth-century corporations, is a poor self-regulator when it comes to environmental and social justice. Though companies such as Interface, Packaging 2.0, and Ecovative are powerful exceptions, from-the-ground-up campaigns are essential to making big shifts stick.

In February 2009, Anna and I were invited to give a talk at Thomas Starr King Middle School in Los Angeles. I remember a twelve-year-old student saying, "We're gonna use reusable trays instead," referring to the three thousand Styrofoam lunch trays the class had collected from the cafeteria. They had washed them, strung them together, and hung them from the tree branches above the playground. It looked like a giant rectangular snake.

"These students noticed how much plastic waste gets generated in the cafeteria," their teacher, Annamarie Ralph, explained. In schools across Los Angeles and the United States, school lunch is often served on Styrofoam plates, with plastic sporks, straws, and napkins packaged in little plastic bags. Even the milk is served in a plastic bag, like a water balloon. Oils from pizza or a leaky burrito absorb unbounded monomers of styrene from new Styrofoam plates, providing a low dose of a suspected human carcinogen. All of it is thrown away, teaching children a hidden curriculum—that waste is acceptable.

For three years those Styrofoam plates hung in the trees, while the school switched to reusable trays and cutlery, saving $12,000 each year in the process. In August of 2012 we returned to Thomas Starr King Middle School with two Los Angeles City Council members and the superintendent of the Los Angeles Unified School District, John Deasy, who said, "From this day forward, LAUSD is off Styrofoam lunch trays." The entire district had opted for compostable trays in light of public pressure.

Four years later, six school districts, including Los Angeles and New York, combined forces to find a single vendor of compostable food trays that could match the price of Styrofoam. Making the case for good business sense made the difference.

As You Sow, led by Conrad MacKerron, engages in corporate dialogue and shareholder advocacy; by becoming a McDonald's shareholder, it voted internally in a successful effort to eliminate Styrofoam hamburger containers. Think Beyond Plastic, founded by Daniella

Russo, is a design competition and business-accelerator program that supports bringing alternatives to plastic to market.

These corporate strategy efforts are working alongside legislative policy campaigns to cast a wider net over the common design flaw inherent in plastic bottles, straws, bags, microbeads, and hundreds of other single-use throwaway products that contaminate the environment with their toxicity and sheer abundance.

Casting a wider net means forming a wider coalition in the plastic pollution movement, operating together with coordination, and using policy to seal the deal.

The movement grows stronger.

We must globalize ideas, not stuff.

EMBRACE

DAY 88: AUG. 27, 2008, MILE 2,600

Midnight. Five miles from Waikiki
(Latitude 21°27', Longitude 157°84')

The glow of Waikiki penetrates the midnight fog. *Junk* is racing through the Molokai Channel at 3.6 knots, a new record for us thanks to the gyre currents squeezing between islands.

"I think I see them," I say. Joel is on the VHF radio talking to his friends on *Ishi*, a sailboat from Ala Wai Harbor, where Joel has his own sailboat sitting by the dock. The red glow of their navigation lights dimly appears.

Two thousand six hundred miles of open ocean crossed in eighty-eight days. From our first week of sinking hopes on a sinking raft, through four hurricanes that swept south of us, to the unbelievable chance meeting with Roz Savage in the middle of nowhere, we return tomorrow, if all goes well, to the world of alarm clocks, calendars, cars, and shoes. I long for family, fresh veggies, and exercise. But will there be days I'll wish to return to the raft, even if only for a minute? Absolutely. So much will happen in the years ahead.

Eight years later, on June 1, 2016, I'll get a letter in the mail from Tomoko in Guam that begins: "Hi Marcus, my son and I found your message in a bottle." It's the one I tossed in the sea off the coast of Mexico when we realized we would be months, not weeks, at sea. The faded note read, "My Dearest Anna, My heart aches for you, here and now, somewhere in the middle of the Pacific Ocean," and ended, "And the night promises another wonderful dream. Till we meet again, my love."

Roz and I will meet again and again at conferences. David de Roth-schild and I will meet after his successful bottle-boat sail to Australia on *Plastiki*, and laugh about the fabricated conflict between us. Joel and I will meet now and then to bring the raft here and there, including to the steps of the state capitol in Sacramento, California, to defend the plastic-bag bans emerging in cities statewide. A year after *Junk Raft*, Anna and I will embark on *Junk* ride, a two-month cycling and lecturing tour down the West Coast. We'll find a good spot overlooking the Pacific in Big Sur and tie the knot wearing a plastic tux and a dress artfully sewn by our friend Dianna Cohen, an artist and cofounder of the Plastic Pollution Coalition. Anna's dad will later pull me aside and say, "That eloping thing doesn't count. I want to walk my daughter down the aisle." And he eventually does.

At the 2011 Netherlands Sustainability Conference in Amsterdam, I'll have the privilege of sharing the stage with Charlie Moore, my friend and mentor, and I will present our latest findings from the first 5 Gyres Institute voyages. From there, Anna and I will travel to France to visit family, and somewhere along the way our daughter Avani's heartbeat will begin. I love this child before I know her. Anna glows. She smiles often and pets her stomach. In her womb this child floats in warmth, protected by the cradle of Anna's body and natural barriers, but some synthetic chemistry gets through. We have an obligation to defend this child, to our death. To care for our child, we must care for the children of our brothers and sisters, and our neighbors. Should our daughter live a full life, by eighty-eight she'll witness the beginning of the twenty-second century, and the longitudinal experiment of synthetic chemistry that Anna discovered after her body-burden test will have played out in Avani's body. What will the result be for her, for her generation?

What will that lifetime witness? Will we have broken through the unprecedented challenges of overpopulation, biodiversity loss, resource scarcity, poverty, and pollution, to collectively embrace the tenets of living in a closed system?

What has our *Junk Raft* adventure meant in the context of these greater issues? Into the wild we went in the early twentieth century with many expedition firsts—climbing mountains, reaching the poles, and circumnavigating oceans. But the wild frontier then is the waste frontier now, as the results of our synthetic century permeate the globe. The *Junk Raft* was about something different. Those early, ambitious expeditions to conquer wild nature have transformed into an urgency to conserve it. The modern adventurer must be part of, and is integral to, communicating the ideals of a larger movement.

Grassroots movements are sharing resources, strategies, and ideas, and they are organizing internationally. So, join in with your time and money, get connected, and fight for a zero-waste life.

We do not want the "fortress societies" some predict could emerge, where isolationism and walled-in countries live amid a greater waste-land of land, sea, and people, all suffering. I don't believe we'll follow this path. The agricultural revolution, followed by the industrial and technological revolutions, will be followed by a revolution of regeneration. Will the industries that make the material that plagues our seas embrace the Age of Regeneration? I offer this open letter.

To: Member companies of the American Chemistry Council

Dear shareholders,

The business model of the past, where those external costs to the environment and the lives of people were either unknown or ignored, must be replaced by a circular economy that does not harm anyone or the ecosystems that sustain our existence. Looking beyond resource scarcity, population density, pollution, and biodiversity loss, the plastics industries can exist without causing harm. Instead, invest in their security.

Why fight the hundreds of community organizations that work to secure a clean environment and common decency and democracy for all? The tobacco industry spent billions of dollars on legal fees, lobbying lawmakers, and public misinformation campaigns, and still lost.

Instead, take that same funding committed to defending the status quo and invest in a business model that builds a circular economy. A true circular economy will have two effects: a legacy of good business, and the betterment of our biosphere.

We must therefore reject the business model that harms other life. To begin, transform your corporate charter to become a B-corporation. Embrace principles of extended producer responsibility and design all plastic with an end-of-life plan.

Your decisions now will affect the remainder of this century, including the unborn generations to come.

Sincerely,
All of us

Anna is aboard *Ishi* now, and heading toward us. She flew in from Los Angeles only an hour ago, all of us underestimating the speedy currents pulling us through the islands. She ran through the Honolulu airport to the curb, where a car was waiting to race her to the dock to join the receiving crew.

"We've got to drop our sails," Joel says, negotiating the approach. Our raft is now aimlessly adrift. Joel is all smiles, knowing he'll have the night of his life with close friends on the North Shore. They approach slowly, coming along our port side. It's a rain of cheers.

I can see Anna on the bow, jumping up and down. By the time I grab hold of the railing I'm at the stern. I climb over and scramble across the deck to the center cockpit, meeting her halfway. My arms find her and wrap around her firmly.

I love her as no other. I think of this rare and perfect moment in the human experience, when two people, driven by moral certainty, may drift away from each other, only to come together again, stronger than imaginable.

ACKNOWLEDGMENTS

There are many people I've shared time at sea with over the last decade to whom I owe a debt of gratitude for guiding my thoughts on this issue. I thank Captain Charles Moore, my friend and mentor, for his patient guidance through my initial work in this field, and Edward Carpenter for paving the way. I'm grateful to Peter Stranger and Michael Brown, who demonstrated that "comply" is not a vision for the future. I'm indebted to Don McFarland for pointing us forward, *imua*, toward Hawaii; to Hamida and Arawa for inviting me to return to Kuwait; and to Steve, Atticus, and Tomoko in Guam for finding and returning my message to Anna, left in a bottle, eight years after I sent it to sea. In 2016 I met Sophie Thomas and have enjoyed with her an invaluable and ongoing design conversation. I must thank Nancy Bryan for her help preparing this book and Will Myers of Beacon Press for taking on this story and for his insightful edits along the way to publication. To the staff of the 5 Gyres Institute, thank you for having my back at all times, proving that together we are stronger; and to my parents, brother, sister, and family, for always supporting my ideas, regardless of where they take me.

I am forever indebted to Joel Paschal for believing in the *Junk* and risking his life for it, and also for the many lessons I've learned from him. He is a true sailor and conservationist. Roz Savage will always have a special place in my heart for our remarkable meeting, which wonderfully continues as our lives seem to frequently intersect.

While many played a role in the success of the *Junk*, I must acknowledge Nicole Chatterson, Jody Lemmon, Randy Olson, David Helvarg, the Skyscrape Foundation, Patagonia, and Surfrider.

When I met Anna in Charlie's kitchen I knew she was the one, if only she would allow me to walk by her side. Thank you for the remarkable journey through life we share.

NOTES

CHAPTER 1: SYNTHETIC SEAS

1. Midway Atoll National Wildlife Refuge and Battle of Midway National Memorial, "Laysan Albatross," US Fish & Wildlife Service, June 2016, https://www.fws.gov/refuge/Midway_Atoll/wildlife_and_habitat/Laysan _Albatross.html.

2. National Academy of Engineering, "Petroleum Technology History Part 1—Background," http://www.greatachievements.org/?id=3677.

3. Curtis C. Ebbesmeyer and Eric Scigliano, *Flotsametrics and the Floating World: How One Man's Obsession with Runaway Sneakers and Rubber Ducks Revolutionized Ocean Science* (New York: Harper Collins, 2009).

4. World Shipping Council, "Survey Results for Containers Lost At Sea— 2014 Update," http://www.worldshipping.org/industry-issues/safety /Containers_Lost_at_Sea_-_2014_Update_Final_for_Dist.pdf.

5. Jeremy Green, "Media Sensationalisation and Science," in *Expository Science: Forms and Functions of Popularisation*, vol. 9, *Sociology of the Sciences*, ed. Terry Shinn and Richard Whitley (Dordrecht: D. Reidel, 1985), 139–61.

6. Edward J. Carpenter and K. L. Smith, "Plastics on the Sargasso Sea Surface," *Science* 175, no. 4027 (1972): 1240–41.

7. David G. Shaw and Steven E. Ignell, "The Quantitative Distribution and Characteristics of Neuston Plastic in the North Pacific Ocean, 1985–88," in *Proceedings of the Second International Conference on Marine Debris, 2–7 April 1989, Honolulu, Hawaii*, ed. R. S. Shomura and M. L. Godfrey (Hawaii: US Department of Commerce, 1990).

8. Mathy Stanislaus, *Advancing Sustainable Materials Management: Facts and Figures 2013; Assessing Trends in Materials Generation, Recycling and Disposal in the United States* (Washington, DC: US EPA, June 2015), https://www.epa.gov/sites/production/files/2015-09/documents /stanislaus.pdf.

9. National Oceanic and Atmospheric Administration, "Marine Debris Research, Prevention, and Reduction Act," http://marinedebris.noaa.gov /sites/default/files/MDAct06.pdf.

CHAPTER 2: JUNK & GYRE

1. United Nations Environment Programme, *Marine Litter: A Global Challenge* (Nairobi: UNEP, 2009), http://www.unep.org/publications/search/pub_details_s.asp?ID=4021.

2. Kathryn J. O'Hara, *A Citizen's Guide to Plastics in the Ocean: More Than a Litter Problem* (Washington, DC: Center for Marine Conservation, 1988).

3. Anthony L. Andrady, "Microplastics in the Marine Environment," *Marine Pollution Bulletin* 62, no. 8 (2011): 1596–1605.

4. Jeannie Faris, "Seas of Debris: A Summary of the Third International Conference on Marine Debris," in *Seas of Debris: A Summary of the Third International Conference on Marine Debris*, ed. Jeannie Faris et al. (Seattle: Alaska Fisheries Science Center, 1994).

5. Christiana M. Boerger, Gwendolyn L. Lattin, Shelly L. Moore, and Charles J. Moore, "Plastic Ingestion by Planktivorous Fishes in the North Pacific Central Gyre," *Marine Pollution Bulletin* 60, no. 12 (2010): 2275–78.

6. Peter Davison and Rebecca G. Asch, "Plastic Ingestion by Mesopelagic Fishes in the North Pacific Subtropical Gyre," *Marine Ecology Progress Series* 432 (2011): 173–80.

7. Amy L. Lusher, Ciaran O'Donnell, Rick Officer, and Ian O'Connor, "Microplastic Interactions with North Atlantic Mesopelagic Fish," *ICES Journal of Marine Science: Journal du Conseil* 73, no. 4 (2016): 1214–25.

8. Murray R. Gregory, "Environmental Implications of Plastic Debris in Marine Settings—Entanglement, Ingestion, Smothering, Hangers-On, Hitch-Hiking and Alien Invasions," *Philosophical Transactions of the Royal Society of London B: Biological Sciences* 364, no. 1526 (2009): 2013–25.

9. Chris Wilcox et al., "Threat of Plastic Pollution to Seabirds Is Global, Pervasive, and Increasing," *Proceedings of the National Academy of Sciences* 112, no. 38 (2015): 11899–904.

10. C. M. Rochman et al., "Anthropogenic Debris in Seafood: Plastic Debris and Fibers from Textiles in Fish and Bivalves Sold," *Scientific Reports* 5 (2015).

11. Mark A. Browne et al., "Ingested Microscopic Plastic Translocates to the Circulatory System of the Mussel, *Mytilus edulis* (L.)," *Environmental Science & Technology* 42, no. 13 (2008): 5026–31.

12. Yukie Mato et al., "Plastic Resin Pellets as a Transport Medium for Toxic Chemicals in the Marine Environment," *Environmental Science & Technology* 35, no. 2 (2001): 318–24.

13. Emma L. Teuten et al., "Transport and Release of Chemicals from Plastics to the Environment and to Wildlife," *Philosophical*

Transactions of the Royal Society B: Biological Sciences 364, no. 1526 (2009): 2027–45.

14. Stephanie L. Wright et al., "Microplastic Ingestion Decreases Energy Reserves in Marine Worms," *Current Biology* 23, no. 23 (2013): R1031–R1033.

15. Kosuke Tanaka et al., "Accumulation of Plastic-Derived Chemicals in Tissues of Seabirds Ingesting Marine Plastics," *Marine Pollution Bulletin* 69, no. 1 (2013): 219–22; Adil Bakir et al., "Enhanced Desorption of Persistent Organic Pollutants from Microplastics Under Simulated Physiological Conditions," *Environmental Pollution* 185 (2014): 16–23.

16. Chelsea M. Rochman et al., "Polybrominated Diphenyl Ethers (PBDEs) in Fish Tissue May Be an Indicator of Plastic Contamination in Marine Habitats," *Science of the Total Environment* 476 (2014): 622–33.

17. Kim G. Harley et al., "PBDE Concentrations in Women's Serum and Fecundability," *Environmental Health Perspectives* 118, no. 5 (2010): 699.

18. Lucio G. Costa and Gennaro Giordano, "Is Decabromodiphenyl Ether (BDE-209) a Developmental Neurotoxicant?," *Neurotoxicology* 32, no. 1 (2011): 9–24.

19. James M. Coe and Donald Rogers, "Impacts of Marine Debris: Entanglement of Marine Life in Marine Debris Including a Comprehensive List of Species with Entanglement and Ingestion Records," in *Marine Debris: Sources, Impacts, and Solutions*, ed. Coe and Rogers (New York: Springer, 1997), 99–139.

20. Susanne Kühn, Elisa L. Bravo Rebolledo, and Jan A. van Franeker, "Deleterious Effects of Litter on Marine Life," in *Marine Anthropogenic Litter*, ed. Melanie Bergmann, Lars Gutow, and Michael Klages (New York: Springer, 2015), 75–116.

21. David K. A. Barnes, "Biodiversity: Invasions by Marine Life on Plastic Debris," *Nature* 416, no. 6883 (2002): 808–9.

22. Dale R. Calder et al., "Hydroids (Cnidaria: Hydrozoa) from Japanese Tsunami Marine Debris Washing Ashore in the Northwestern United States," *Aquatic Invasions* 9, no. 4 (2014): 425–40.

23. Sam Chan et al., *Non-Indigenous Species Transported on the 2011 Japanese Tsunami Debris: Considerations for a Natural Disaster Driven AIS Pathway of Emerging Concern* (Corvallis: Oregon State University, 2013), http://www.icais.org/pdf/2013abstracts/4Thursday/B-10/0950_Chan.pdf, accessed September 30, 2016.

24. Miriam C. Goldstein, Henry S. Carson, and Marcus Eriksen, "Relationship of Diversity and Habitat Area in North Pacific Plastic-Associated Rafting Communities," *Marine Biology* 161, no. 6 (2014): 1441–53.

25. Miriam C. Goldstein and Deborah S. Goodwin, "Gooseneck Barnacles (Lepas spp.) Ingest Microplastic Debris in the North Pacific Subtropical Gyre," *PeerJ* 1, no. 12 (2013): e184.

CHAPTER 3: IMUA

1. *Cola Kayak*, online video, Amphibious Productions, January 1, 2005, https://www.youtube.com/watch?v=nZY9rlEHYi8, accessed October 1, 2016.
2. Togeir Higraff, *Rafting to Easter Island*, 2016, viewed January 1, 2016, http://www.kontiki2.com/.
3. Joseph Smith, *The Book of Mormon* 1 Ne. 18:5, 8, 23 (Carlisle, MA: Applewood Books, 2009).
4. DeVere Baker, *The Raft Lehi IV: 69 Days Adrift on the Pacific Ocean* (Long Beach, CA: Whitehorn Publishing, 1959).
5. Santiago Genovés, *The Acali Experiment: Five Men and Six Women on a Raft Across the Atlantic for 101 Days* (New York: Crown, 1980).
6. Carpenter and Smith, "Plastics on the Sargasso Sea Surface," 1240–41.
7. National Research Council, *Petroleum in the Marine Environment* (Washington, DC: 1975), 6; K. G. Brummage, *What Is Marine Pollution? Symposium on Marine Pollution* (London: Royal Institute of Naval Architects, 1973), 1–9.
8. R. Michael M'gonigle and Mark W. Zacher, *Pollution, Politics, and International Law: Tankers at Sea* (Berkeley: University of California Press, 1981).
9. Andrew J. Peters and Ans Siuda, "A Review of Observations of Floating Tar in the Sargasso Sea," *Oceanography* (2014): 217.
10. George Lakoff, *Don't Think of an Elephant! Know Your Values and Frame the Debate: The Essential Guide for Progressives* (White River Junction, VT: Chelsea Green, 2004).
11. National Oceanic and Atmospheric Administration, *The Honolulu Strategy: A Global Framework for Prevention and Management of Marine Debris* (2011).

CHAPTER 4: JUNK-O-PHILIA

1. "Throwaway Living," *Life*, August 1, 1955, 43–44.
2. Teresa Davis and David Marshall, "Methodological and Design Issues in Research with Children," in *Understanding Children as Consumers*, ed. David Marshall (London: Sage, 2010), 61–78.
3. T. Bettina Cornwell et al., "Children's Knowledge of Packaged and Fast Food Brands and Their BMI: Why the Relationship Matters for Policy Makers," *Appetite* 81 (2014): 277–83.
4. Daniel Hoornweg and Perinaz Bhada-Tata, "What a Waste: A Global Review of Solid Waste Management," Urban Development Series Knowledge Papers 15 (2012): 1–98.
5. Stanislaus, *Advancing Sustainable Materials Management*.
6. DuPont USA, "Innovation Starts Here," http://www.dupont.com/corporate-functions/our-company/dupont-history.html, accessed October 6, 2016.

7. Don Whitehead, *Dow Story: The History of the Dow Chemical Company* (New York: McGraw-Hill, 1968).

8. "Bioplastic Feedstock Alliance," accessed October 06, 2016, http://bioplasticfeedstockalliance.org/who-we-are/.

9. "Bottle Bills in the USA: Michigan," *Bottle Bill Resource Guide*, http://www.bottlebill.org/legislation/usa/michigan.htm, accessed October 6, 2016.

10. Container Recycling Institute, *Container and Packaging Recycling Update*, newsletter, Fall 2000, http://www.container-recycling.org/assets/pdfs/newsletters/CRI-NL-2001Fall.pdf, accessed October 6, 2016.

CHAPTER 5: THROWN AWAY

1. David H. Guston, "Boundary Organizations in Environmental Policy and Science: An Introduction," *Science, Technology, & Human Values* 26, no. 4 (2001): 399–408.

CHAPTER 7: "JUNK IN, JUNK OUT"

Roger Pielke Jr., *The Honest Broker: Making Sense of Science in Policy and Politics* (Cambridge, UK: Cambridge University Press, 2007), 62.

1. "AB 2058: Not a Tax, a Choice. Make the Best Choice and Bring Reusable Bags," Bag Monster, http://www.bagmonster.com/2008/08/ab-2058-not-a-tax-a-choice-make-the-best-choice-and-bring-reusable-bags.html, accessed October 6, 2016.

CHAPTER 8: GUADALUPE LOOP

Thor Heyerdahl, *Kon-Tiki: Across the Pacific by Raft* (Chicago: Rand McNally, 1950), 1.

1. Office of the United States Trade Representative, "The People's Republic of China: US-China Trade Facts," accessed October 6, 2016, https://ustr.gov/countries-regions/china-mongolia-taiwan/peoples-republic-china.

2. Jeff Gearhart, Karla Peña, and HealthyStuff.org, *The Chemical Hazards in Mardi Gras Beads & Holiday Beaded Garland* (Ann Arbor, MI: Ecology Center, December 5, 2013), http://www.ecocenter.org/sites/default/files/beadreport2013_lowres.pdf.

3. John Tierney, "The Reign of Recycling," *New York Times*, October 3, 2015, http://www.nytimes.com/2015/10/04/opinion/sunday/the-reign-of-recycling.html.

4. Jack Buffington, *The Recycling Myth: Disruptive Innovation to Improve the Environment* (Santa Barbara, CA: Praeger, 2015).

5. Henry Fund, *Waste Collection & Disposal Services,* Henry B. Tippie School of Management, February 10, 2016, accessed October 6, 2016, http://tippie.biz.uiowa.edu/henry/reports16/Waste_Management.pdf.

6. Buffington, *The Recycling Myth*, 11.

7. Thomas C. Kinnaman et al., "The Socially Optimal Recycling Rate: Evidence from Japan," *Journal of Environmental Economics and Management* 68, no. 1 (2014): 54–70.

8. Rick Orlov, "Eric Garcetti Signs Waste Franchise Plan to Expand Recycling," *Los Angeles Daily News*, April 15, 2014, http://www.dailynews .com/government-and-politics/20140415/eric-garcetti-signs-waste-franchise -plan-to-expand-recycling.

9. Jillian Jorgensen, "Bill de Blasio Calls for the End of Garbage by 2030," *Observer* (New York), April 22, 2015, http://observer.com/2015/04/bill -de-blasio-calls-for-the-end-of-garbage-by-2030/.

10. Buffington, *The Recycling Myth*, 15.

11. "President Bachelet Enacts the Recycling and Extended Producer Liability Law," press release, Gobierno de Chile, May 26, 2016, http://www .gob.cl/president-bachelet-enacts-the-recycling-and-extended-producer -liability-law/.

12. Closed Loop Fund, http://www.closedloopfund.com/, accessed October 7, 2016; Conrad MacKerron, "You Say 'Recycling Is Garbage?' Trash That Argument," GreenBiz, October 12, 2015, https://www.greenbiz .com/article/you-say-recycling-garbage-trash-argument.

CHAPTER 9: TOO WASTEFUL TO VALUE

1. "Lobbying Database," OpenSecrets.org, accessed October 07, 2016, https://www.opensecrets.org/lobby/.

2. Jim Wook, "Joe Garbarino: For More Than 50 Years, Garbage Collection Has Been His Business. Today, What He Collects Is Considered a Commodity," *Marin*, December 2011, http://www.marinmagazine.com /December-2011/Joe-Garbarino/.

3. Eoin O'Carroll, "Industry Group Fighting Seattle Plastic-Bag Tax," *Christian Science Monitor*, September 15, 2008, http://www.csmonitor .com/Environment/Bright-Green/2008/0915/industry-group-fighting -seattle-plastic-bag-tax.

4. "Seattle Plastic Bag Tax, Referendum 1, 2009—Ballotpedia," *Ballotpedia: The Encyclopedia of American Politics*, https://ballotpedia.org /Seattle_Plastic_Bag_Tax,_Referendum_1,_2009, accessed October 7, 2016.

5. Chris Grygiel, "Big $: Anti-Seattle Bag Tax Bucks Break Fundraising Records," *Seattle PI*, August 9, 2009, http://blog.seattlepi.com/seattlepolitics /2009/08/09/big-anti-seattle-bag-tax-bucks-break-fundraising-records /?source=rss.

6. Stanislaus, *Advancing Sustainable Materials Management*.

7. Richard Shomura and Howard Yoshida, *Proceedings of the Workshop on the Fate and Impact of Marine Debris: 27–29 November 1984* (Honolulu: US Department of Commerce, National Oceanic and Atmospheric Administration, 1985).

8. Qamar Schuyler et al., "Global Analysis of Anthropogenic Debris Ingestion by Sea Turtles," *Conservation Biology* 28, no. 1 (2014): 129–39.

9. Dorothy A. Drago and Andrew L. Dannenberg, "Infant Mechanical Suffocation Deaths in the United States, 1980–1997," *Pediatrics* 103, no. 5 (1999), http://pediatrics.aappublications.org/content/pediatrics /103/5/e59.full.pdf

10. *Smoking and Health Proposal*, Brown & Williamson Records, 1969, Truth Tobacco Industry Documents, https://www.industrydocuments library.ucsf.edu/tobacco/docs/mtfg0138.

11. "Environmental Hazards Control of Pesticides and Other Chemical Poisons," statement before Congress, June 4, 1963, http://rachelcarson council.org/about/about-rachel-carson/rachel-resources/rachel-carsons -statement-before-congress-1963/.

12. Eliza Griswold, "How 'Silent Spring' Ignited the Environmental Movement," *New York Times Magazine*, September 21, 2012, http://www .nytimes.com/2012/09/23/magazine/how-silent-spring-ignited-the -environmental-movement.html?_r=1.

CHAPTER 10: WAVES AND WINDMILLS

1. "Former Cabinet Member's Advice: 'Keep Out of Politics,'" *Fresh Air*, National Public Radio, October 5, 2006, http://www.npr.org/templates /story/story.php?storyId=6202342.

2. Emma Marris, *Rambunctious Garden: Saving Nature in a Post-Wild World* (New York: Bloomsbury, 2013).

CHAPTER 11: WASTING AWAY

William McDonough, *Cradle to Cradle: Remaking the Way We Make Things* (New York: North Point Press, 2002).

1. Ronald Clark, *Einstein: The Life and Times* (New York: World Publishing, 1971). Remark made during Einstein's first visit to Princeton University, April 1921.

2. Jenna R. Jambeck et al., "Plastic Waste Inputs from Land into the Ocean," *Science* 347, no. 6223 (2015): 768–71.

3. Marcus Eriksen et al., "Plastic Pollution in the World's Oceans: More Than 5 Trillion Plastic Pieces Weighing over 250,000 Tons Afloat at Sea," *PLOS ONE* 9, no. 12 (2014): e111913.

4. Andrés Cózar et al., "Plastic Debris in the Open Ocean," *Proceedings of the National Academy of Sciences* 111, no. 28 (2014): 10239–44.

5. Peter Sherman and Erik van Sebille, "Modeling Marine Surface Microplastic Transport to Assess Optimal Removal Locations," *Environmental Research Letters* 11, no. 1 (2016), http://iopscience.iop.org/article /10.1088/1748-9326/11/1/014006/pdf.

6. Kim Martini, "The Ocean Cleanup, Part 2: Technical Review of the Feasibility Study," *Deep Sea News*, July 14, 2014, http://www.deepseanews.com/2014/07/the-ocean-cleanup-part-2-technical-review-of-the-feasibility-study/, accessed October 7, 2016.

7. "Interactive Panel Discussion on Utility and Feasibility of Cleaning Up Ocean Plastics," online video, posted July 22, 2014, https://vimeo.com/101430245, accessed October 1, 2016; Marinedebris.info.

8. "Fishing for Litter," KIMO: Local Authorities International Environmental Organisation, accessed October 7, 2016, http://www.kimointernational.org/fishing-for-litter/.

9. Eriksen et al., "Plastic Pollution in the World's Oceans," e111913.

10. Ibid.

11. Emma Watkins et al., "Marine Litter: Socio-Economic Study," *Scoping Report* (London: Institute for European Environmental Policy, June 2, 2015), https://www.bundesregierung.de/Content/DE/_Anlagen/G7_G20/2015-06-01-marine-litter.pdf?__blob=publicationFile&v=4.

12. J. R. A. Butler et al., "A Value Chain Analysis of Ghost Nets in the Arafura Sea: Identifying Trans-Boundary Stakeholders, Intervention Points, and Livelihood Trade-Offs," *Journal of Environmental Management* 123 (2013): 14–25.

13. Mark Anthony Browne et al., "Accumulation of Microplastic on Shorelines Worldwide: Sources and Sinks," *Environmental Science & Technology* 45, no. 21 (2011): 9175–79; Lisbeth Van Cauwenberghe et al., "Microplastic Pollution in Deep-Sea Sediments," *Environmental Pollution* 182 (2013): 495–99.

CHAPTER 12: SYNTHETIC DRIFT

1. Kühn et al., "Deleterious Effects of Litter on Marine Life."

2. Lusher et al., "Microplastic Interactions with North Atlantic Mesopelagic Fish."

3. Matthew Cole et al., "Microplastic Ingestion by Zooplankton," *Environmental Science & Technology* 47, no. 12 (2013): 6646–55.

4. Marc Long et al., "Interactions Between Microplastics and Phytoplankton Aggregates: Impact on Their Respective Fates," *Marine Chemistry* 175 (2015): 39–46.

5. Jiana Li et al., "Microplastics in Commercial Bivalves from China," *Environmental Pollution* 207 (2015): 190–95.

6. Nate Seltenrich, "New Link in the Food Chain? Marine Plastic Pollution and Seafood Safety," *Environmental Health Perspectives* 123, no. 2 (2015): A34–A41.

7. Paul Farrell and Kathryn Nelson, "Trophic Level Transfer of Microplastic: *Mytilus edulis* (L.) to *Carcinus maenas* (L.)," *Environmental Pollution* 177 (2013): 1–3.

8. Chelsea M. Rochman et al., "Ingested Plastic Transfers Hazardous Chemicals to Fish and Induces Hepatic Stress," *Scientific Reports* 3 (2013).

9. Mark Anthony Browne et al., "Microplastic Moves Pollutants and Additives to Worms, Reducing Functions Linked to Health and Biodiversity," *Current Biology* 23, no. 23 (2013): 2388–92; Wright et al., "Microplastic Ingestion Decreases Energy Reserves in Marine Worms."

10. Rossana Sussarellu et al., "Oyster Reproduction Is Affected by Exposure to Polystyrene Microplastics," *Proceedings of the National Academy of Sciences* 113, no. 9 (2016): 2430–35.

11. Louis J. Guillette Jr. et al., "Reduction in Penis Size and Plasma Testosterone Concentrations in Juvenile Alligators Living in a Contaminated Environment," *General and Comparative Endocrinology* 101, no. 1 (1996): 32–42.

12. Sylvain De Guise et al., "True Hermaphroditism in a St. Lawrence Beluga Whale (*Delphinapterus leucas*)," *Journal of Wildlife Diseases* 30, no. 2 (1994): 287–90.

13. Éric Dewailly et al., "Inuit Exposure to Organochlorines Through the Aquatic Food Chain in Arctic Québec," *Environmental Health Perspectives* 101, no. 7 (1993): 618.

14. Jeanett Louise Tang-Péronard et al., "Endocrine-Disrupting Chemicals and Obesity Development in Humans: A Review," *Obesity Reviews* 12, no. 8 (2011): 622–36.

15. Marijke de Cock et al., "Does Perinatal Exposure to Endocrine Disruptors Induce Autism Spectrum and Attention Deficit Hyperactivity Disorders? Review," *Acta Paediatrica* 101, no. 8 (2012): 811–18.

16. Sascha C. T. Nicklisch et al., "Global Marine Pollutants Inhibit P-glycoprotein: Environmental Levels, Inhibitory Effects, and Cocrystal Structure," *Science Advances* 2, no. 4 (2016): e1600001.

17. International Seafood Sustainability Foundation, *Status of the Stocks Report: Tracking Progress*, accessed October 7, 2016, http://iss-foundation.org/about-tuna/status-of-the-stocks/.

18. Dongqi Yang et al., "Microplastic Pollution in Table Salts from China," *Environmental Science & Technology* 49, no. 22 (2015): 13622–27.

19. John L. Pauly et al., "Inhaled Cellulosic and Plastic Fibers Found in Human Lung Tissue," *Cancer Epidemiology, Biomarkers & Prevention* 7, no. 5 (1998): 419–28.

20. Rachid Dris et al., "Synthetic Fibers in Atmospheric Fallout: A Source of Microplastics in the Environment?," *Marine Pollution Bulletin* 104, no. 1 (2016): 290–93.

21. P. T. Williams, "Dioxins and Furans from the Incineration of Municipal Solid Waste: An Overview," *Journal of the Energy Institute* 78, no. 1 (2013): 38–48.

22. Suh-Woan Hu and Carl M. Shy, "Health Effects of Waste Incineration: A Review of Epidemiologic Studies," *Journal of the Air & Waste Management Association* 51, no. 7 (2001): 1100–09.

23. Jeremy Thompson and Honor Anthony, "The Health Effects of Waste Incinerators," *Journal of Nutritional & Environmental Medicine* 15, nos. 2–3 (2005): 115–56.

24. Committee to Review the Styrene Assessment in the National Toxicology Program 12th Report on Carcinogens, *Review of the Styrene Assessment in the National Toxicology Program on the 12th Report on Carcinogens* (Washington, DC: National Academies Press, 2014).

25. Lawrence Fishbein, "Exposure from Occupational Versus Other Sources," *Scandinavian Journal of Work, Environment & Health* (1992): 5–16.

26. T. D. Lickly et al., "A Model for Estimating the Daily Dietary Intake of a Substance from Food-Contact Articles: Styrene from Polystyrene Food Contact Polymers," *Regulatory Toxicology and Pharmacology* 21, no. 3 (1995): 406–17.

27. Bum Gun Kwon et al., "Regional Distribution of Styrene Analogues Generated from Polystyrene Degradation Along the Coastlines of the North-East Pacific Ocean and Hawaii," *Environmental Pollution* 188 (2014): 45–49.

28. National Toxicology Program, *13th Report on Carcinogens* (Research Triangle Park, NC: US Department of Health and Human Services, Public Health Service, October 2, 2014), https://ntp.niehs.nih.gov/pubhealth /roc/roc13/index.html, accessed October 7, 2016.

29. Anna Biró et al., "Lymphocyte Phenotype Analysis and Chromosome Aberration Frequency of Workers Occupationally Exposed to Styrene, Benzene, Polycyclic Aromatic Hydrocarbons or Mixed Solvents," *Immunology Letters* 81, no. 2 (2002): 133–40.

30. José Antonio Brotons et al., "Xenoestrogens Released from Lacquer Coatings in Food Cans," *Environmental Health Perspectives* 103, no. 6 (1995): 608.

31. "World BPA Production Grew by over 372,000 Tonnes in 2012," Merchant Research & Consulting, https://mcgroup.co.uk/news /20131108/bpa-production-grew-372000-tonnes.html, accessed October 7, 2016.

32. E. Burridge, "Bisphenol A: Product Profile," *European Chemical News* 17 (2003): 14–20.

33. Guergana Mileva et al., "Bisphenol-A: Epigenetic Reprogramming and Effects on Reproduction and Behavior," *International Journal of Environmental Research and Public Health* 11, no. 7 (2014): 7537–61.

34. Stephen J. Gould, "The Spice of Life," *Leader to Leader* 15 (2000): 14–19.

35. Elizabeth Kolbert, "A Warning by Key Researcher on Risks of BPA in Our Lives," *Environment 360*, November 24, 2010, http://e360.yale .edu/feature/a_warning_by_key_researcher_on_risks_of_bpa_in_our _lives/2344/, accessed October 7, 2016.

36. Frederick S. vom Saal et al., "Chapel Hill Bisphenol A Expert Panel Consensus Statement: Integration of Mechanisms, Effects in Animals and Potential to Impact Human Health at Current Levels of Exposure," *Reproductive Toxicology* 24, no. 2 (2007): 131.

37. US Environmental Protection Agency, "Summary of the Toxic Substances Control Act," https://www.epa.gov/laws-regulations/summary -toxic-substances-control-act, accessed October 7, 2016.

38. Clark Mindock and Viveca Novak, "Toxic Substance Control Act," OpenSecrets.org, May 2015, http://www.opensecrets.org/news/issues /chemical/, accessed October 7, 2016.

39. Elana Schor, "Industry Opposition Scuttles Bipartisan Senate Bid for BPA Curbs," *New York Times*, November 17, 2010, http://www .nytimes.com/gwire/2010/11/17/17greenwire-industry-opposition -scuttles-bipartisan-senate-18943.html.

40. Frederick S. vom Saal and Wade V. Welshons, "Evidence That Bisphenol A (BPA) Can Be Accurately Measured Without Contamination in Human Serum and Urine, and That BPA Causes Numerous Hazards from Multiple Routes of Exposure," *Molecular and Cellular Endocrinology* 398, no. 1 (2014): 101–13.

41. Schor, "Industry Opposition Scuttles Bipartisan Senate Bid for BPA Curbs."

42. Jeong-Hun Kang and Fusao Kondo, "Bisphenol A Degradation in Seawater Is Different from That in River Water," *Chemosphere* 60, no. 9 (2005): 1288–92.

43. Lucio G. Costa et al., "Polybrominated Diphenyl Ether (PBDE) Flame Retardants: Environmental Contamination, Human Body Burden and Potential Adverse Health Effects," *Acta Biomedica* 79, no. 3 (2008): 172–83.

44. Beth C. Gladen et al., "Development After Exposure to Polychlorinated Biphenyls and Dichlorodiphenyl Dichloroethene Transplacentally and Through Human Milk," *Journal of Pediatrics* 113, no. 6 (1988): 991–95.

45. Nuria Ribas-Fito et al., "In Utero Exposure to Background Concentrations of DDT and Cognitive Functioning Among Preschoolers," *American Journal of Epidemiology* 164, no. 10 (2006): 955–62.

46. Coming Clean Inc., "Campaign for Healthier Solutions," http://www .comingcleaninc.org/projects/chs, accessed October 7, 2016.

47. Chris Gennings et al., *Chronic Hazard Advisory Panel on Phthalates and Phthalate Alternatives* (Bethesda, MD: US Consumer Product Safety Commission, July 2014), https://www.cpsc.gov/PageFiles/169876/CHAP -REPORT-FINAL.pdf, accessed October 7, 2016.

48. Chelsea M. Rochman et al., "The Ecological Impacts of Marine Debris: Unraveling the Demonstrated Evidence from What Is Perceived," *Ecology* 97, no. 2 (2016): 302–12.

CHAPTER 13: LITTLE FISH BITES BIG FISH

1. Christopher Rootes, "Environmental Movements," in *The Blackwell Companion to Social Movements*, ed. David A. Snow, Sarah Anne Soule, and Hanspeter Kriesi (Malden, MA: Blackwell, 2004), 67–93.
2. Kyle Stanley and Matt Nejad, "Microbeads in Toothpaste & Face Wash," *Beverly Hills Dentist* (blog), July 15, 2014, http://www.beverly hillsladentist.com/blog/microbeads-toothpaste-face-wash/&source =gmail&ust=1465031888677000&usg=AFQjCNENZfO-X8KLyuSy Mzp9S5Pve-OFRQ, accessed October 7, 2016.
3. Center for Media and Democracy, *ALEC Exposed*, http://www.alec exposed.org/wiki/ALEC_Exposed, accessed October 7, 2016.
4. Richard Bloom, "AB 888 (Bloom)—Microbeads OPPOSE Concurrence, Assembly Floor—File Item # 15," http://blob.capitoltrack.com/15blobs /d7132b11-0537-449e-af99-455f1e2b9b39, accessed Nov. 30, 2016.
5. Chelsea M. Rochman et al., "Scientific Evidence Supports a Ban on Microbeads," *Environmental Science & Technology* 49, no. 18 (2015): 10759–61.
6. Alexander Kaufman, "Obama's Ban on Plastic Microbeads Failed in One Huge Way," *Huffington Post*, May 23, 2016, http://www.huffingtonpost .com/entry/obama-microbead-ban-fail_us_57432a7fe4b0613b512ad76b.

CHAPTER 14: A PLASTIC SMOG

Alan Weisman, *The World Without Us* (New York: Picador, 2007), 83.
1. Delphine Lobelle and Michael Cunliffe, "Early Microbial Biofilm Formation on Marine Plastic Debris," *Marine Pollution Bulletin* 62, no. 1 (2011): 197–200.

CHAPTER 15: THE GREAT DIVIDE

Paul Ormerod, *The Death of Economics* (New York: John Wiley & Sons, 1994).
1. Molly A. Timmers, Christina A. Kistner, and Mary J. Donohue, *Marine Debris of the Northwestern Hawaiian Islands: Ghost Net Identification* (Honolulu: US Department of Commerce, National Oceanic and Atmospheric Administration, National Sea Grant College Program, 2005).
2. Plastics Europe, *Plastics—the Facts 2014/2015: An Analysis of European Plastics Production, Demand and Waste Data* (Brussels: Plastics Europe, February 27, 2015), accessed October 7, 2016, http://www .plasticseurope.org/documents/document/20150227150049-final_plastics _the_facts_2014_2015_260215.pdf.

3. Stanislaus, *Advancing Sustainable Materials Management.*
4. Martin Engelmann/Plastics Europe, "Zero Plastics to Landfill by 2020," September 2013, accessed October 7, 2016, http://www.plasticseurope .org/documents/document/20131017112406–03_zero_plastics_to _landfill_by_2020_sept_2013.pdf.
5. Baishali Adak, "South-East Delhi Residents Demand Toxic Waste Plant Be Shut Down," *India Today,* May 1, 2016, http://indiatoday.intoday.in /story/south-east-delhi-residents-demand-waste-plant-to-be-shut/1 /656184.html, accessed October 7, 2016.
6. M. Zafar and B. J. Alappat, "Landfill Surface Runoff and Its Effect on Water Quality on River Yamuna," *Journal of Environmental Science and Health, Part A* 39, no. 2 (2004): 375–84.
7. Chintan: Environmental Research and Action Group, "No Child in Trash," http://chintan-india.org/initiatives_no_child_in_trash.htm, accessed October 8, 2016.
8. Ocean Conservancy, *Stemming the Tide: Land-Based Strategies for a Plastic-Free Ocean* (2015), http://www.oceanconservancy.org/our-work /marine-debris/mckinsey-report-files/full-report-stemming-the.pdf.
9. Jenna R. Jambeck et al., "Plastic Waste Inputs from Land into the Ocean," *Science* 347, no. 6223 (2015): 768–71.
10. "Open Letter to Ocean Conservancy Regarding the Report 'Stemming the Tide,'" October 2, 2015, http://www.no-burn.org/downloads/Open _Letter_Stemming_the_Tide_Report_2_Oct_15.pdf, accessed October 7, 2016.
11. Zhao Yusha and Liu Xin, "Incinerators Flout Standards," *Global Times,* July 7, 2016, http://www.globaltimes.cn/content/992772.shtml?from =groupmessage&isappinstalled=0, accessed October 7, 2016.
12. Pascal Fabre et al., *Study of the Incidence of Cancers Close to Municipal Solid Waste Incinerators* (Saint-Maurice: French Institute for Public Health Surveillance, July 2009), http://opac.invs.sante.fr/doc_num .php?explnum_id=676, accessed October 7, 2016.
13. Cecilia Allen et al., *On the Road to Zero Waste: Successes and Lessons from Around the World* (Berkeley, CA: Global Alliance for Incinerator Alternatives, 2012), http://www.no-burn.org/on-the-road-to-zero-waste -successes-and-lessons-from-around-the-world, accessed October 8, 2016.
14. Cecilia Allen, *Community Action Leads Government Toward Zero Waste* (Berkeley, CA: Global Alliance for Incinerator Alternatives, June 2012), http://www.no-burn.org/downloads/ZW Taiwan.pdf, accessed October 7, 2016.
15. Allen et al., *On the Road to Zero Waste.*
16. Ruby Ray and R. B. Thorpe, "A Comparison of Gasification with Pyrolysis for the Recycling of Plastic Containing Wastes," *International Journal of Chemical Reactor Engineering* 5, no. 1 (2007).

17. World Economic Forum/Ellen MacArthur Foundation/McKinsey & Company, *The New Plastics Economy: Rethinking the Future of Plastics* (Cowes, UK: Ellen MacArthur Foundation, January 19, 2016), https:// www.ellenmacarthurfoundation.org/publications/the-new-plastics -economy-rethinking-the-future-of-plastics, accessed October 7, 2016.

18. "Plastic Pollution Policy Project (P4)," *Upstream*, http://upstreampolicy .org/projects/plastic-pollution-policy-project-p4/, accessed October 8, 2016.

CHAPTER 16: A REVOLUTION BY DESIGN

Ray Anderson, *Business Lessons from a Radical Industrialist* (New York: St. Martin's Press, 2009).

1. Paul Anastas and Julie Zimmerman, "Design Through the 12 Principles of Green Engineering," *Environmental Science and Technology* 37, no. 5 (April 2003): 94A–101A.

2. Andrew S. Winston, *The Big Pivot: Radically Practical Strategies for a Hotter, Scarcer, and More Open World* (Boston: Harvard Business Review Press, 2014).

INDEX

Acali (raft), 33–34, 35
Adrift (Callahan), 86
Advance Polybag, 97–100
Age Unlimited (raft), 32
Agin, Dan, 76
Algalita Marine Research and Education (AMRE), 3, 8, 57–58, 70, 149
Alguita (ORV): scientific voyages of, x, 5, 8, 15, 23–24, 46; towing *Junk*, 55–56, 61; in Transpacific Yacht Race, 3. *See also* Moore, Charles
Alvarenga, Salvador, 32
American Beverage Association, 53
American Chemistry Council (ACC): about, 11, 95, 166, 185; on California Assembly Bill 2058, 75–76; lobbying by, 12, 13, 38, 95, 97, 141, 166–67; on microbead legislation, 155–56; open letter to, 195–96; response to plastic studies, 8, 11, 17, 57–59, 60, 75–76, 136–37. *See also* Plastics Europe
American Legislative Exchange Council (ALEC), 152, 183
American Plastics Council. *See* American Chemistry Council (ACC)
Anastas, Paul, 188
Anheuser-Busch company, 52
Aquarium of the Pacific, 40, 55

Arntz, Ray, 70
ASTM standards, 154, 155
As You Sow, 89–90, 191
Atlantis II (ORV), 8
Auman, Heidi, 2
AXYS Analytical Services, 139

Bachelet, Michelle, 89
bad science vs. junk science, 76–78, 140
Backcland, Leo, 49
bag bans. *See* plastic-bag ordinances
Bakelite, 49–50
Baker, DeVere, 32, 43, 82, 86
Baker, James, III, 110–11
barnacles, 19, 23–24, 112, 125, 130, 161
Bay of Bengal, 123, 161, 162
B-corporation model, 188, 195
Be Water Wise, 184
The Big Pivot (Winston), 188
biodegradation, 48, 51–52, 153, 155, 189. *See also* recycling
biodiesel, 179
biophilia, 110, 113–15
bioplastic, 51–52, 153
Bioplastic Feedstock Alliance, 51
birds. *See* seabirds
bisphenol A (BPA), 68, 75–76, 134, 135–38, 140
Bloom, Richard, 152, 154
Blue Mind (Nichols), 20
Boerger, Christiana, 130

Bombard, Alain, 32
Boogaard, Rob, 187
Borrero, Jose, 161
bottle redemption programs, 53, 89, 174
Bottle Rocket (plastic-bottle boat), 2–3, 30
Boyle, Lisa, 151
Braskem, 51
"Break Free from Plastic" campaign, 149, 184
Breast Cancer Fund, 153
Brocade (rowing vessel), 146. *See also* Savage, Roz
Brown, Jerry, 105
Brown, Michael, 188–89
brown algae, 22
Buck, Phil, 35
Buffington, Jack, 87, 88–89
buoys. *See* fishing industry waste
Burbank Recycling, 39–40
Bureo Skateboards, 126

California: bottle redemption program in, 89; import regulations in, 85; legislative bills of, 58, 75–76, 96, 105, 152–56; plastic-bag ordinances in, 8, 42, 75–76, 96–98, 101, 105; public education on waste, 12, 57, 150–51; recycling initiatives in, 11, 57, 88, 191; waste management in, 39–40, 46
California League of Conservation Voters, 153–54
Californians Against Waste, 153
Callahan Stephen, 86
camels, 163–64, 185
Campaign for Safe Cosmetics, 154
Canada, 138, 180
cancer, 101–2, 134, 135, 136, 139, 177. *See also* public health issues
Capellano, Mark, 40

Care2, 100
Carnival Cruise Lines, 180
Carpenter, Edward J., 8–10, 34, 103
Carson, Hank, 23, 60, 161
Carson, Rachel, 102, 105, 149
"The Case for a Ban on Microplastics in Personal Care Products," 151–52
Center for Biological Diversity, 154
Center for Responsive Politics, 95
Central Veterinary Research Laboratory, 163
Cervantes Saavedra, Miguel de, 107
Chatterson, Nicole, 70
Chaturvedi, Bharati, 174–75
ChicoBag, 97–100
children: chemical burden of, 4, 22, 133, 134, 138–40, 194; education on waste for, 57–58; school cafeteria waste, 191; as supporters of *Junk*, 29–30, 41; as waste managers, 173–76
Chile, 76, 77, 89, 176, 179
China, 82–84, 87, 172, 176, 177
Chintan, 174–76
cholorofluorocarbon (CFC), 50, 114
Christman, Keith, 155
circular vs. linear economy, xi, 85, 88–89, 167, 171–73. *See also* design of plastic products; planned obsolescence
circumpolar gyre, 5
citizen brigades, 105, 149, 183–84. *See also* environmental advocacy
citizen science, 12
Clean Seas Coalition, 151
Clean Water Action, 153
Close, Ann, 70
Closed Loop Fund, 89–90
Coalition to Stop the Seattle Bag Tax, 97
Coca-Cola company, 11, 51, 52, 176

Cody, Iron Eyes, 52
Cohen, Dianna, 194
Cola Kayak (plastic-bottle boat), 29–30
Colborn, Theo, 129, 140
Colgate-Palmolive, 89
collodion, 49
composting: in Chile, 179; in India, 175; in Philippines, 178; in Taiwan, 179; in United States, 47, 51–52, 88, 189, 191; vs. waste-to-energy systems, 170, 172, 178, 181. *See also* recycling
Confessions of an Economic Hitman (Perkins), 177
Consumer Product Safety Improvement Act (2008), 141
consumer responsibility, 11, 52, 95, 190. *See also* extended producer responsibility (EPR)
Conway, Erik M., 1, 101
coral reefs, 16, 17, 23, 59
Coriolis effect, 6
Crate and Barrel, 189
"crying Indian" advertisements, 52, 167, 177
Cummins, Anna: background of, 26; communication with Eriksen, 62, 65, 90, 193; expeditions on *Alguita* (ORV), 15, 24–27; *Junk* ride of, 148, 194; on love and justice, 42–43; marriage of, x, 26–27, 194; as mission control of *Junk*, x, 90, 113; Operation *Junk*-sunk by, 69–71; on Our Oceans conference, 178; planning of *Junk* and, 38–39; pregnancies and child of, 138–40, 194. *See also* Eriksen, Marcus; 5 Gyres Institute; *Junk* (plastic-bottle boat and expedition)

Danone, 51
Day, Robert, 10–11, 58
DDT, 22, 101, 102, 133, 138
Deasy, John, 191
De Blasio, Bill, 88
Defenders of Wildlife, 154
Delhi, India, 173–75
Dell Computer, 189
De Rothschild, David, 31, 35–36, 43, 194
design of plastic products, 185–90. *See also* circular vs. linear economy; planned obsolescence
"Design Through the 12 Principles of Green Engineering" (Anastas and Zimmerman), 188
Don Quixote (Cervantes), 107, 131
Don't Think of an Elephant (Lakoff), 37
Don't Waste LA, 88
Dow Chemical, 9, 11, 50–51, 95, 134, 136–37, 176
Doyle, Miriam, 58
Dubai, UAE, 163–65
Dumanoski, Dianne, 129, 140
DuPont chemical company, 9, 11, 50–51, 95

Earth Resource Foundation, 100
Ebbesmeyer, Curtis, 3, 6
eco-pragmatism, 113–15
Ecovative, 189, 191
education initiatives, 3, 57–58. *See also specific institutions*
Einstein, Albert, 120
Ellen MacArthur Foundation (EMF), 84, 182–83
Enck, Judith, 38
endocrine disrupting chemicals (EDCs), 68, 133–34, 136, 138
end-of-life vs. unregulated design, 171, 185–88. *See also* circular vs. linear economy; design of

plastic products; extended producer responsibility (EPR)

entanglement and ingestion of plastic, 18–22, 99, 101, 130–33, 140

environmental advocacy: citizen brigades, 100, 105, 149, 183–84, 195–96; eco-pragmatism, 113–15; industry strategies vs., 12, 38, 52, 99–103, 105, 166–67; microbead campaign, 150–56; science and, 8, 76–78, 141–42. *See also* 5 Gyres Institute; scientific community; *specific organizations and individuals*

Environmental Charter High School, California, 29–30, 41

Environmental Working Group (EWG), 8, 100, 138, 139

Environment California, 154

EPA. *See* US Environmental Protection Agency (EPA)

Eriksen, Marcus: advice from Moore, 59, 115, 116; background of, 1–3, 8, 110; child of, 194; collecting hobby of, 48, 91, 114; communication with Cummins, 62, 65, 90, 193; on eco-pragmatism, 113–15; education of, 113; expeditions on *Alguita* (ORV), 5, 8, 15, 23–27; fishing by, 130, 144; Gulf War memories and mementos, 48, 109–11, 165–66; lectures by, 30, 42, 58, 96, 113, 176, 194; on love and justice, 42–43, 62, 166; marriage of, x, 26–27, 194; open letter to ACC by, 195–96; post-*Junk* work of, 148, 193–96, 194; river expeditions by, 2–3, 29–30; self-reflections aboard *Junk*, 90–92, 93–94,

108–11. *See also* Cummins, Anna; 5 Gyres Institute; *Junk* (plastic-bottle boat and expedition)

Ernst, Jeff, 15, 24, 70

Ever Laurel (cargo ship), 6

Explorer Satellite, 41

Explorers Club, 113

export industry of trash, 83, 84–85, 87, 181

extended producer responsibility (EPR), 11, 84, 88–90, 95, 167, 172

Exxon Valdez (oil tanker), 38

Feinstein, Dianne, 138

fish: as food aboard *Junk*, 112, 127, 130–31, 144, 147; human ingestion of toxins from, 133–34, 140, 141; plastic entanglement and ingestion by, 18–22, 99, 101, 130, 131–32

Fishing for Litter, 125, 126

fishing industry waste, 16–18, 125–26, 161

5 Gyres Institute: campaigns of, 150–56, 183–84; equipment loans by, 149–50; establishment of, x, 148; expeditions and studies by, 21–22, 23, 148–49, 160–61; publications of, 13, 77–78, 159–60. *See also* Cummins, Anna; Eriksen, Marcus

flame retardants, 21, 22, 133, 138, 139

Florida, 152, 153

Fluke (plastic-bottle boat), 30

Folsom, Geoff, 39, 40

Ford Motor Company, 51

Freon, 50

Galgani, Francois, 161

Garbage Project, 46

Garbarino, Joe, 83, 96–97
garbology, 46
Garcetti, Eric, 88
Garrett, Jim, 181
gasification, 172, 180
genetic alteration due to plastic
    exposure, 135–36; epigenetic
    effects, 136
Genovés, Santiago, 33–34, 35
Germany, 76, 89, 126
GhostNet project, 18
Global Alliance for Incinerator
    Alternatives (GAIA), 149, 175,
    178–80, 184
Gold, Mark, 156
Goldman Sachs, 89–90
Goldstein, Miriam, 23, 24, 58
Goodyear, Charles, 49
Gould, Stephen J., 136
Grate, Frolian, 178, 184
Great Lakes project, 149–50
Great Pacific Garbage Patch trope,
    3–4, 11, 76–78, 162
Great Recovery, 185–86
Green, Jeremy, 7
Green Bag Campaign, 97
Green Cities California, 100
Green Fence, 84, 87
Greenfire Law, 152
Greenpeace, 18
Groh, Holly, 85
Guadalupe Island, 81–82, 86, 90
Guston, David, 60
gyres, 5. See also specific gyres;
    specific regions

Hansa Carrier (cargo ship), 6
Hawaii: Junk's arrival in, 169, 193,
    196; Kamilo Beach, 60, 160,
    185–86; Papahānaumokuākea
    Marine National Monument,
    1–2, 115, 144; plastic-bag ban
    in, 183; Polynesian settlement

history of, 32; waste-to-energy
    power, 170
health. See public health issues
Heal the Bay, 100, 149, 154
Healthy Stuff report, 85
Heller, Kyaa, 70
Heyerdahl, Thor, 31, 33, 81
high density polyethylene (HDPE),
    39
Higraff, Torgeir Sæverud, 31
Hilex Poly Company, 97–100
"Hitting the Bottle" (skit), 46
H. J. Heinz Company, 51
The Honest Broker (Pielke), 73, 74
The Honolulu Strategy, 38
H-Power, 170
hurricanes, 103–4, 108, 115–17
Hyatt, John W., 49
hydrocarbon gas liquids (HGL), 4

Illinois, 154
incineration of trash, x, 17, 87,
    88, 134, 167, 170. See also
    Global Alliance for Incinerator
    Alternatives (GAIA); waste
    management
India, 84–85, 173–76, 179
Indian Ocean Gyre, 124, 149, 160
Indonesia, 176
ingestion. See entanglement and
    ingestion of plastic
Interface, Inc., 187, 191
Intergovernmental Maritime Consul-
    tative Organization (IMCO), 34
International Marine Debris Con-
    ference, 38
Inuit, 133
Iraq War, 110, 114
Ishi (sailboat), 193, 196

Jambeck, Jenna, 17, 176–77
Japanese earthquake and tsunami
    (2011), 22, 23, 129, 160

jellyfish, 18, 123
Johnson & Johnson, 152, 154–55
Joseph, Stephen, 96
Junk (plastic-bottle boat and expedition): communication with Cummins, xi, 64, 69, 104, 144; communication with others, 73–74, 78–79, 111, 115, 140, 145; description of, x, 29, 121–22; drinking water on-board, 36, 145; fishing aboard, 82, 111–13, 127, 130–32, 143–44, 147; food aboard, 33, 82, 104, 108, 111–13, 119; Guadalupe Island, 81–82, 86, 90; Hawaiian arrival of, 169, 193, 196; launch and first days on, 55–57, 61–64; mission control of, x, 90, 113; onboard repairs of, 90, 93–95, 107, 120; Operation *Junk*-sunk, xi, 64–65, 67–71, 70–71; planning and building, x, 38–42; post-voyage display of, 194; purpose of, 56, 93–94; rendezvous with Savage, 144–48; San Nicholas Island, 62–71; trawling samples on, 5, 122–23, 129, 147
Junk ride, 148, 194
Junk Science (Agin), 76
junk science vs. bad science, 76–78, 140

Kamilo Beach, Hawaii, 60, 160, 185–86
Keep America Beautiful campaign, 52
Keith, Christie, 178
Keller, Andy, 97–100, 101, 104
Kellert, Stephen, 113
Kerry, John, 176
Kevlar, 50
Kinnaman, Thomas, 88

Kon-Tiki I and *II* (Heyerdahl), 31, 81
Kopcho, Blake, 154, 155
Kuwait, 110, 163, 165

Lake Erie sampling, 149–50
Lakoff, George, 37
land debris. *See* plastic land pollution
landfills, 46–47, 170, 174–75. *See also* waste management
Langmuir cells, 16
Laursen, Duane, 70, 71, 119
Lebreton, Laurent, 161
Lehi IV (raft), 32–33, 36, 82. *See also* McFarland, Don
Lemmon, Jody, 5
L'Hérétique (dinghy), 32
life-cycle assessments (LCA), 100–101
linear vs. circular economy, xi, 85, 88–89, 167, 171–73
Los Angeles Alliance for a New Economy, 88
Los Angeles Times, 98
Los Angeles Waterkeeper, 154
Louisiana, 85, 91
Lycra, 50

MacArthur, R. H., 23
Machleder, Herb, 15
MacKerron, Conrad, 89, 191
mahi mahi, 112, 127, 130–31, 144, 147
Maine, 53
Mallos, Nick, 125
Mango Materials, 154
Marin County Recycling, 83, 96–97
marine debris, as term, 37–38. *See also* plastic marine pollution
Marine Debris.info, 184
marine worms, 21, 23, 130, 132, 133
MARPOL, 16, 34–35, 126

Marris, Emma, 115
Mason, Sam, 149–50
Mata Rangi (raft), 35
material recovery facilities (MRFs),
 87–88, 178
McDonald, Bob, 190
McDonald's, 191
McFarland, Don, 33, 43, 111–12,
 143. *See also Lehi IV* (raft)
McKinsey Center for Business De-
 velopment, 176
media coverage of plastic pollution,
 3–4, 7–8, 76–77
"Media Sensationalisation and
 Science" (Green), 7
Mediterranean Sea, 123, 161, 162
Merchants of Doubt (Oreskes and
 Conway), 1, 101
Metabolix, 189
Michigan, 53
microbead campaign, 150–56
Microbead-Free Waters Act (2015),
 155
microplastics. *See under* plastic
Midway Atoll, 1–2, 115, 144
Mississippi River, 2–3, 30, 91
MOL Comfort (cargo ship), 6–7
monomers, 4. *See also* styrene
Monsanto, 9, 11, 95
Moore, Charles: advice to Eriksen
 from, 59, 115, 116; discovery
 of, 3, 10–11, 12; lectures by,
 176, 194; opinions of, 5, 59;
 publications of, 9, 60, 77, 161.
 See also Alguita (ORV)
Morlet, Andrew, 182
Morris, Robert, 10
Morse, Molly, 154
Mother Earth Foundation, 178
mothers, chemical transmission by,
 22, 133, 134, 138–40
Muñoz, Kitin, 35
mycelium, 189

Myctophidae, 19
Myers, John Peterson, 129, 140
Mylar, 50
Mystic (ship), 162

nanoplastics. *See under* plastic
Nantucket, Massachusetts, 96
National Academy of Engineering, 5
National Academy of Sciences
 (NAS), 34
National Center for Ecologi-
 cal Analysis and Synthesis
 (NCEAS), 12–13
National Geographic Society,
 30–31, 98
National Resources Defense Coun-
 cil (NRDC), 8, 138, 154
National Soft Drink Association, 53
Natural Resources Defense Council,
 154
Nature (journal), 60
neoprene, 50
Netherlands Sustainability Confer-
 ence, 194
nets. *See* fishing industry waste
New Jersey, 153
The New Plastics Economy (Ellen
 MacArthur Foundation), 83–84,
 182
New York, 88, 149, 153, 163, 183
New Yorker, 102
New York Times, 86–87, 88, 138
Nichols, Wallace J., 20
Nike, 51
NOAA (US National Oceanic and
 Atmospheric Administration),
 12, 18, 63, 159
No Child in Trash, 175
North Atlantic Subtropical Gyre,
 12, 160, 162, 189
North Pacific Subtropical Gyre, 3,
 5, 10–11. *See also* Great Pacific
 Garbage Patch trope

nurdles, 34, 58. *See also* microbead campaign
nylon, 50
NY/NJ Baykeepers, 149

Oahu, 170
Obama, Barack, 115, 155
Ocean Champions, 150–51
Ocean Cleanup Project (OCP), 124, 125–27
Ocean Conservancy, 12–13, 38, 125, 154, 176–78
Ocean Detox, 70
oceanic current systems, 5–6
ocean plastic. *See* plastic marine pollution
Ockels, Wubbo Johannes, 124
oil pollution. *See* petroleum marine waste
oil tankers, 16, 34–35, 38, 126
Olson, Randy, 90
Operation Clean Sweep, 58
Oregon, 53
Oreskes, Naomi, 1, 101
Organisation for Economic Co-operation and Development, 89
Our Ocean conference, 176–78, 184
Our Stolen Future (Colborn, Dumanoski, Myers), 129, 140
oysters, 133

Packaging 2.0, 188, 191
Pallone, Frank, Jr., 155
Pangaea Exploration, 149, 160
Papahānaumokuākea Marine National Monument, 1–2, 115
Parkes, Alexander, 49
Parkesine, 49
Paschal, Amity, 72
Paschal, Joel: background of, 63, 72; as co-navigator on *Junk*, x,

38–39, 55, 103–4, 107; expeditions on *Alguita* (ORV), 15, 24; fishing by, 82, 111–13, 127, 130, 147; on ocean pollution, 16; post-voyage work of, 194. See also *Junk* (plastic-bottle boat and expedition)
Patagonia, 68
PepsiCo, 11, 52
Perkins, John, 177
Persian Gulf research trip, 163–64
Persian Gulf War memories, 48, 109–11, 165–66
persistent organic pollutants (POPs), 133, 138
Personal Care Products Council (PCPC), 152, 154–55
Peterson, Strom, 97
petroleum interests and war, 109–11
petroleum marine waste, 8, 33, 34, 126
Philip Morris company, 52
Philippines, 176, 178, 184
phthalates, 133, 134, 141. *See also* plasticizers
Pielke, Roger, Jr., 73, 74
planned obsolescence, x, 9–10, 45, 50, 171–72, 187. *See also* circular vs. linear economy; design of plastic products
Plastic Bag Laws, 96
plastic-bag ordinances, 8, 42, 75–76, 95–98, 101, 104–5, 183
Plastic Change, 149
"Plastic Debris, Rivers to Sea" conference, 57–58
plastic industry: ASTM standards, 154, 155; beginning of, 49–50; bottle redemption programs, 53, 89, 174; core strategies of, 99–103, 105, 166–67; extended producer responsibility (EPR), 84, 88–90, 95, 167, 172;

lawsuits by, 97–100; lobbying and public campaigns for, 8–12, 22, 52–54, 137; microbead campaign against, 150–56; planned obsolescence and, x, 9–10, 45, 171–72, 187; politics of language and, 37–38, 52, 177; regulation of, 137–38, 141, 150–56; response to scientific studies by, 8, 9, 12; ubiquitousness of plastic, 48–49, 100–101, 133–34, 164; water bottles, 29, 39–40. *See also* American Chemistry Council (ACC); plastic production

plasticizers, 133, 134

plastic land pollution: camels and, 163–64, 185; consumer responsibility vs. EPR, 11, 52, 95, 167, 177, 190. *See also* plastic-bag ordinances; recycling; waste management

plastic marine pollution: conferences on, 11, 12, 38, 57, 176–78, 184; distribution of, 160–63; entanglement and ingestion of, 18–22, 99, 101, 130–33, 140; fishing industry waste, 16–18, 125–26, 161; floating hitchhiking on, 21–23; language and, 37–38; life cycle of, 5; media attention on, 3–4, 7–8, 76–77; microbead campaign, 150–56; on Papahānaumokuākea Marine National Monument, 1–2; proposed solutions for, 123–25, 185–90; regulations on, 16, 34–35, 155; scientific studies on, 8–11, 13, 20, 60, 77–78, 159–60, 161; from shipping container accidents, 3, 6–7; statistics on, 124–25, 161;

"Texas-sized garbage patch" trope, 3–4, 11, 76–78, 162. *See also* environmental advocacy; plastic industry; scientific community; *specific plastics*

Plastic Movement Alignment Project (PMAP), 184

Plastic Poison (plastic-bottle boat), 30

Plastic Pollution Coalition, 100, 149, 151, 184, 194

plastic production: circular vs. linear economy and, xi, 85, 88–89, 167, 171–73; cycle and statistics on, x, 11, 45–46, 98, 171–73; design interventions, 185–90; planned obsolescence of, x, 9–10, 45, 171–72, 187; process and products of, 4–5, 100–101, 171. *See also* plastic industry; *specific types*

Plastics Europe, 45, 172, 173, 182, 185. *See also* American Chemistry Council (ACC)

Plastic Soup Foundation, 150, 151

"Plastics: Too Valuable To Waste" campaign, 57–58

Plastiki projects, 30–31, 35–36, 194

Plymouth University, 60

pollution. *See* plastic land pollution; plastic marine pollution

polybrominated diphenyl ethers (PBDEs), 21, 22, 133, 138–39

polychlorinated biphenyls (PCBs), 22, 133, 134, 138, 139

polycyclic aromatic hydrocarbon (PAHs), 133

polyethylene, 4–5, 21, 34, 50, 51, 122, 124

polyethylene terephthalate (PET), 39, 47, 52, 53, 188–89

polyhydroxyalkanoate (PHA), 51–52, 154, 189

polylactic acid (PLA), 51–52, 153
polymers, 4, 47, 51. *See also specific types*
polyporopylene, 4, 50, 122, 124
polystyrene, 50, 96–97, 125, 133, 134–35, 183, 191
PolyTalk conference, 182, 185
polyurethane, 4
polyvinyl chloride (PVC), 21, 47, 134, 186
Potomac Attack (plastic-bottle boat), 30
Prindiville, Matt, 177
Pristine Seas, 115
Procter & Gamble, 51, 89, 152, 190, 191
Progressive Bag Alliance, 8
pteropods, 18
public health issues: BPA and, 135–38; cancer, 101–2, 134, 135, 136, 139, 177; Consumer Product Safety Improvement Act (2008), 141; from fish consumption, 133–34, 140, 141; infants and toxins, 22, 133, 134, 138–40; of waste management in India, 173–76. *See also specific chemicals*
Puente Hills Landfill, California, 46
Pyrogenesis, 180
pyrolysis, 124, 172, 180–81

rafting adventures, 31–36. *See also specific raft names*
Ra I (raft), 33
Ra II (raft), 33
Rambunctious Garden (Marris), 115
Rathje, William, 46
recycling: bottle donations for *Junk*, 39–40; bottle redemption programs, 53, 89, 174; Green Fence, 84, 87; in India, 173–76;

initiatives on, 11–12, 54, 57–58; of plastics, 83–90, 96–97; pyrolysis, 124, 180; vs. waste management, 87–90, 171–73; waste-pickers, 173–76, 178–79. *See also* composting; waste management
Recycling and Extended Producer Liability Law (Chile), 89
The Recycling Myth (Buffington), 87, 88–89
Reed, Dwight, 53
Reeve, Susan, 31
"The Reign of Recycling" (Tierney), 86–87, 88
Reisser, Julia, 161
Reproductive Toxicology, 137
Republic Act 9003 (Philippines), 178
Republic Services, 87
Rhode Island, 153
Ritter, Ron, 149, 160
river expeditions, 2–3, 29–30, 91, 163
Rochman, Chelsea, 21–22, 59–60, 61, 142, 155
Romer, Jennie, 96
Roosevelt, Theodore, 113
Russell, Steve, 97, 159, 166
Russo, Daniella, 191–92
Ryan, Peter, 161

Sala, Enric, 115
San Francisco, 83, 96–97, 183
San Nicholas Island, 62–71
Santa Monica High School, California, 41
Saran Wrap, 10, 51
Sauers, Len, 152, 190
Savage, Roz, 144–48, 194
Save the Plastic Bag Coalition, 8, 96–97, 101, 103
Schubel, Jerry, 40

Schwarzenegger, Arnold, 96
Sciences International, 137
scientific community: barriers and channels of engagement in, 12, 59–61, 78; environmental advocacy and, 8, 76–78, 141–42, 150–56; junk science vs. bad science, 76–78, 140; plastic industry response to, 8, 9, 12; policymaking and, 61, 74–76; publication strategies of, 13; rise in studies on ocean plastics, 8–9, 20. *See also* environmental advocacy
Scripps Institution of Oceanography and SEAPLEX, 7, 12, 20, 58, 60, 77
seabirds, 2, 4, 18, 20, 21, 90, 144
Sea Dragon (ship), 149, 160
Sea Education Association (SEA), 10, 12, 60
seals, 71, 90, 99
Seattle, 97, 104–5
sea turtles, 1, 4, 20, 122
self-storage industry, 48
Seven Little Sisters (raft), 32
sharks, 19, 86
Sheavly, Seba, 58
Shell Oil, 11
shipping containers, 3, 6–7, 82
Sierra Club, 8, 154
Silent Spring (Carson), 102, 149
skeletal eroding band disease, 23
Skyscrape Foundation, 40
SLAPP suits, 98–100, 103
Slat, Boyan, 124, 125, 126–27
Smith, Kenneth L., Jr., 8, 34
Society of the Plastics Industry (SPI), 9, 10, 50–51, 103, 137
South Atlantic Subtropical Gyre, 21, 160, 161
South Carolina, 98
South China Sea, 123, 161, 162

South Pacific Subtropical Gyre, 77, 160, 161
Spastic Plastic (plastic-bottle boat), 30
squid, 143–44
Stad Amsterdam, 124, 149
Standard Oil, 9
Stanley, Kyle, 151
Stemming the Tide (OC), 176–78, 182
Stockholm Convention on Persistent Organic Pollutants (POPs), 22
Story of Stuff, 149, 154, 184
styrene, 134–35. *See also* polystyrene
styrofoam. *See* polystyrene
subpolar gyres, 5, 161
subtropical gyres, x, 5–6. *See also* specific gyres
Sun Diver (powerboat), 70, 71
Superbag Operating, 97–100
Surfrider Foundation, 8, 100, 149, 151, 154
syngas, 180

"Tackling Marine Debris" conference, 57–59
Taiwan, 179
Takada, Hideshige, 7, 60
Tamminen, Leslie, 30
tar balls, 8, 33, 34, 126
Teflon, 50, 51
Thailand, 176
Thiel, Martin, 161
thermoplastics. *See specific types*
thermosets, 4
Think Beyond Plastic, 191–92
Thomas, Sophie, 185–86, 187–88, 189
Thomas Starr King Middle School, California, 191
Thompson, Richard, 7, 60, 190

"Throwaway Living" (*Life* maga-zine), 45
Tierney, John, 86–87, 88, 89
tobacco industry, 8, 101–2, 159, 195
toxicology, 60, 132–34, 135. *See also specific toxins*
Toxic Substance Control Act (1976), 137
Trash-Free Waters, 184
tsunami (Japan, 2011), 22, 23, 129, 160
Tulane Environmental Law Journal, 151–52
Tulane Summit on Environmental Law and Policy, 151

Unilever, 51, 151
United Arab Emirates, 163–65
United Nations Development Pro-gramme (UNDP), 38, 159
United Nations Environment Pro-gramme (UNEP), 17, 38, 159
University of Hawaii at Hilo, 60
University of Tokyo, 60
University of Washington, 58
Upstream Policy Institute, 149, 177, 183–84
Upton, Fred, 155
US Coast Guard, 73–74, 78–79
US Consumer Product Safety Com-mission, 85
US Department of State, 83
US Environmental Protection Agency (EPA), 11, 38, 47, 99, 137, 159
US Fish and Wildlife Service, 2
US Food and Drug Administration (FDA), 137
USS *Niagara*, 150

Vadxx Energy, 181
Van Walsem, Johan, 189

Velsicol, 102
Verdi Gras, 85
Vermont, 153
Vietnam, 176
Viracocha (raft), 35
Vom Saal, Frederick, 135–37
Vulcanite Court, 49
vulcanization, 49

Walmart, 89
war, 48, 109–11, 114, 165–66
Washington, 97
Waste Connections, 87
waste management: in Chile, 179; diversion vs. cleanup, 171, 181; exportation of US trash, 83, 84–85, 87, 181; failures in United States, 11–12; gasifica-tion, 172, 180; incineration, x, 17, 87, 88, 134, 167, 170–78; in India, 173–76; landfills, 46–47, 170, 174–75; MRFs, 87–88, 178; public education on, 57–58, 86, 150–51, 178–79; pyrolysis, 124, 172, 180–81; in Taiwan, 179; of technology, 186, 187; zero waste vs. waste-to-energy, 170, 172, 176–81. *See also* circu-lar vs. linear economy; compost-ing; recycling
Waste Management (company), 87
waste pickers, 173–76, 178–79
water, drinking, 29, 32, 36, 145
water bottles, 29, 39–40
Weisman, Alan, 121, 157
Werner, Ulli, 163
Westerbos, Maria, 151
whales, 133
White, Angelique, 76–77
Whole Foods, 41–42, 188
Willis, William, 32
Wilson, E. O., 23, 113, 183
Wilson, Monica, 178

Wilson, Stiv, 151
windrow, 15–16
Winston, Andrew, 188
Wisconsin, 153
women: childbearing and toxic
    transmission by, 22, 133, 134,
    138–40; EDCs and, 68, 133–34,
    136, 138; risks of waste pickers,
    174–75, 179
Woods Hole Oceanographic Institu-
    tion (WHOI), 7, 9–10, 12, 60
World Bank, 46
World Shipping Council, 6
World Wildlife Fund, 51

The World Without Us (Weisman),
    121, 157
worms. *See* marine worms

yellowfin tuna, 134

"Zero Plastics to Landfill by 2020"
    (Plastics Europe), 173
Zero Waste LA, 88
zero waste vs. waste-to-energy pro-
    grams, 170, 172, 176–81. *See
    also* circular vs. linear economy;
    waste management
Zimmerman, Julie, 188